Constitutional Conventions

I0894797

This book analyses constitutional conventions as a powerful but largely neglected framework for studying the law and politics of constitutions.

Constitutional conventions are the unwritten rules that inform and circumscribe the political behaviour of individuals, organisations, and a political system. They are as important as the formal legal rules that define written constitutions and shape modern states; yet, unlike formal written rules, conventions have received only limited scholarly attention. This book considers conventions as a lens to theorise and to analyse the institutional dynamics of contemporary constitutions. Interrogating constitutional conventions in a wide variety of contexts – including in Westminster parliamentary systems, in presidential systems, and in non-democratic regimes – the book offers new perspectives for understanding diverse aspects of constitutional politics such as the capacity of conventions to constrain populists, how conventions influence constitutional transformation, how they reflect and reshape core democratic values such as citizenship and constitutional identity, and what they reveal about the character of authoritarian regimes. The book thus demonstrates how the dynamics of conventions shape the very character of constitutions.

The book will be of interest to legal theorists, constitutional lawyers, and political scientists.

Nicholas Barry is Senior Lecturer in Politics at La Trobe University, Australia.

Narelle Miragliotta is Associate Professor in Politics and Policy at Murdoch University, Australia.

Zim Nwokora is Associate Professor in Politics and Policy Studies at Deakin University, Australia.

Haig Patapan is Professor in the School of Government and International Relations at Griffith University, Australia.

Constitutional Conventions

Theories, Practices and Dynamics

Edited by Nicholas Barry,
Narelle Miragliotta, Zim Nwokora
and Haig Patapan

Routledge
Taylor & Francis Group
a GlassHouse Book

First published 2025
by Routledge
4 Park Square, Milton Park, Abingdon, Oxon OX14 4RN

and by Routledge
605 Third Avenue, New York, NY 10158

Routledge is an imprint of the Taylor & Francis Group, an informa business
A GlassHouse book

British Library Cataloguing-in-Publication Data
A catalogue record for this book is available from the British Library

Library of Congress Cataloging-in-Publication Data
Names: Barry, Nicholas, editor. | Miragliotta, Narelle, editor. | Nwokora, Zim G., 1983– editor. | Patapan, Haig, 1959– editor.
Title: Constitutional conventions : theories, practices, and dynamics / edited by Nicholas Barry, Narelle Miragliotta, Zim Nwokora, and Haig Patapan.
Description: Abingdon, Oxon [UK] ; New York, NY : Routledge, 2025. | Includes bibliographical references and index.
Identifiers: LCCN 2024044435 (print) | LCCN 2024044436 (ebook) | ISBN 9781032828336 (hardback) | ISBN 9781032828367 (paperback) | ISBN 9781003506577 (ebook)
Subjects: LCSH: Constitutional conventions. | Constitutional amendments. | Constitutional law.
Classification: LCC K3168 .C66 2025 (print) | LCC K3168 (ebook) | DDC 342.02/4—dc23/eng/20240920
LC record available at https://lccn.loc.gov/2024044435
LC ebook record available at https://lccn.loc.gov/2024044436

ISBN: 978-1-032-82833-6 (hbk)
ISBN: 978-1-032-82836-7 (pbk)
ISBN: 978-1-003-50657-7 (ebk)

DOI: 10.4324/9781003506577

Typeset in Sabon
by Apex CoVantage, LLC

Contents

About the Contributors

Frank Algra-Maschio is a final year PhD candidate in political science and a teaching associate in the School of Social Sciences at Monash University, Australia. Frank's PhD research focuses on the making and fulfilment of election promises in Australia.

Nicholas Barry is Senior Lecturer in Politics at La Trobe University, Australia and Course Coordinator of the Bachelor of Arts. His research interests are in the areas of political theory, comparative political institutions, and Australian politics. His work has been published in outlets such as the *Journal of Politics*, *Governance*, *Parliamentary Affairs*, *Journal of Applied Philosophy*, *Canadian Journal of Political Science*, and *Australian Journal of Political Science*.

Baogang He is Alfred Deakin Professor at Deakin University, Australia, and Fellow of the Academy of Social Sciences in Australia. He is widely known for his work in Chinese politics, in particular the deliberative politics in China, as well as in regionalism, international relations, federalism, and multiculturalism in Asia. His publications are found in top journals including *Science*, *British Journal of Political Science*, *Journal of Peace Research*, *Political Theory*, *Political Studies*, and *Perspectives on Politics*. His two papers ("Authoritarian Deliberation: The Deliberative Turn in Chinese Political Development", co-authored with Mark Warren, and "The Domestic Politics of the Belt and Road Initiative and its Implications") are in the top 1% of the highly cited research papers in the Web of Sciences as of 11 February 2021. His published books include *The Democratisation of China*, *The Democratic Implications of Civil Society in China*, *Rural Democracy in China*, and *Governing Taiwan and Tibet*. He co-edited and published *Deliberative Democracy in Asia* (with Michael Breen and James Fishkin) in 2021, and *China and North Korea's Human Rights* (with David Hundt and Chengxin Pan) in 2021.

David Kosař is Professor of Constitutional Law at Masaryk University (MUNI), Czechia. He researches constitutional law and theory, judicial studies, transitional justice, and human rights. He studied law at MUNI in

Brno, at the CEU in Budapest, and at NYU Law School in New York. His current project (ERC Consolidator Grant) studies informal judicial institutions. He authored 'Perils of Judicial Self-Government in Transitional Societies' (2016), co-authored 'Domestic Judicial Treatment of European Court of Human Rights Case Law' (2020) and 'The Constitution of Czechia' (2021), and edited the special issue on 'Informal Judicial Institutions' (*German Law Journal*, Vol. 24, No. 8, pp. 1239–1595). His work appeared in *International Journal of Constitutional Law*, *European Constitutional Law Review*, *American Journal of International Law*, *European Journal of International Law*, *Hague Journal of the Rule of Law*, *German Law Journal*, *Feminist Legal Studies*, *Law & Policy*, *Law & Social Inquiry*, and *Regulation & Governance*.

Narelle Miragliotta is Associate Professor in Politics and Policy at Murdoch University, Australia. Her research interests include comparative constitutionalism, political parties, elections and electoral systems. Miragliotta's work has been published in *Governance*, *Government and Opposition*, *Party Politics*, *Parliamentary Affairs*, and *Electoral Studies*, among other outlets.

Sarah Murray is a professor at the University of Western Australia, where she teaches constitutional law and researches in public law, electoral law, and court innovation. She is a Fellow of the Australian Academy of Law, co-Chair of the International Society of Public Law AUS-NZ Chapter and a co-Convenor of the WA Chapter of the Electoral Regulation and Research Network. She has published widely in Australia and internationally and is an editor of *Constitutional Perspectives on an Australian Republic – Essays in Honour of Professor George Winterton* (2010), co-editor of *Regulating Preventive Justice – Principle, Policy and Paradox* (2017) and a co-author of *The Constitution of the Commonwealth of Australia – History, Principle and Interpretation* (2015).

Zim Nwokora is an associate professor in politics and policy studies at Deakin University, where he currently serves as course director of the bachelor of politics, philosophy and economics (PPE). A comparative political scientist by background, his research focuses on constitutions, political parties, and political finance. His work has been published in journals such as the *British Journal of Political Science*, *Governance*, *International Journal of Constitutional Law*, *Party Politics*, *Political Research Quarterly*, and *Political Studies*.

Graeme Orr is a professor of law at The University of Queensland, Australia, specialising in the law and norms of electoral democracy. His books include *The Law of Politics* (2nd edition, 2019), one on elections as rituals *Ritual and Rhythm in Electoral Systems* (2015) and *The Law of*

Deliberative Democracy (2016, co-authored). Graeme is a Fellow of the Australian Academy of Law and the Australian Social Sciences Academy.

Haig Patapan is a professor in the School of Government and International Relations, Griffith University, Australia. His research interests are in democratic theory and practice, political philosophy, political leadership, and comparative constitutionalism. Professor Patapan is a Fellow of the Academy of Social Sciences in Australia. He has received a number of awards, including an Australian Prime Ministers Centre Fellowship; a Senior Fulbright Scholarship at the Center for Public Leadership, Harvard Kennedy School of Government; an Isaac Manasseh Meyer Fellowship, the National University of Singapore; and most recently a Visiting Fellowship, Australian Center for Federalism, Australian National University. His latest book, *Modern Philosopher Kings: Wisdom and Power in Politics* (2023), explores modern attempts to resolve the enduring question of the philosopher king – whether it is possible to combine wisdom and power to secure justice.

James P. Pfiffner is University Professor emeritus in the Schar School of Policy and Government at George Mason University, United States. His major areas of expertise are the presidency, U.S. national government, public management, and the national security policy process. He has lectured on these topics at universities in Europe and throughout the United States, as well as at the Federal Executive Institute, the National War College, the U.S. Military Academy, and the Departments of State, Justice, and Defense. He has written or edited 16 books on the presidency and U.S. national government, including *The Strategic Presidency: Hitting the Ground Running* (2nd edition, 1996), *The Character Factor: How We Judge Our Presidents* (2004), *Power Play: The Bush Administration and the Constitution* (2008), and *Torture as Public Policy* (2010). He has also published more than 100 chapters and articles in books and scholarly journals.

Attila Vincze is Senior Lecturer in the Judicial Studies Institute at Masaryk University MUNI. He studied law in Budapest, Heidelberg, Munich, and Vienna; he holds a JD, an LL.M. in German law, and a PhD in European law; and he was also granted *venia docendi* in European and comparative law. Before moving to Masayrk University Brno in 2021, he was reader in law at the German-speaking Andrassy University, lecturer in Hull, and research fellow in Budapest, and he acted as counsel in two boutique law firms in Budapest, as well. Attila focuses on comparative public law, the law of the European Union, and the judicial system. He has around 150 publications in five languages.

Acknowledgements

This edited volume has been long in the making, and it would not have been possible without the support of many individuals and several organisations at key stages in its development. The project originated out of conversations that the editors were having about constitutional conventions in late 2020, which led them to submit a proposal to the Australian Political Studies Association (APSA) for a grant to fund a workshop on 'The Soft Rules of Governance'. The workshop would aim to bring together an interdisciplinary group of scholars – in particular, constitutional lawyers/theorists and political scientists/theorists – to explore constitutional conventions, a topic that raised many interesting and pressing questions that seemed to be relatively understudied in the existing scholarship. Our suspicion was that a wide-ranging discussion that unearthed and interrogated some of these understudied issues – and which did so drawing from different disciplines, methodologies, countries, and regions – could be intellectually productive. We are grateful to APSA for seeing the value in this initial idea, and for providing the seed funding to convene a workshop to discuss them.

Unfortunately, our plans for an in-person workshop in Melbourne in late 2021 were interrupted by the COVID19 pandemic and the rolling lockdowns that ensued across Australia, especially in the state of Victoria where three of the editors were based. With some shuffling of the deck, we were able to host a vibrant online version of the workshop in February 2022. It was at that two-day workshop that the idea of an edited volume was mooted, and we began to imagine its shape. Most of the papers that were presented at the online workshop would also be discussed, as more advanced manuscripts, at a subsequent in-person workshop that took place at Deakin University in September, 2022. At this second workshop, we were also able to bring in a couple of additional contributors to give presentations addressing themes and country cases that would be valuable for a collection but which were missing from the first workshop.

The contributors who presented papers at these workshops have been marvellous to work with. The individuals who are now listed as chapter authors in this volume have not only supplied their chapter manuscripts; they have also been lively and insightful contributors to a wider discussion about conventions from which we have all benefited. That collective thinking has also been greatly advanced by the generosity of others who participated in the workshops as discussants, chairs, and audience members. In addition to the chapter authors, we would like to acknowledge the contributions of Farrah Ahmed, Scott Brenton, Rowan Callick, Tom Daly, Rosalind Dixon, Bjoern Dressel, Patrick Emerton, Tadesse Melaku, John Morss, Yee-Fui Ng, Jayani Nadarajalingam, Raul Sanchez-Urribarri, Ben Saunders, Cheryl Saunders, Scott Stephenson, Adrienne Stone, Robert Thomson, Anne Twomey, Miguel Vatter, and Edward Willis.

One of the editors (Zim Nwokora) would like to thank the facilities team at Deakin University for support in hosting the in-person workshop, and all of the editors would like to acknowledge the support of their institutions in supplying a conducive environment for work on this project. The editorial team at Routledge have taken the project through its final stages, organising two valuable reviews of sections of the manuscript and working with the editors to finalise the volume. We are grateful to the Routledge team and the reviewers they commissioned.

Chapter 1

Introduction

New Research Directions in Constitutional Conventions

Nicholas Barry, Narelle Miragliotta, Zim Nwokora and Haig Patapan

Constitutional conventions are the unwritten norms and rules that inform, guide, empower and curtail the actions of individuals and the operation of political organisations and institutions. They are widely recognised and respected, and they are no less important than written constitutions and the formal rules that define and shape modern states. Yet "constitutional conventions" are the poor cousins of the extensive scholarship on "constitutional laws," receiving much less attention from constitutional lawyers and political scientists. While there has been growing interest in conventions in recent years, this research has largely neglected the theoretical dimensions of this phenomenon; it has focused more on their legal rather than their political functions and utilised individual case studies (typically drawn from crisis situations in Westminster countries) rather than deriving lessons based on a more comparative approach.

In this book, we argue that conventions are a valuable conceptual lens for understanding modern constitutions and political systems. To demonstrate the merits of our approach, we undertake a new theoretical engagement with the question of the nature of conventions; examine their provenance, development and application; investigate their efficacy in shaping, guiding and restraining politics; and finally, contemplate their potential to reveal new insights into contemporary comparative constitutionalism. This book aims to highlight conventions as a feature of constitutions of all kinds. Animating the volume is a view of conventions as a *vital* and *dynamic* class of rules within a constitution, intersecting with constitutional laws and embedded in a wider society with its unique political characteristics, culture and traditions. This focus on the dynamics of conventions and their interdependence with legal, political, cultural and social contexts directs our attention to the ways conventions shape and are, in turn, moulded by political and legal ideas, various kinds of institutions, specific traditions and historical contexts. The theoretical and conceptual issues raised by this perspective, and the range of countries examined to illuminate how conventions work and change in different and evolving contexts, make this volume a significant contribution to the emerging scholarship on constitutional conventions.

DOI: 10.4324/9781003506577-1

In this introduction, we situate conventions within the scholarly literature and explain why they matter. In particular, we argue that conventions provide a powerful lens through which to understand and analyse constitutional systems, and we summarise how each of the book's chapters contribute to the development of this approach. We conclude by identifying some of the new research directions that are made possible by the insights of these contributions.

What are Conventions and Why Do They Matter?

Defining Constitutional Conventions

Defining a "constitutional convention" is deceptively difficult. According to a common view, constitutional conventions are the unwritten, informal rules which emerge from the practical workings of a constitution, and which prescribe and/or prohibit certain actions or conduct that are generally not enforced via official (i.e., formal legal) channels. While this definition captures some of the important qualities of conventions, namely their character as binding rules and their location within and relationship to a wider constitutional system, it requires some qualifications and leaves a number of critical conceptual and practical issues unresolved.

In the first place, to describe a convention as an *unwritten* device is not, as some scholars have observed, strictly accurate. Conventions can be captured in various written forms, including in official documents such as cabinet manuals, legislative handbooks and legislative committee reports, as well as in influential scholarly texts. Such renderings are generally not enforceable by the courts, though even this notion that all conventions are non-enforceable via official channels has been persuasively challenged.[1]

Second, defining conventions as *binding* rules – a property which distinguishes them from non-obligatory customary practices – can also pose problems. The fact that numerous tests have been devised to address this issue speaks to the complexities of capturing what makes a convention distinctive in comparison to other kinds of informal rules and practices that impose expectations on actors.[2]

Third, there is some laxity in relation to when a norm might deserve the status of a constitutional convention. The lines drawn in this regard depend

1 See Ahmed et al. (2019) and also Jaconelli (1999: 26), who points out that constitutional conventions are sometimes incorporated into law as a reference, such as "the legal powers of a designated official (for example) are defined or limited in the statute by reference to the constitutional conventions relating to the exercise of his functions," thereby placing the convention within the purview of the courts.

2 See, for example, Marshall and Moodie (1967); de Smith 1977; Jaconelli 1999; Ahmed (2022), though Jennings' (1938) test continues to be used more often than any other.

very much on the boundaries that scholars place around their idea of a "constitution." If a constitution is understood as furnishing the meta rules from which all political rules emerge, then a constitutional convention may be defined as any norm that relates to any of those practices and offices created by the constitution, whether directly or indirectly. But if a narrower standard is applied to delineate a "constitution" – for example, when this term is used to describe one specific document (i.e., a country's formal written constitution) – then each constitutional convention must be directly traced to particular provisions within that special, entrenched document (Ahmed 2022; Siegel 2018), and the scope of what should be considered a convention will be considerably narrower.

The Ubiquity and Significance of Conventions

While conceptual ambiguities about constitutional conventions abound, the more basic point that such rules exist, and indeed emerge as a constitution becomes more established, is less in doubt. As a category within the broader class of "informal norms,"[3] conventions seem to inevitably arise in any political system. Their appearance – and, we argue, their *necessity* – emerges from the intrinsic limitations of the written word and thus of formal constitutional texts. Rules cannot be written to convey with precision all the intents of their crafters, nor to capture every contingency or circumstance in the present – let alone the future. When combined with the often high hurdles imposed to thwart ill-considered constitutional amendment, some constitutional clauses will slip into redundancy, or an event will occur that will expose a gap, which will then necessitate some shared understanding about how to deal with such matters (Albert 2015: 391).

Yet it would be incorrect to regard conventions as mere by-products of the challenge of inscribing rules or the failure of constitutional framers to see around "constitutional corners." Rather than treating them as incidental to a constitutional system, conventions have sometimes been intentionally cultivated as a system property. The reasons for this intentionality might be rooted in a country's constitutional culture. For example, conventions may be the preferred way to manage political relations in some countries, or because, as Michael Foley (2011) has argued, resolving disputes and practical problems through conventions is often less likely to result in conflict than when actors attempt to use written laws for this purpose. Indeed, some constitutional clauses are framed to make room for conventions to regulate aspects of their practice because these matters are thought to be best managed via

3 Helmke and Levitsky (2004: 727) define informal rules in a manner which chimes with most standard definitions of constitutional conventions: "socially shared rules, usually unwritten, that are created, communicated, and enforced outside of officially sanctioned channels."

political negotiation. For example, the office of the Australian Prime Minister cannot be found in the text of the Australian federal constitution. This was no accident on the part of the framers, who determined that this singularly important office should not be conceived in law but rather emerge and operate through convention (see, for example, Appleby 2018: 215). In seeking to avoid addressing certain matters in the text, constitutional drafters might employ a particular type of omission that Michael Foley (2011) refers to as "constitutional abeyances." Abeyances, according to Foley, are "packages of aggregated positions" that "include contradictions, tensions, anomalies and inequities" that cannot be explicitly addressed without undermining the entire constitutional edifice (2011: 9). Foley contends that these abeyances are properties of the constitution that "remain unspoken by convention" (2011: 10) because they cannot be explicitly embraced or declared without undermining the political and constitutional system.

That myriad reasons give rise to conventions means that they manifest in every type of political system. Whether they are referred to as conventions or informal constitutional norms, the presence of such rules has been observed across the full spectrum of political systems from non-democracies to democratising states to fully consolidated democracies (Helmke and Levitsky 2004: 725). However, while conventions are naturally occurring phenomena, they are not regarded in the same way, or valued to the same degree, across systems. In the United States, conventions have struggled to gain recognition, prominence and respect in law and politics (Vermeule 2015). Not only are they subordinated to the formal written constitution, they have also often been ignored over other, more controversial "unwritten rules" that arise from "judicial extrapolation from text and principle" (Appleby 2018: 211). Consequently, as Siegel observes (2018: 187), "the character of the U.S. Constitution leads to constitutional conventions being underenforced by elected officials and underappreciated by scholars," suggesting that conventions are, at best, undervalued and, at worst, lacking legitimacy.

In Westminster systems, by contrast, conventions are viewed as necessary (because, in the case of the United Kingdom (UK), there is no entrenched constitutional text) and desirable (because they provide flexible but binding rules) properties of the constitutional order. The same is true of Westminster offshoots such as Australia (Barry and Miragliotta 2015). Conventions in these settings tend to be accepted as authoritative and of comparable constitutional legitimacy to written law, even if they are also recognised as being a qualitatively different sort of rule (Barber 2010; Feldman 2013).[4]

4 See, for example, David Feldman, who notes: "The UK is peculiar in that the values of this tradition are generally accepted without conscious thought, and deviations from them are regarded as pathological rather than normal behaviour" (2013: 91).

Outside of Westminster contexts, however, conventions are more likely to be conceived of as an inferior or even a dangerous class of rule (note for example, Grzymala-Busse 2010; Lauth 2000).[5] The concerns here emerge largely from the mechanism of their enforcement, namely "political" rather than "legal" sanctions. This feature generates two sets of related concerns about informal rules: what they permit and what they fail to prohibit. In the case of the former, such rules, even if we accept that they may be desirable and useful, exist in tension with the rule of law, which assumes that rules are material, stable and enforceable by the courts. That informal rules permit departures from sanctioned written laws strains against this important constitutional principle. By contrast, in the case of the latter, these rules seem rather precarious because their enforcement depends on the particular sensitivity of an agent to political sanction. Exacting political consequences on agents for non-adherence is more difficult in settings where respect for the rule of law is weak, and political institutions are weakly institutionalised.

Nevertheless, regardless of their prominence in a country's constitutional debates and whether (or not) they are perceived to be a desirable property of the system, conventions play an important role in the functioning of political systems *of all kinds*. At the height of their power, these devices possess the ability to cancel, violate and supplement the entrenched constitutional text (Elster 2014: 50), an outcome which Heard (2005: 19) contends is vital because "we could scarcely live if we had to abide by all the formal laws and rules that apply" (see also Stephenson 2015). In doing so, conventions perform a great deal of invisible heavy lifting within any political system. They offer guidance to political elites about when and how to use their discretionary powers (Dicey 1897), they fill omissions when a written constitution is silent or unclear (Jennings 1938: 80), and they change – albeit informally – the meaning and application of formal constitutional rules (Albert 2015). They create an avenue for the constitutional system to evolve organically, by-passing the formal change process (Azari and Smith 2012). Conventions also clarify and implement the abstract principles that undergird the wider constitutional system (Ahmed 2022). The importance of conventions to the stability of the political system is perhaps most apparent when they are transgressed without sufficient reason or good cause. The violation of certain conventions is as destabilising as violations of written law, and perhaps even

5 Grzymala-Busse (2010: 311) observes that "formal institutions might be weakened or reinforced by informal rules, but the effectiveness of formal institutions is an outcome, not a precondition, of formal-informal interactions." See also her concerns that, "in transitional settings, informal institutions can replace, undermine, and support formal institutions irrespective of the latter's strength" (p. 331).

more so because a judicial umpire is not expected (as well as generally reluctant) to resolve such disputes (Barry and Miragliotta 2015).[6]

The Study of Constitutional Conventions

Despite the critical role of constitutional conventions and the consequences that non-observance of them can engender, they have not always attracted sustained attention from scholars. Much of the formative scholarship on constitutional conventions was concerned with describing their properties in terms of positive law. The classical texts on conventions, such as those by Dicey (1897), Jennings (1933) and Wheare (1951), sought to characterise and explain the nature and distinctive properties of these unwritten rules in relation to formal constitutional laws. Moreover, much of the formative literature was written specifically about these devices in Westminster contexts.

The emphasis on conventions in Westminster systems was sustained even in the 1980s, which witnessed renewed interest on the topic, exemplified by Geoffrey Marshall's (1987) influential book. Marshall's focus was on the status of conventions in the UK as a consequence of changes in the structures of government, electoral politics and party politics. Much of the literature which emerged in this period,[7] while still debating the classical questions about conventions, shifted attention to the ways in which long-standing constitutional norms were evolving in response to political, social and legal forces.

Several decades later, the scholarship became increasingly animated about the future of conventions in light of the trend towards the judicialisation of politics and the formalisation of conventions more specifically[8] (Galligan and Brenton 2015: 20–22; Blick and Hennessy 2011: 13). Formalisation refers to forms of enshrinement that occur outside of the formal constitutional text, whereas codification is used here to refer to the incorporation of conventions into the consolidated constitutional document. Formalisation is typified by the proliferation of "codes and circulars, guidance, official notices and memoranda" that replace "discretion" with "rules" (Rawlings 2000: 257; see also McHarg 2008; Bowden and MacDonald 2012), the imposition of statutory constraints on the executive (Blick 2016: 105) and creating what many regarded as unfavourable judicial incursions into the political

6 Andrew Heard (1989) argues that this is particularly true of what he terms *fundamental* and *meso conventions* of the constitution – the former because they "embody or buttress vital constitutional principles and are supported by general agreement on the existence and value of the principle involved, as well as on the terms of the rule itself" and the latter, which are "rules [that] ultimately protect widely accepted and important constitutional principles, but do not necessarily incorporate those principles closely" (1989: 72). Heard concludes that either type of convention, if breached, would cause significant upheaval.

7 See, for example, Forsey 1984.

8 Note earlier scholarship by Sampford (1987), for example.

constitution (Dodek 2011). Formalisation also led to questions about the suitability of these devices to hold modern political elites to account (Brazier 1992). Several important scholarly defences of the capacity of conventions to constrain relative to written law were published (Jaconelli 1999; Waldron 1999) while others raised concerns about the implications of formalisation practices for the development of conventions (McHarg 2008; Bowden and MacDonald 2012; Blick 2014; Barber 2010, chapter 6).[9]

Since the 2000s, U.S. scholars have increasingly turned their attention to conventions (Tushnet 2004; Balkin 2017; Posner and Vermeule 2008; Seigel 2018; Huq and Ginsburg 2018). This interest was sparked by the problem that Tushnet referred to as "constitutional hardball" (2004), which he defined as "political claims and practices – legislative and executive initiatives – that are without much question within the bounds of existing constitutional doctrine and practice but that are nonetheless in some tension with existing pre-constitutional understandings" (2004: 523). Concerns about unyielding polarisation among elites, and its implications for the observance of long-standing conventions, has been characterised as both a symptom and a cause of democratic malaise in the United States.

As this general overview suggests, conventions are not a new object of study. However, they are underdeveloped and underutilised as an analytical tool. There is, in short, value in putting conventions front and centre in the analysis of constitutions (see also Dixon and Stone 2018). It is a view that sheds new light both on constitutional law and politics, on the one hand, and on the role of conventions for system stability, on the other hand.[10]

A New Lens on Constitutional Law and Politics

The approach that this book advances, whereby conventions are highlighted and interrogated as a prism to understand law and politics, promises a number of valuable insights. Adopting a synoptic view of the chapters, we suggest there are at least three areas where this convention-centred approach yields clear and significant insights into the politics and law of modern constitutions.

9 For example, see Waldron's reasoning that little separates written law and conventions to the extent that: "in the end they amount to an interlocking set of rules and practices that depend on nothing more concrete and nothing more secure than those involved in political life to regulate and judge their own and others' behaviour by certain standards" (1999: 68). However, this does not mean that Waldron rejects entrenched constitutional text (see especially pp. 86–87).

10 An approach endorsed by the recent international project led by Vanessa MacDonnell that examines conventions from a comparative and interdisciplinary perspective is described at https://www.uottawa.ca/research-innovation/news-all/professor-vanessa-macdonnell-co-leads-major-17-million-international-project.

Mapping Conventions and Their Contexts

As a result of this volume's contributions, we gain a clearer understanding of what conventions are, how they differ from law and how to make sense of the variety of conventions and their effects on constitutional law and politics. This, we acknowledge, is not a new line of inquiry. As noted previously, earlier generations of scholarship have engaged with these questions. However, our analysis makes a number of novel contributions to the question of how we should think about the mapping of conventions.

First, it suggests the need to attend to conventions in different regime settings. The volume's chapters consider the operation of conventions in a variety of countries that represent significantly different political systems. These include established Westminster democracies, an established presidential democracy, an emerging presidential democracy and authoritarian states. The cases are, of course, not fully representative of these contexts. For instance, the class of Westminster democracies includes Australia, Canada and the United Kingdom, which display important legal and political differences – yet there are also deep commonalities connecting these three countries stemming from their Westminster origins. Likewise, the other classes that are relevant to the comparative aspect of this project also have their defining qualities. Cutting across these groups, we can understand the variation that this book taps as comprising the variables of "age" (i.e., old and new constitutional systems), "democratic credentials" (high, medium or low) and "separation of powers" (strong or weak).

Each of these dimensions might conceivably have some bearing on conventions and their relationship to law and politics. For example, age might be expected to affect conventions. However, although this hypothesis might be prompted by a reading of the volume, its main aim is something different. The chapters, especially the empirical ones, capture particular configurations of these variables, in which conventions are then analysed in depth. None of the chapters aims to be comprehensive with respect to all the conventions in that country. Mostly, they provide a snapshot. It is, however, a revealing and instructive snapshot, not only because the conventions selected are interesting in their own right, but also because the context in which they constrain is important. We learn about the broader context by knowing whether the convention in focus is adhered to (i.e., what are the general expectations regarding following conventions?), whether the convention is fully aligned with law (i.e., what is the relationship (complementary/clashing) between law and conventions?) and who has the power to change the convention (an individual, small collective, or large collective)? In these and other respects, the study of a specific convention can provide valuable and more general insights about that specific context as an environment for conventions.

The analyses of conventions *in their contexts* yields some important implications, several of which are counter-intuitive from the standpoint of the extant literature. To begin with, the analyses in the volume lead strongly to the conclusion that *conventions matter across all major forms of constitutional regime.*[11] This is an important qualification of the dominant view in the literature, which has tended to assume that conventions matter in the Westminster context but not elsewhere. Our analyses show, however, that conventions are detectable across highly varied contexts and have real effects – constraining actors, encouraging them to take some actions instead of others and carrying social, political and potential legal consequences for those who breach them. This observation is standard fare for Westminster democracies, but it is somewhat counter-intuitive for the other contexts that this volume considers, including authoritarian regimes. It may be surprising that conventions matter in these contexts because authoritarian leaders are often portrayed as being quite unconstrained – even hard laws and constitutions are unable to keep them in check. This volume shows, though, that conventions can have a constraining effect, even in an authoritarian context.

Likewise, we might not expect conventions to do much constraining work in new and democratising countries. Based on the existing scholarship on constitutions and political institutions, we might expect that the rules of democracy will be no more than weakly institutionalised in such contexts. Conventions take time to become well-established, and this process may not yet have had time to occur. What is more, in a new democracy, the regime may not hold much value as a constraint – and therefore, actors may be prepared to jettison and ignore emerging conventions in order to advance their political goals. The chapters in this volume suggest that conventions operate even in these challenging contexts, though perhaps in a different way from the way they do in established Westminster democracies. For example, the conventions in new democracies less consistently prevent actors from doing something they would otherwise do or compel them to do something they might otherwise resist. Yet they still shape the context in which decisions are made. Conventions provide the infrastructure around which expectations – and ultimately rules – are created, and they raise the stakes and costs of transgressing a rule. They also provide a rallying point for opposition actors. We might expect conventions to play a limited role in the U.S. presidential system for different reasons, because of the high status of the written constitution and the prominent role of judges in the interpretation of constitutional controversies. Again, our analyses reveal that conventions matter in this context, as well.

Cutting across these "unusual" contexts – autocratic, new democratic and presidential – we therefore see that the conventions lens brings something new, and that constitutional law and politics in these countries can be

11 In making this claim, we extend the growing interest in constitutionalism in authoritarian contexts (see e.g., Ginsburg and Simpser 2013)

analysed in terms of conventions, using a prism that has traditionally been thought to be useful only in the context of a Westminster democracy. Just as conventions help us to analyse these non-Westminster contexts in interesting ways, comparative analysis can also be productive for our understanding of conventions in the Westminster context where their role is clearer, they are relied upon to do a wider range of functions, and they seem to carry greater moral force. We might say that conventions matter more in the Westminster context and putting them centre stage in comparative analysis with non-Westminster regimes makes clear how and why this is the case. In short, what emerges from the perspective that we propose is a more nuanced understanding of the role conventions play in different systems.

The Condition and Dynamics of Conventions

Another novel theme that emerges out of this project is the need to take account of the *condition of conventions*. A convention can be robust – stable, legitimate, observed and feature prominently in the decision-making of political elites. Yet, conventions can come under strain even in established democracies. The actors who are meant to be bound by the convention may not be constrained by it; the transgressions may be so frequent and egregious that it stands to reason to ask whether the convention still exists. Of course, as previously noted, this scenario may be endemic in a democratising or autocratic context. More generally, however, there may be myriad causes of the weakening of a convention. It may be that there is an unprecedented crisis that is unmanageable through the existing web of conventions (and laws); it may be that broader social, institutional or political change has made the convention untenable; or the strain may come from the actions of a single, significant constitutional actor. Whatever the cause, it is clear from our volume that conventions may be in good health, poor health or somewhere between these poles.

The variability of causes of convention strain is matched by the range of potential consequences that can flow from this situation. A convention under strain might, in some cases, lead to the convention being replaced by a law or a new convention; it might also, alternatively, simply produce an unfilled gap in the system as the functional work that the convention used to do is not replaced. Another possibility is that the convention might bounce back, perhaps in a slightly modified way.

Taking conventions, their contexts and their conditions seriously opens up a thicker notion of conventions, which takes account of not only the conventions themselves but also the settings in which they operate, their robustness and stability as guidance for action, and the consequences of these matters for the broader constitutional system. Our approach encourages a focus on conventions and suggests that there is particular value in thinking about them from this perspective. In this richer, expanded view of conventions, the question of the dynamics of conventions then needs to be revised. It has two basic aspects. First, we can identify stability and change at the core – that is, in the convention itself (including its health). The relevant questions on this level might include the following: Is the convention rule applied as it used to be? Do elites observe it? Is the convention new? Does it appear to be relevant? Crucially, however, there is also a second aspect that is specifically concerned with the institutional conditions that support the convention. Is the convention supported to perform its normative purposes? Or are there features of the institutional and political context that have eroded the efficacy of the convention?

Conventions and Constitutions

The perspective on conventions that we advance also has implications for how we think about constitutions. Of course, we are not the first to regard conventions as being vital, and probably indispensable, to a functioning constitution. As noted earlier, this has been a prominent view of constitutionalism in the Westminster democracies. However, we want to take this well-rehearsed argument to the next level by bringing more clarity to the work that conventions do in a constitutional system. In this way, we highlight the advantages that close scrutiny of conventions brings for our conception of a constitution by placing them at the centre of constitutional analysis.

For this purpose, it is useful to consider how constitutions and conventions are related *historically*. While there are many different accounts of the origins of constitutions, we are drawn to accounts which elaborate the view that conventions may often predate written constitutions (e.g., Weingast 1997). From this standpoint, it is the conventions that represent the essence or heart of the constitution – the written document aims to codify the conventions (or at least a particular interpretation of them) into written form. The process will necessarily be an imperfect one. For example, the conventions may be somewhat fuzzy and disputed. Still, the written constitution aims to capture much of what many would consider the principles of the governmental system. In other words, its conventions. It is necessary to be more precise than this, however, so let us describe these pre-constitution conventions (following Heard) as the system's *fundamental conventions*. This kind of convention can tell us a great deal about the values underlying a constitutional system, especially when those are agreed upon since these are the principles that are likely to become the new basic law of the constitution. An interesting set of questions arises when the values shift, yet the written constitution remains unchanged. To the extent that the new set of values impinge on government, it can be said that the conventions underlying the constitution have shifted, and we have in this situation a scenario whereby the laws of the constitution and its conventions are no longer in sync.

Once the constitution has been crafted, ratified and promulgated, conventions also matter in other, practical ways. While the constitution may try to prescribe and proscribe many actions and behaviour, it is inevitable that it will leave gaps. If constitutional actors worked strictly, and only, to the rules of the constitution, there are many important actions that could not happen (or would not occur in a timely, efficient manner). Another kind of convention is therefore needed to smooth the operation of the constitutional system in practice. We might describe these as *operational conventions*.

From this perspective, then, the constitution depends on conventions in two senses – both for its founding and grounding, but also for its day-to-day functioning. Conversely, seen through the prism of conventions, the written constitution is an attempt at making conventions legible. Why is this valuable? One reason is that this can be efficient, which is an outcome that is highly prized by the modern state (Scott 1998). Having flexible, open-ended rules can be a liability to the many tasks that a modern state seeks to perform and for which standardised processes are necessary (or at least beneficial). However, there are risks associated with the attempt to control through comprehensive planning and the technicalities of written law. At one extreme, the effort to exert maximum control through formal rules and their policy equivalent, micro-management, has been the root cause of the biggest disasters in social engineering, as James Scott (1998) observes. Although these disasters usually arise in the context of "an authoritarian state that is willing and able to use the full weight of its coercive power to bring [the] high-modernist designs into being" (Scott 1998: 5), even without going to this extreme, the effort to exercise to control through codification can create obstacles to spontaneity, organic development and improvisation in the face of unpredictable events.

A focus on conventions therefore raises questions about how a constitutional system manages crisis. Is it by searching within an authoritative rulebook for relevant provisions and precedents, as the paradigm of written constitutionalism suggests, supported by the authority given to judges? Or is it by entrusting mostly political actors with the responsibility to deal with crises on the basis of the system's conventions? This difference in the management of crisis hints at another important contrast that a focus on conventions relates to. This is the contrast between legal constitutionalism, whereby the constitution is managed by judges (which is what written law enables and indeed typically requires), and forms of political constitutionalism (which are more salient in convention-dominated constitutional areas), whereby politicians play the leading role in navigating constitutional questions.

New Insights Into Constitutional Conventions

The chapters in this book engage with conventions through diverse theoretical and empirical analyses. What emerges is a body of new insights into the nature of conventions and their impact on political and legal systems. Four clear themes are revealed which in turn inform the new approach to conventions that we develop, providing the structure and organisation of this book. First, the volume proposes a more nuanced theoretical view of what constitutes a convention and how conventions relate to other core concepts in law and political science. Second, instead of the static view of conventions that dominates in the existing literature, we take seriously their flexible and adaptive nature, examining how they evolve over time. Third, we interrogate the rigour of conventions by analysing their resilience when they come under pressure from politicians who seek to challenge the constitutional status quo. Finally, we explore the political and jurisprudential value of the concept of constitutional conventions by examining the insights they yield not only in the long-standing liberal democratic contexts in which they are usually studied but also in democratising and autocratic states. In these ways, the book aims to deepen and broaden our understanding of conventions, demonstrating our core contention that conventions should be regarded as a crucial feature of a constitutional system, and thereby their significance in comparative studies of constitutional law and politics.

The book explores, as its first theme, new conceptual and theoretical ground in the study of conventions. Existing accounts have often adopted a narrow approach to analysing conventions, with a concentration on conceptual questions about the relationship between conventions and the law, while giving much less attention to the deeper theoretical and historical contexts that inform these questions, and the distinct but related questions about the way in which conventions shape the behaviour of political actors. The chapters in the book's first section explore these themes. Haig Patapan's Chapter 2 examines the theoretical, historical and political assumptions about law and constitutions that underpin different understandings of conventions. It argues that these deeper differences help explain why there is such persistent disagreement over the legitimacy and efficacy of conventions. Zim Nwokora's Chapter 3 examines the dominant theoretical assumptions about political actors that underpin existing academic research on conventions. The chapter identifies two distinct approaches – the moral and the strategic – that have not been brought into dialogue with each other, arguing that these approaches can be brought together, and that doing so generates new insights into the effects of conventions and helps set an agenda for future research.

The book is also marked by a focus on the dynamic analysis of conventions, the second theme that delineates the book's distinctive approach. Scholars have long noted the flexible nature of constitutional conventions, which can more readily adapt to changing social and political circumstances than the provisions of an entrenched constitution. However, there have been relatively few attempts to study and explain systematically how and why constitutional conventions change over time. In contrast to the tendency to provide a static account of conventions, focused on a single point in time, our dynamic approach shifts the analysis onto the evolution of conventions in changing social and institutional conditions. These issues are explored in the second section of the book, in which the chapters examine various stages and features in what Barry et al. (2019: 672–673) have called the "life cycle" of a convention (see also Jaconelli 2013). Graeme Orr's Chapter 4 is a detailed case study of the emergence of a new convention regarding the eligibility of members of parliament (MPs) to sit in the Australian federal parliament. This case study reveals important insights into how conventions emerge, how they relate to political power and how pervasive they are in politics and constitutionalism. Narelle Miragliotta and Frank Algra-Maschio examine in Chapter 5 how actors interpret and justify convention departures. Focusing on the UK's Salisbury-Addison convention, this chapter identifies instances of elite resistance to the convention between 1945 and 2021, and finds that some political actors attempt to circumvent this convention by invoking the principles on which it rests. This reveals that acts of resistance can strengthen a convention, thereby ensuring its ongoing relevance. Sarah Murray's Chapter 6 examines how conventions are affected by broader shifts in a country's constitutional framework. As a case study, the chapter focuses on the debate over whether constitutional conventions should be codified if Australia were to become a republic. Her analysis reveals that constitutional conventions are a crucial feature of constitutional identity in Westminster systems like Australia, which explains why the debate over codification – and, in part, the republic – is so fraught.

The third major theme of the book explores the power, influence and resilience of conventions in hostile political conditions when they are placed under intense strain – for example, by populist politicians who resist and even undermine or overturn constitutional constraints. The dynamic approach adopted in this collection enables us to analyse how conventions operate under pressure. Building on the distinction between moral and strategic accounts of conventions developed in the first part, and the account of convention evolution outlined in the second, Nicholas Barry's Chapter 7 develops a theoretical account of the ways in which conventions are affected by different forms of populism. Barry's account helps strengthen our understanding of an under-explored aspect of the populist threat to constitutionalism, while giving us a clearer theoretical standpoint from which to judge its long-term implications for constitutional democracy. James P. Pfiffner examines in Chapter 8 the issue of strained conventions through a case study of conventions during the Donald Trump presidency in the United States. His chapter outlines the ways in which Trump violated long-standing conventions, most notably by repeatedly – and falsely – claiming that he won the 2020 election. These chapters reveal that the effects of populist leaders on conventions is often part of a longer-term trend of constitutional erosion, and that it has adverse consequences for the future of constitutional government.

The fourth major theme of the book is the relevance of constitutional conventions beyond the Anglo-American world. Although case studies of Westminster democracies and, increasingly, the United States dominate the existing literature on constitutional conventions and norms, this volume's scope extends beyond these long-standing liberal democracies. Baogang He's Chapter 9 examines the role of constitutional conventions in China's authoritarian political system. He finds that succession rules do have some of the characteristics of constitutional conventions and may even act as constraints within an authoritarian state. David Kosař and Attila Vincze's Chapter 10 investigates how conventions shape law and politics in central Europe, and particularly post-communist Czechia and Hungary. Their chapter shows that conventions have played different roles in the political discourse in both of these countries, and they have been conceptualised in different ways in these countries – including by the courts. Focusing on the different paths in the dynamics of conventions in these countries provides important insights into the post-communist constitutional legacy in Europe. The case studies in this final part yield insights into how conventions operate in very different social and political conditions, and they suggest the value of incorporating conventions into comparative analyses of constitutional governance.

Conclusion

In this book, we argue that conventions are a valuable lens through which modern constitutions can be understood. To demonstrate the merits of such a convention-centred approach, we undertake a new theoretical engagement with the question of the nature of conventions; examine their provenance, development and application; investigate their efficacy in shaping, guiding and restraining the contours of politics; and, finally, show their potential to reveal new insights into contemporary comparative constitutionalism. Once the salience of constitutional conventions is acknowledged, then a series of compelling questions emerge for future research and examination. We suggest that these insights into constitutional conventions provide the conceptual foundations and architecture for new research directions into the politics and law of constitutions. These new research questions include, for example, the best means of managing conventions in the course of constitutional reform or innovation, the important yet little examined question of the relationship between conventions and regime type, the nature of conventions in different religious and cultural settings, and the extent to which conventions foster or limit innovation and progress.

Consider, for instance, the question of how conventions – and, more generally, constitutions – can shape civic culture, which is a complex and profound question. But for our purposes it is useful to distinguish between "liberal" and "classical" conceptions of constitutions to show the variety of approaches regarding the educative role of constitutions. For influential thinkers of the liberal approach, constitutions are typically devised as forms of social contract intended to protect individual rights and limit governments. They therefore defray authority, institutionalise checks and balances, and are in effect "power maps," or rules intended to instruct citizens of their rights and "players" or elites of acceptable or permitted ranges of actions. In contrast, the classical approach to constitutions regards them not as means to limit or confine power, but as organic expressions or foundational articulations of civic principles and aspirational goals and visions of the community. They are, therefore, not only legal measures but fundamentally political, social, cultural and religious in character, devised to educate and instruct both individuals and leaders in civics, and more comprehensively, the appropriate vision of citizenship informed by civility, duty, trust and amity favoured and endorsed by each community. This admittedly broad and general dichotomy allows us to see that conventions have different purposes and roles in each form of constitution, which in turn determines their status and importance. A proper understanding of the educative role of constitutions therefore requires an appreciation of conventions. In turn, in examining the educative role of conventions, we surmount disciplinary demarcations to provide a much richer account of the politics and law of the modern constitutions.

The focus on the educative role of conventions and the other research themes we have identified show the rich potential for scholarship opened up by our focus on constitutional conventions. Adopting conventions as a theoretical lens will also make possible many other new research directions. Whatever their ultimate findings and insights, the potential for these research directions reveals and confirms the importance of constitutional conventions as an innovative lens for the study of the politics and law of modern constitutions.

References

Ahmed, A. (2022). A theory of constitutional norms. *Michigan Law Review*, 120(7): 1361–1418.

Ahmed, F., Albert, R., & Perry, A. (2019). Judging constitutional conventions. *International Journal of Constitutional Law*, 17(3): 1146–1165.

Albert, R. (2015). How unwritten constitutional norms change written constitutions. *Dublin University Law Journal*, 38: 387.

Appleby, G. (2018). Unwritten rules. In: C. Saunders & A. Stone (Eds.), *The Oxford handbook of the Australian constitution*. Oxford University Press, 209–236.

Azari, J. R., & Smith, J. K. (2012). Unwritten rules: Informal institutions in established democracies. *Perspectives on Politics*, 10(1): 37–55.

Balkin, J. (2017). Constitutional crisis and constitutional rot. *Maryland Law Review*, 77(1): 147.

Barber, N. W. (2010). *The constitutional state*. Oxford University Press.

Barry, N., & Miragliotta, N. (2015). Australia. In B. Galligan & S. Brenton (Eds.), *Constitutional conventions in Westminster systems: Controversies, changes and challenges*. Cambridge University Press.
Barry, N., Miragliotta, N., & Nwokora, Z. (2019). The dynamics of constitutional conventions in Westminster democracies. *Parliamentary Affairs*, 72(3): 664–683.
Blick, A. (2014). The cabinet manual and the codification of conventions. *Parliamentary Affairs*, 67: 191–208.
Blick, A., & Hennessy, P. (2011). *The hidden wiring emerges: The cabinet manual and the working of the British Constitution*. Institute for Public Policy Research.
Bowden, J., & MacDonald, N. (2012). Writing the unwritten: The officialization of constitutional convention in Canada, the United Kingdom, New Zealand and Australia. *Journal of Parliamentary and Political Law*, 6: 365–398.
Brazier, R. (1992). The non-legal constitution: Thoughts on convention, practice and principle. *Northern Ireland Legal Quarterly*, 43(3): 262–287.
de Smith, S. A. (1977). *Constitutional and administrative law*. Penguin.
Dicey, A. V. (1897). *Introduction to the study of the law of the constitution*. Macmillan, 5th ed.
Dixon, R., & Stone, A. (Eds.). (2018). *The invisible constitution in comparative perspective*. Cambridge University Press.
Dodek, A. M. (2011). Courting constitutional danger: Constitutional conventions and the legacy of the patriation reference. *Supreme Court Law Review*, 54: 117–142.
Elster, J. (2014). Political norms. *YWN*, 63: 47–59.
Feldman, D. (2013). Constitutional conventions. In: M. Qvortrup (Ed.), *The British constitution: Continuity and change*. Bloomsbury Publishing, 93–120.
Foley, M. (2011). *The silence of constitutions (Routledge revivals): Gaps, 'abeyances' and political temperament in the maintenance of government*. Routledge.
Forsey, E. (1984). The courts and the conventions of the constitution. *University of New Brunswick Law Journal*, 33: 11–42.
Galligan, B., & Brenton, S. (Eds.). (2015). *Constitutional conventions in Westminster systems*. Cambridge University Press.
Ginsburg, T., & Simpser, A. (Eds.). (2013). *Constitutions in authoritarian regimes*. Cambridge University Press.
Grzymala-Busse, A. (2010). The best laid plans: The impact of informal rules on formal institutions in transitional regimes. *Studies in Comparative International Development*, 45: 311–333.
Heard, A. (1989). Recognizing the variety among constitutional conventions. *Canadian Journal of Political Science/Revue Canadienne De Science Politique*, 22(1): 63–82.
Heard, A. (2005). Constitutional conventions and parliament. *Canadian Parliamentary Review*, 28(2): 19–22.
Helmke, G., & Levitsky, S. (2004). Informal institutions and comparative politics: A research agenda. *Perspectives on Politics*, 2(4): 725–740.
Huq, A., & Ginsburg, T. (2018). How to lose constitutional democracy. *UCLA Law Review*, 65(1): 78–169.
Jaconelli, J. (1999). The nature of constitutional convention. *Legal Studies*, 19(1): 24–46.
Jennings, W. I. (1933). *The law and the constitution*. University of London Press.
Jennings, W. I. (1938). *The law and the constitution*. University of London Press.
Lauth, H.-J. (2000). Informal institutions and democracy. *Democratization*, 7(4): 21–50.
Marshall, G. (1987). *Constitutional conventions: The rules and forms of political accountability*. Oxford University Press.

Marshall, G., & Moodie, G. C. (1967). *Some problems of the constitution.* Hutchinson University Library.

McHarg, A. (2008). Reforming the United Kingdom constitution: Law, convention, soft law. *The Modern Law Review*, 71(6): 853–877.

Posner, E., & Vermeule, A. (2008). Constitutional showdowns. *University of Pennsylvania Law Review*, 156(4): 991–1048.

Rawlings, R. (2000). Concordats of the constitution. *Law Quarterly Review*, 116: 257–286.

Sampford, C. J. (1987). Recognize and declare: An Australian experiment in codifying constitutional conventions. *Oxford Journal of Legal Studies*, 7(3): 369–420.

Scott, J. (1998). *Seeing like a state: How certain schemes to improve the human condition have failed.* Yale University Press.

Siegel, N. S. (2018). Political norms, constitutional conventions, and President Donald Trump. *Indiana Law Journal*, 93: 177–205.

Stephenson, S. (2015). When constitutional conventions fail. *Dublin University Law Journal*, 38(2): 447–464.

Tushnet, M. (2004). Constitutional hardball. *The John Marshall Law Review*, 37(2): 523.

Vermeule, A. (2015). Conventions in court. *Dublin University Law Journal*, 38(2): 283–310.

Waldron, J. (1999). *Law and disagreement.* Oxford University Press.

Weingast, B. (1997). The political foundations of democracy and the rule of law. *American Political Science Review*, 91(2): 245–263.

Wheare, K. C. (1951). *Modern constitutions.* Oxford University Press.

Chapter 2

What Are Constitutional Conventions?

Common Law, Legal Positivism and Liberal Perspectives

Haig Patapan

On 2 October 1980, Prime Minister Pierre Trudeau of Canada announced that Ottawa would make a unilateral request to the British Parliament to amend Canada's constitution, allowing Canada to modify the constitution itself, and to entrench the Charter of Rights and Freedoms. Eight provinces opposed the plan and sought the Canadian Supreme Court's judgment regarding the constitutionality of the federal government's attempt to 'patriate' the constitution, making Canada independent of Britain. In the *Patriation Reference*, the Canadian Supreme Court unanimously held the proposed changes to the Constitution would affect the 'powers, rights, or privileges' of the provinces and a majority held that there was a constitutional convention obliging the federal government to seek the consent of the provinces before asking the Parliament of the United Kingdom to modify the constitution.[1] But a majority also found that the federal government had the *legal* authority to unilaterally seek the amendment without consent of the provinces as the requirement of provincial consent 'had not crystallized into law'. As it was not the role of the courts to enforce constitutional conventions, in cases of conflict, 'the courts are bound to enforce the legal rules'.[2] The Supreme Court's *Patriation Reference* revealed a puzzling approach to constitutional conventions. It confirmed the complexity of constitutions by recognising both their 'written' and 'unwritten' aspects. Yet in acknowledging the 'unwritten' constitution, it simultaneously seemed to depreciate it, by deciding that it was a matter of 'politics' and not 'law'; the court was unwilling to adjudicate the 'unwritten', and where there was a conflict between the written and the unwritten, the court would always favour the written. The Supreme Court's *Patriation Reference* decision thereby exposed complex and equivocal views

1 *Re Resolution to Amend the Constitution* [1981] 1 SCR 753. The Chief Justice and Estey and McIntyre JJ. dissenting that there was such a convention (760).
2 Per Laskin C.J. and Dickson, Beetz, Estey, McIntyre, Chouinard and Lamer JJ. (759).

DOI: 10.4324/9781003506577-2

regarding the nature of constitutional conventions, their relationship to law and the role of the judiciary in adjudicating them.[3]

This diversity of views and opinions is evident in the political and legal scholarship on the nature and significance of constitutional conventions. Constitutional conventions have been defined as the 'nonlegal, or informal, rules that regulate how political actors and institutions interact'.[4] But the variety in the alternative terms for conventions – as 'morality' of the constitution, 'soft law', 'norms' and 'informal institutions' – attest to the complexity of the phenomenon and to the range of disciplinary approaches in attempting to understand it.[5] This complexity finds its way to the core debates on the nature of conventions. Whether unwritten conventions are legal and therefore justiciable remains a contested question in the scholarship.[6] Equally problematic has been the efficacy and legitimacy of conventions.[7] Finally, there is a variety of attempts to provide a typology of conventions, sociological examinations of why they bind and how they evolve – in effect a life-cycle of conventions from their origins to their 'decomposition' and 'deterioration'.[8] These discussions often take place and therefore are inflected by the constitutional and jurisprudential questions concerning specific countries, especially England and Westminster-based regimes such as Australia, Canada and New Zealand, while the American scholarship concedes that it is a question that has received insufficient attention.[9] There is therefore a continuing contestation in the scholarship

3 The Supreme Court verdict resulted in negotiations and a conference, which culminated in the patriation of the Constitution on 17 April 1982. On conventions in Canadian constitutionalism, see Heard (1991). See, however, Ahmed et al. (2019) on the judicial enforcement of conventions in India, the UK and Canada.

4 Barry et al. (2019, 1). See also the definitions in Jaconelli (1999); McHarg (2008); Blick (2014); Feldman (2013).

5 On 'morality', see Dicey as cited in Jaconelli (1999). On 'soft law' and 'hard law', see McHarg (2008). On 'norms', see the American scholarship, especially Chafetz and Pozen (2018), Renan (2018) and Siegal (2018). On 'informal institutions', see Helmke and Levitsky (2004) and Azari and Smith (2012); on rational choice institutionalism, see Strong (2021).

6 See Jaconelli (2005); McHarg (2008); Renan (2018) and Whittington (2013).

7 For critical approaches to the efficacy of conventions and constitutional norms, see Chafetz and Pozen (2018); Fleming and Schleiter (2020). On the question of legitimacy, see Perry and Tucker (2018).

8 For typologies, see Azari and Smith (2012), who look at functions of informal institutions; Jaconelli (2005), who distinguishes between power conferring and duty imposing conventions; and Perry and Tucker (2018), who distinguish between 'top down' and 'bottom up' conventions. On typologies of change, see Barry et al. (2019), and on destruction and decomposition of norms in the American context, see Chafetz and Pozen (2018); Helmke and Levitsky (2004).

9 On Westminster influenced countries, see generally, Galligan and Brenton (2015); Duncan (2015); McHarg (2008); Menzies and Tiernan (2014); Mulherin (2020); Strong (2021). On the American scholarship, see Siegel (2018); Renan (2018); Azari and Smith (2012).

regarding the nature of constitutional conventions, whether they are laws or not, and therefore whether they are subject to judicial review or a matter of political adjudication. In spite of this diversity of the scholarship, there is nevertheless a general consensus on the importance of constitutional conventions, not only theoretically, as a question of jurisprudence and political philosophy, but as a matter of political consequence, both in shaping contemporary political practice and for their far-reaching salience for future constitutional change and innovation. There are therefore compelling theoretical and practical reasons for gaining a clearer understanding of constitutional conventions.

In this chapter, I explore this diversity of views to provide greater clarity regarding the nature, legitimacy and efficacy of constitutional conventions. My core argument is that different theoretical presuppositions and the specific constitutional context inform and shape our understanding of constitutional conventions. More specifically, and focusing on what I consider are the most influential jurisprudential approaches and traditions for understanding conventions, I argue that disputes concerning the nature of constitutional conventions have their theoretical origins in the way the English common law understanding was challenged and transformed by new schools of political and legal thought, in particular legal positivism and liberal constitutionalism that questioned the origin, form and justiciability of 'unwritten' constitutional laws. In terms of constitutional practice, I propose that our understanding of the contending views regarding constitutional conventions is shaped by the way these theoretical conceptions were employed and in turn transformed by the unique constitutionalism of specific states that took their bearings from Westminster, either in adopting and modifying its political and juridical principles – such as Australia, Canada and New Zealand – or in repudiating important aspects as in American republicanism.

In the discussion that follows, I outline how the common law – informed by classical and scholastic influences – conceived constitutional conventions as law subject to adjudication by judges. I then examine a major challenge to this common law understanding in the form of legal positivism and how this approach reconceived law as the command of the sovereign, and in doing so, questioned the authority of 'unwritten' laws and of the 'artificial reasoning' of common law judges. The third major source I explore is liberal constitutionalism that derived its conception of politics and law from the natural rights of individuals and posed a challenge to both the common law and positivistic conceptions of constitutional conventions. This necessarily synoptic discussion of these contending jurisprudential conceptions of conventions provides the basis for examining the extent to which these ideas shaped subsequent thought and practice, noting in particular how the confluence and conflict of these views account for the scholarship on conventions in England, the United States and those countries that have drawn on both English and American constitutionalism for their founding.

Common Law

To gain a better insight into the nature of constitutional conventions, it is instructive to start with the English common law that favoured 'unwritten' laws and conventions. The historical roots of the common law can be traced to the innovations in the institutions of justice such as the central courts that administered the common law, as well as the rise of the writ and jury systems.[10] The common law was distinctive for being *ius non scriptum*, or unwritten law, based on the view that law was discerned or emerged in the course of oral arguments within a procedural framework.[11] Thus, central to the common law were the concepts of 'deliberative reasoning' and 'reasonable usage'. The best-known statement of this view was Coke's description of the common law in his famous and influential *Institutes* (1832, 97b) as 'perfection of reason':

> for reason is the life of the law, nay the common law itselfe is nothing else but reason; which is to be understood of an artificiall perfection of reason gotten by long study, observation, and experience, and not every man's naturall reason.[12]

For contemporary scholars who presume that a law must be written, its existence and validity determined by its 'source', and its meanings and provisions to be evaluated by abstract theoretical speculation, this formulation can seem puzzling. It is therefore important to understand what is meant by 'artificial reason', not only because it is central to understanding of the common law and its preference for the 'unwritten', but also to appreciate how the common law engaged with custom, precedent and parliamentary enactments.

A valuable insight into complex and multilayered notion of 'artificial reason' can be found in the overview by Postema (2003a, 2003b), who notes six distinguishing aspects of the common law reason. Artificial reason, according to Postema (2003b, 3–4), was pragmatic, so that common law lawyers sought to resolve immediate problems with materials to hand, within the larger context of a public mission, with due regard to justice and the commonweal. Relying on experience and practice, artificial reason drew on contextual competence, acquired through long years of immersion in the particularity of law

10 See generally Caenegem (1973), Milson (1969), Postema (2011), Stoner (1992).

11 See in particular Hale's *The History of the Common Law of England* cited in Postema (2003a, 174).

12 As Siegel (1981, 31) puts it,

> In sum, since Coke conceives English law as so exclusively rooted in immemorial custom and usage, he, even more than St. German and Fortescue, views English law as consisting of and drawn from an unsystematic mass of ancient rules which, nonetheless, are unfathomably wise.

rather than the study of abstract elements or principles of a systematic body of knowledge. Accordingly, common law adjudication did not seek to find a relevant rule and apply it but used analogical reasoning drawing on experience, resisting the reduction of the law to axioms. The law was to be found in the accumulated experience recorded in the books and memories of common law jurists, not in any theory or articulation of this experience (6). This meant that the artificial reason of the common law was essentially 'discoursive', a matter of deliberative reasoning and argument in an interlocutory and forensic setting, where argument permitted the light of reason to disclose the law (7). Consequently, though previous argumentation and judgment shaped the nature and formulation of the claims that could be put forward, it was cross examination that determined public standards of success in pursuing common judgment in the face of partial disputes. Finally, common law reason was considered common or shared but required the practice of forensic argument in court. Though it drew on settled common law and custom and authorities in past cases, it was not an exercise in abstract reasoning that sought general principles. It did not seek the moral vision of an individual or the partial perspective of the litigants; it was 'artificial' not because of any special insight, but because 'it is the disciplined practice of argument and disputation in a public forum' or a 'product of reflexive practical experience' (10). It is on this basis that the common law drew on custom or unwritten law that was immemorial though also variable.[13] This conception of reason also accounted for its complex and contradictory treatment of Acts of Parliament, whereby legislation was regarded as declaratory or remedial, and its treatment of precedent as instructive but not binding.[14]

This view of the common law reason, according to Postema (2003b, 10), 'challenged both natural law and positivist views of law'. It did so, I suggest, by drawing upon classical political philosophy, especially of Aristotle's conception of the regime and the importance of *phronesis* or prudence. Each *polis* or city, according to Aristotle's *Politics* (1278b10), is constituted by a *politeia* or regime that comprehends both written and unwritten laws, whereby the regime is defined as the governing body or the arrangement of

13 Whether immemorial meant unchanging, see Postema (2003a, 168–176), who contrasts the Coke–Davies approach with that of Hale–Selden, who endorsed a constantly evolving common law.

14 The common law questioned the integrity of enactments as an exercise of particular wills, or as in *lex facit legem*, viewed parliament as deriving its authority from the common law, so that the continued validity of legislative declaratory and remedial enactments were subject to their incorporation, accommodation and use by common law judges and the people (Postema 2003b, 20). As Postema (2003b, 11–17) shows, the common law emphasis on particulars meant that rules or maxims pointed to the law, rather than settling it. But there was a notion of precedent in a more general sense, understood as prior decisions requiring judicial respect, inviting and focusing on reasoning employed in previous decisions.

the authoritative offices in the city. Aristotle's conception of regime denies that it can be a neutral or merely administrative arrangement. Because a city aims at living well or noble actions, it is not merely a 'defensive alliance' or only 'a partnership in a location and for the sake of not committing injustice against each other and of transacting business'. Each regime, with its institutions, offices and laws, will therefore pursue a distinctive vision of the good life. Aristotle acknowledges the tension between the rule of the wise and rule of law in his extended discussion of the benefits of each form of rule, concluding that the rule of law – especially when the laws are made by the wise – is necessary, provided there is scope for individuals to adjudicate, deliberate and judge regarding particulars (*Politics*, 1286a–1288b). This form of adjudicating required *phronesis* or prudence. Aristotle in his *Nicomachean Ethics* (1103a15) considers prudence to be an intellectual virtue that differs from *theoria* or science with its universal and invariable rules, *poiesis* or 'making' whose end was fabrication, and mere 'cleverness' (114a10; 1144a26). The aim of prudence is *praxis* or considered, virtuous action (1140b6–7). Prudence required virtue but also extensive experience, and it was especially concerned with making good decisions in specific cases, taking into account the unique aspects of each case (1142a11–15). It was therefore a virtue that drew on theoretical insights as well as the moral virtues, such as magnanimity, liberality and courage. Recognising the demands of specific circumstances, it acknowledged the need to reconcile principle with the claims of contingency and necessity.[15] The Aristotelian – and later scholastic – conception of law was influential in the development of English common law.[16] As Siegel (1981) shows, the leading common law jurists, the medieval judge Sir John Fortescue (1400–1476), Renaissance lawyer Christopher St. German (1460–1540) and Elizabethan judge, Privy Councillor and Parliamentarian

15 See *Nicomachean Ethics*, 1143a35–b5. To the extent that prudence could not be simply reduced to laws or rules, it showed the limitations of written enactments. Note in this context Socrates's famous and detailed critique of writing in Plato's *Phaedrus* (274e), intended to show its limitations compared to the advantages of conversation and dialogue that he considers the only true form of philosophical engagement. Plato seems to concur, noting the limitations of writing in his *Second Letter* (314c–d) and in particular in the *Seventh Letter* (341c–342; 344c–d) where he denies that philosophical insights can ever be captured in writing that is unalterable, contrasting it to conversations that like a blaze kindled by a spark, yield insights that are self-sustaining. On the philosophical superiority of writing over oral or recitative approaches, see Gee (1988, 199–200). For an overview of the political role of writing see, for example, Fisher (1966), Hyland (1968), Griswold (2008), Scott (2009), Patapan (2023, 171–190).

16 This classical conception of politics and law was altered by revealed religion. Thus, Thomas Aquinas, who profoundly shaped scholastic thought, called classical and especially Aristotelian philosophy *ancilla theologiae* or handmaiden to theology in his attempt to reconcile natural reason with divine revelation. Consequently, we find Aristotelian conceptions of law inform Thomistic theology and jurisprudence; see in particular the 'Treatise of Law', Questions 90–108 of the First of Second Part of the *Summa Theologiae* (Aquinas 1952).

Sir Edward Coke (1552–1634) drew on natural law and Aristotelian epistemology in their reflections and explication of the common law. For example, Aristotelian right reason, general and particular customs, maxims, statutes and equity were seen as guides to God's eternal law. The common law was therefore regarded as an Aristotelian practical science, whereby judgment rather than the formulation of abstract principles was necessary for determining controversies. This approach to adjudication meant that the ancient laws and determinations provided a matchless aggregate of experience and wisdom. Common law reason therefore recalls Aristotle's phronesis, applied to the specific sphere of the law, making it into a *juris*prudence.

In sum, the common law approach – drawing on classical and scholastic traditions – rejected laws as creatures of contract or agreement, with limited purposes and ends. Rather, the authority, wisdom and justice of law derived from a variety of sources, attested by their ancient lineage. The common law's constitution was not simply a written enactment; it acknowledged both written and unwritten laws. Consequently, judges were required to use their judgment, refined over years of study, to discern how the general wisdom of these laws could be interpreted to apply to the specific circumstances.

Legal Positivism

This common law approach would in time be challenged by new perspectives that would attempt to overturn both the classical and religious foundations of the common law.[17] Francis Bacon's scientific method was appropriated and deployed in politics by his secretary Thomas Hobbes, who attempted to found a politics and jurisprudence on wholly new principles. Starting with the individual rights of nature, Hobbes argues that to secure peace and prosperity, each individual in the state of nature authorises the actions of the sovereign who will enforce a foundational social contract to establish a Levithan state. This new commonwealth, an attempt to solve political instability though law and constitutionalism, has far-reaching implications for common law and natural law, as is evident from Hobbes' early political works, *De Cive* (1642) and the *Leviathan* (1651) as well as his *A Dialogue between a Philosopher and Student of the Common Laws of England* (1681), a polemic against Sir Edward Coke.[18] The general tenor of Hobbes' arguments challenging the common law approach can be seen in his 'Of Civill Lawes', Chapter XXVI of the *Leviathan* (1981, 311–335). According to Hobbes, the civil laws are rules

17 For a detailed examination of the nature of this confrontation, see Siegel (1981, 21ff) and more generally Stoner (1992).

18 For his argument in *De Cive*, see in particular Chapters II, V, VI and XI. For the discussion of the common law in the *Dialogue*, see especially his critique of the common-lawyer and his rejection of artificial reason: 'the reason of the common law is not a special treasure of a single guild': Hobbes (1978, 54–55, 61–62).

of right and wrong commanded by the commonwealth. As the legislator in all commonwealths is the sovereign, laws are the commands of the sovereign and therefore the sovereign can never be subject to the law. Hobbes denies that there can be unjust laws, since it is the law that determines what is right and wrong. He accepts that length of usage or custom may be a source of law, but only if authorised by the sovereign, whose will is the only source of law. He therefore denies the 'foolish opinion of Lawyers' that the common law can only be changed by parliament or that it requires 'Artificiall perfection of Reason' – it is the reason and command of the sovereign and not the '*Juris prudentia*, or wisedome of subordinate Judges' that make laws. Finally, unwritten laws are laws of nature summarised as 'Do not that to another, which thou thinkest unreasonable done by another to thy self', otherwise, commands must be written and published to become law (311–318).

Such a positivistic notion of law would continue to clash with the common law approach as we can see from Jeremy Bentham's (1789) *An Introduction to the Principles of Morals and Legislation* in which he castigates the 'sinister interest' of rulers, lawyers and religious leaders, rejects rights as 'nonsense on stilts', defends egalitarian hedonism as a moral foundation for reforming laws and advocates codification of all common law as the essential means for initiating legal and economic reform. The Benthamite approach to politics and law was influential in subsequent English jurisprudence, evident in John Austin's (1832) *The Province of Jurisprudence Determined* where Austin attempts to introduce a science of law by separating morality and law and defining positive laws as commands by a sovereign backed up sanctions. Bentham and Austin informed Dicey's (1915) *Introduction to the Study of the Law of the Constitution*, described by Sir Ivor Jennings (1936, xiv) as the 'great classical authority on the British Constitution' and H. L. A. Hart's (1961) *The Concept of Law* wherein he attempted to refine legal positivism by distinguishing between primary and secondary legal rules, and differentiating between internal and external points of view of law and rules.[19] For a recent expression of this view, consider Jaconelli (2005, 153) who argues there is a 'conceptual gap between Law and Conventions' based on the fact that conventions are not law because they are not enforced by the courts.

The legal positivist approach, as noted previously, differs in important ways from the common law approach to politics and law. For legal positivism, the determination of the sovereign marks a moment of transition from political contestation to legal and in particular constitutional certainty. Sovereignty, once established, becomes the source of all political and legal

19 For 'continental' variations of this Hobbesian influence, see Carl Schmitt's (1932) *The Concept of the Political*, and Kelsen's (1960) *Pure Theory of Law*, whose concept of 'grundnorm' influenced H.L.A. Hart. On positivism and natural law, see the Hart/Dworkin debates (Ball 1984).

authority. The origin and authority of laws therefore derive from the will of the sovereign. As the sovereign's will would be discerned in enacted laws and legislation, conventional, unwritten or ancient rules were denied authority, unless declared and recognised by the sovereign. Moreover, the paramountcy of the sovereign meant that justice of the laws was determined by their legality so that all laws – and only laws – were just. The authority of the sovereign also meant that judges were servants of the sovereign, interpreting the sovereign's will in the determination of legal disputes. Judges could never legally challenge the authority of the sovereign and therefore the legality of laws.

Liberal Constitutionalism

The common law and legal positivistic conceptions of law, politics and constitutionalism needs to be contrasted with the liberal constitutionalism that predominates in contemporary politics. Though liberal constitutionalism has a number of theoretical sources, its distinctive aspects – especially its reliance on written constitutions – can be seen when we turn to John Locke and Montesquieu, two major thinkers who influentially shaped its defining features. John Locke's (1689) *Second Treatise on Government* traces the origins of political society to inconveniences of the state of nature, which include the absence of known and settled laws, indifferent judges and common power to enforce sentences. The state of nature, 'full of fears and continual dangers', drives free, equal and independent individuals to establish political society by consenting to give up their natural liberty for the 'mutual *Preservation* of their Lives, Liberties and Estates', which Locke designates with the general name '*Property*' (*Second Treatise*, §123). Consequently, political societies have a specific purpose: 'the great and *chief end* therefore, of Mens uniting into Commonwealths, and putting themselves under Government, *is the Preservation of their Property*' (§124). The supreme power of government, according to Locke, is in the legislative, though the people retain the power to remove or alter it when there is a breach of trust (§149; §221–222). He also distinguishes among the legislative, executive and federative powers (§143–148), though the legislative power is limited by four requirements: that government must be by 'promulgated establish'd Laws'; that these laws must be for 'the good of the People'; that taxes cannot be raised on the Property of the People 'without the Consent of the People'; and finally, that the legislative 'neither must nor can transfer the Power of making Laws to any Body else' (§142). An additional constraint advocated by Locke in his *Letter Concerning Toleration* (1689) was a limitation on the 'magistrate's authority' to enforce religious belief, advocating separation of Church and state as necessary for liberty and religious toleration.

Montesquieu's (1748) *Spirit of the Laws* draws upon English laws and government to refine his insights into political liberty. His starting point is the need to acknowledge the importance of mores and the variety of factors, from the nature of the people, their religion, history and origin, to the character of country including its climate, soil, situation and extent that influence the character and efficacy of laws (SL 1.3). Distinguishing among republican, monarchic and despotic governments that are moved by their specific passions, Montesquieu advocates laws in favour of political liberty, 'a tranquillity of mind arising from the opinion each person has of his safety' (SL 11.6, 157). Drawing on and refining the English model, Montesquieu argues that liberty requires governments where 'power should be a check to power' (SL 11.4, 155), to be achieved by the separation of the executive, legislative, and judicial powers of government. Liberty also requires that the laws concern only threats to public order and security, requiring laws that are clear, and concern outward conduct (SL 12.6).

Lockean and Montesquieuian conceptions of politics, law and constitutionalism influenced Blackstone's (1765) *Commentaries on the Laws of England* that attempted to renovate the 'old Gothic castle' of the common law by expounding a new conception of rights. All three works were especially influential in the American founding, which according to Publius in *The Federalist Papers* represented a political experiment, not only for the benefit of Americans, but for all of humanity (*Federalist 1*; Hamilton et al. 1788).[20] The modern republicanism they proposed was to be founded upon natural rights, which were discerned by unassisted human reason ('self-evident' truths) and 'inalienable', and included the individual liberty to pursue happiness.[21] Accordingly, they determined the character, extent and end of government, founded on a social contract or 'instituted' by the consent of equal, rights-bearing individuals, to secure these rights, and no more. Where governments exceeded this authority, natural rights also guaranteed a right of revolution.[22] Presuming the safe political maxim that men are not angels (*Federalist 51*), the modern republic also included 'Inventions of prudence' such as distribution of power, checks and balances, the institution of courts, and popular representation (*Federalist 9*). To this list Publius added the enlargement of the republic into a 'one great confederacy' – that is, federalism to overcome the perennial problem of 'faction'. Federalism itself, in this account, was one part of a much more ambitious experiment in republicanism, an innovation to test the possibility of people ruling over themselves by election and choice, without descending to constant dissolution and war. Each aspect of American founding, assembled and enacted, inaugurated a comprehensive political device to solve the problem of securing republicanism.

20 On the status of the *Federalist Papers* as a rhetorical and philosophical work, see generally Epstein (1986).

21 The revolutionary nature of the American founding can be seen in the introductory words of the Declaration of Independence, which inaugurated a *novus ordo seclorum*, or a 'new order of the ages'.

22 On the Lockean influence on the founding, see generally Zuckert (1998), Pangle (1988).

These insights into politics and law at the origin of the U.S. Constitution were later transformed in the course of the American founding. Notable in this respect was a Bill of Rights amendment to the Constitution favoured by the anti-Federalists, with the First Amendment protecting religious freedom as well as freedom of speech and peaceful assembly, revealing the new understanding of government. These rights would in turn encourage a new international perspective on rights, which the United Nations relied on to proclaim Universal Declaration of Human Rights (1948). The other notable American innovation was judicial review that gave the judiciary the power to strike down laws, statutes and some government actions that they judged violated the Constitution of the United States (see *Marbury* v. *Madison*, 5 U.S. 137). Judicial review gave the judiciary an unprecedented authority in determining the nature of liberal constitutionalism and laid the foundations for subsequent political and jurisprudential debates regarding how they should exercise their power.[23]

As this necessarily brief overview reveals, though liberal constitutionalism draws on the common law and legal positivism, it is distinctive in significant respects. In the spirit of legal positivism, liberal constitutionalism proposes a foundational constitutional agreement or contract to determine who is sovereign and therefore favours the written over conventional laws. Yet contrary to the positivistic tradition that presumed unlimited power of the sovereign, liberal constitutionalism proposes limited government, so that separation of powers, federalism and later a new conception of bills of rights become constraints on sovereign will and ambition. Limited government also means the judiciary, in the spirit of the common law, exercise an authority independent of the sovereign, though the source and legitimacy of this authority become new grounds for contestation in modern liberal democracies.

Conventions in Theory and Practice

The argument of this chapter is that our understanding of constitutional conventions has been shaped by the common law, which has in turn been challenged and altered by the major alternative approaches of legal positivism and liberal constitutionalism. These conceptions have been contested, refined and reformulated theoretically, in the works of scholars and jurists, and practically, in the context of constitutional foundings and judicial adjudication of specific states. Thus, the theoretical conceptualisation of constitutional conventions reveals the importance of individual scholars who nevertheless had to confront important limitations shaped by previous schools of thought. This form of dialogic contestation can be seen in the way the common law responded

23 These debates ranged from the appropriate theories of interpretation, ranging from 'originalism' to 'realism', to the accusation of 'juristocracy': see, for example, Hirschl (2004).

to classical conceptions of judgment and scholastic natural law, just as legal positivism sought to counter the common law conception of law and liberalism proposed new theoretical foundations for limited government. Moreover, inherent theoretical features of each approach and body of thought shaped their mutual interaction and influence. The concept of right, for example, was understood differently by each approach, varying from the immemorial common law rights to the positivistic will of the sovereign to liberal conceptions of innate, natural or human rights. The common law favours conventions because it adopts an Aristotelian conception of politics that seeks to empower virtuous and prudent leaders, while positivistic and liberal approaches will tend to insist on writing and codification, but each on a fundamentally different basis, with positivism to defend sovereign authority, while liberalism favours it to make sovereignty limited and accountable. Justiciability also raises a complicated response, with the common law willing to review conventions, while again positivism resists it to enhance the sovereign will and liberalism seeks to circumscribe it to reconcile it with the principle of popular sovereignty. Consequently, each school of thought views constitutional conventions differently, so that in distinguishing among ancient, contractual and natural law, it ascribes different roles for the judiciary, with the common law defending judicial judgment and discretion, positivism insisting the judiciary are servants and agents of the sovereign, and liberal constitutionalism compelled to reconceive a new independent role for judges.

The other significant factor in determining the way the different schools of thought have engaged with each other and in their interactions determined the meaning of constitutional conventions is the distinctive political, legal and historical character of each state where specific conventions are debated and contested in practice. As the historical trajectory of the development of the three approaches reveals, English constitutionalism is dominated by a common law approach that is largely founded on constitutional conventions, while at the other extreme we find U.S. jurisprudence that celebrates the specific terms of the constitution and therefore leaves little or no room for conventions as constitutive provisions. Between these two extremes, we find those countries that in the course of their founding and development took from both jurisdictions, typically combining their common law origins with liberal innovations that were introduced with U.S. federalism. Legalism asserts itself in all these jurisdictions in specific though important ways, typically by favouring codification and denying the judiciary a more expansive legal and political in the development of constitutionalism. A brief overview of the constitution of each country shows how constitutional conventions are defined by interaction of jurisprudential approaches and the specific architecture of each constitution.

The continuing centrality and influential reach of the common law explains the prevalence and prominence of constitutional conventions in English law and politics. These conventions range from the core aspects of cabinet accountability to foundational notions of responsible government. This common law approach coexists and is confronted by a legal positivism that favours codification on the basis that it considers conventions are not laws as they are unwritten and will not be enforced by the judiciary (see, for example, Jaconelli 1999, 2005). Because the common law conventions govern crucial aspects of political power and executive discretion, few have attempted to undertake comprehensive codification of the constitution in the spirit of legal positivism. There is, however, an increasing emphasis on the need to replace the 'political' with a 'written' constitution, driven by mutually reinforcing sources 'including membership of the European Union, the expansion of judicial review and the rise of common law constitutionalism, and, in particular, the raft of constitutional reform measures put in place by the Labour Government since 1997' (McHarg 2008, 853). The difficulty of codification has tended to temper, if not counter, such initiatives.[24] Where codification has been proposed, the focus has been on specific topics, most of which have attracted attention due to their political salience. Consider in this context the discussion of the codification of Cabinet Manuals,[25] prorogation of parliament[26] and the war powers convention.[27] The predominance of the common law understanding of constitutional conventions has faced its most significant challenge indirectly, with the introduction of liberal notions of rights by the enactment of the UK Human Rights Act 1998. The confrontation between liberalism and common law can therefore be found in those debates attempting to reconcile parliamentary sovereignty with European and international human rights codes (Young et al. 2019). The confluence of the three jurisprudential approaches can be seen in the English tendency to acknowledge the importance of constitutional conventions, its view of constitutions as empowering rather than limiting provisions, its distinction between written laws and unwritten conventions, and its resistance to liberal constitutionalism defined by an emphasis on individual rights, limited government and expansive judicial review.

The American experience is at the other extreme. The radical nature of the American founding was especially evident in the centrality of its written

24 Partly because, as McHarg (2008, 853) observes, 'the new legal arrangements have themselves given rise to new political practices which modify or supplement the letter of the law'. See also Blick (2014, 205): 'Constitutional conventions often do not lend themselves readily to codification. Their frequently indeterminate nature cannot necessarily be captured in precise words'.

25 See Blick (2014) on the UK Cabinet Manual. Cabinet Manuals have been a focus in other jurisdictions: see, for example, Duncan (2015) on the New Zealand experience, and Galligan and Brenton (2015) for a comparative analysis.

26 See Schleiter and Fleming (2020) and Fleming and Schleiter (2020) for a comparison of British and European procedures.

27 See Strong (2021) on the parliamentary debates on the war powers convention.

constitution, which seemed to leave little scope for English common law (Stoner 2003). The constitution as an enactment to manage ambition by fragmenting power meant that it was no longer possible to rely on conventions to determine authority – precise written provisions were needed to demarcate the separation of powers as well as federalism. In this way, the spirit of natural rights seemed to coexist with – and in some cases favour – the spirit of legalism. This emphasis on a written constitution explains the absence of constitutional conventions in American constitutionalism, as acknowledged in the scholarship.[28] It also explains why scholars have fashioned new terms in their attempts to introduce the concept of constitutional conventions to American jurisprudence. 'Norms', for Renan (2018, 2187), are 'unwritten or informal rules of political behavior' that provide the 'infrastructure that any particular President inhabits'. As Renan shows, they are valuable for understanding the nature of the U.S. presidency (the so-called Article II norms). Yet it is clear that these rules are not laws, that they can change and that they are not justiciable by the Supreme Court, raising the question of the extent to which they can be said to approximate common law conventions.[29] Similarly, the curious locution 'informal institution' seems to represent another attempt to recognise constitutional conventions in American constitutionalism.[30] But the very definition of 'informal institution' as 'socially shared rules, usually unwritten, that are created, communicated, and enforced outside of officially sanctioned channels' shows that though these rules are valuable for understanding political behaviour, they – just like norms – lack constitutional authority and therefore are not constitutional conventions in its English signification (see Azari and Smith 2012, 38). Finally, the dominance of the U.S. constitution accounts for the absence of demands for codification that is an important aspect of the Westminster scholarship.

Between the English and American approaches we find an admixture of common law, positivism and liberal constitutionalism in those countries originally founded on English legal tradition but which subsequently adopted aspects of American constitutionalism.[31] Countries such as Canada and Australia trace their origins to common law principles and therefore the flexibility of constitutional conventions, even when their foundings were secured by

28 See Azari and Smith (2012), who note that 'unwritten' laws have received little attention in American scholarship, and Siegel (2018), who makes a persuasive case that constitutional conventions are underappreciated by scholars and warrant closer attention.

29 See Siegel (2018), who usefully distinguishes among political norms, political conventions and constitutional conventions.

30 See Azari and Smith (2012), who draw on Helmke and Levitsky (2004) to develop the notion of 'informal institutions'.

31 See in this context Hartz's (1969) 'fragment' thesis of constitutional development and, more recently, Jacobsohn and Roznai (2020).

written constitutions.[32] Yet to the extent that they also incorporated federalism and subsequently bills of rights, they also introduced a liberal constitutionalism that challenged important aspects of the common law founding.[33] Complicating this tension was the influence of legal positivism that predominated in English jurisprudential thought at the founding of Westminster colonies, which was consistent with the common law approach in favouring a powerful notion of sovereignty – yet in its insistence on the primacy of written laws also seemed to endorse liberal constitutionalism. The conflict in these approaches helps explain important aspects of Australia's major constitutional crisis of 1975, when constitutional conventions of responsible government and the nature of the reserve powers of the Governor-General confronted the principle of federalism enshrined in the constitution.[34] It also explains the disparate positions adopted in the Canadian Supreme Court's *Patriation* case, whereby the common law acceptance of the existence of constitutional conventions is countered by a legal positivism that insists only the written is legal and justiciable, devising a significant yet delineated role for a judiciary that after patriation would be responsible for adjudicating a new Charter of Rights and Freedoms.[35]

Conclusion

Though the importance of constitutional conventions is accepted by all, there is significant diversity and contestation in how we define them. This chapter has argued that our understanding of constitutional conventions is shaped by two related factors. The first is the political and legal schools of thought that inform our attempts to explore the nature of conventions. The second is the way these theoretical and jurisprudential premises were adopted and altered in the specific context of the political and legal evolution of each country. The complexity and diversity of scholarship on constitutional conventions can therefore be traced to one's theoretical perspective and the specific jurisdiction under consideration – on the relative authority of the common law, legal positivism and the liberalism within the larger political, legal and historical

32 There was therefore an ambiguity regarding these provision, which appeared to be social contract constitutive enactments but as is evident from the Canadian BNA Act and Commonwealth of Australia Constitution Act derived their authority from Imperial legislation.

33 On the tension between the common law and liberal constitutionalism in Australia, see Patapan (2001, 2005)

34 For the nature of the crisis, see the views of the protagonists Kerr (1978) and Whitlam (1979).

35 *Re Resolution to Amend the Constitution* [1981] 1 SCR 753. For recent debates, see MacDonnell and Lagasse (2023) and Macfarlane (2022) regarding the Supreme Court's reference to 'constitutional architecture' and its recent decision in the *City of Toronto* case [2021] S.C.J. No 34, where it held that unwritten constitutional principles cannot be used to invalidate legislation.

context of English, American and Westminster 'fragment' constitutionalism that combined both. The variety in definitions regarding conventions, ranging from soft law to norms and informal systems, the contests over whether conventions are laws or not, and whether laws should empower or constrain the sovereign can be traced to theoretical and constitutional contests concerning their legitimacy, justiciability and efficacy. Constitutional conventions are enduring and important aspects of modern constitutionalism. Our attempt to gain greater clarity regarding their nature and reach has been mandated not only to support and enhance good governance, but above all to secure the foundations for democratic constitutional resilience and innovation.

References

Ahmed, Farah, Albert, Richard and Perry, Adam (2019). 'Judging Constitutional Conventions'. *International Journal of Constitutional Law*, 17 (3), pp. 787–806.

Aquinas, St. Thomas (1952 [1265]). *Summa Theologica*. Chicago: Encyclopaedia Britannica.

Austin, John (1832). *The Province of Jurisprudence Determined*. London: John Murray.

Azari, Julia R. and Smith, Jennifer K. (2012). 'Unwritten Rules: Informal Institutions in Established Democracies'. *Perspectives on Politics*, 10 (1), pp. 37–55.

Ball, Stephen W. (1984). 'Bibliographical Essay/Legal Positivism, Natural Law, and the Hart/Dworkin Debate'. *Criminal Justice Ethics*, 3 (2), pp. 68–85.

Barry, Nicholas, Miragliotta, Narelle and Nwokora, Zim (2019). 'The Dynamics of Constitutional Conventions in Westminster Democracies'. *Parliamentary Affairs*, 72 (3), pp. 664–683.

Bentham, Jeremy ([1789] 1996). *An Introduction to the Principles and Morals of Legislation*. Oxford: Oxford University Press.

Blackstone, Sir William ([1765] 1884). *Commentaries on the Laws of England*, 3rd edn. Callaghan.

Blick, Andrew (2014). 'The Cabinet Manual and the Codification of Conventions'. *Parliamentary Affairs*, 67 (1), pp. 191–208.

Caenegem, R. C. V. (1973). *The Birth of the English Common Law*. Cambridge: Cambridge University Press.

Chafetz, Josh and Pozen, David E. (2018). 'How Constitutional Norms Breakdown'. *UCLA Law Review*, 65 (6), pp. 1430–1459.

Coke, Edward (1832 [1628]). *The First Part of the Institutes of the Laws of England; or, a Commentary Upon Littleton*, ed. Charles Butler, volume 1, 19th edn. Clarke.

Dicey, A. V. (1982 [1915]). *Introduction to the Study of the Law of the Constitution*, ed. Roger E. Michener, reprint 8th edn. Indianapolis: Liberty Fund.

Duncan, Grant (2015). 'New Zealand's Cabinet Manual: How Does It Shape Constitutional Conventions'. *Parliamentary Affairs*, 68, pp. 737–756.

Epstein, David F. (1986). *The Political Theory of The Federalist*. Chicago: The University of Chicago Press.

Feldman, D. (2013). 'Constitutional Conventions'. In: Matt, Q. (ed.), *The British Constitution: Continuity, Change and the Influence of Europe – a Festschrift for Vernon Bogdanor*. Oxford: Hart Publishing, pp. 94–119.

Fisher, John (1966). 'Plato on Writing and Doing Philosophy'. *Journal of the History of Ideas*, 27 (2), pp. 163–172.

Fleming, Thomas G. and Schleiter, Petra (2020). 'Prorogation: Comparative Context and Scope for Reform'. *Parliamentary Affairs*, pp. 1–15.

Galligan, Brian and Brenton, Scott (2015). *Constitutional Conventions in Westminster Systems*. Cambridge: Cambridge University Press.

Gee, James Paul (1988). 'Essay Reviews: The Legacies of Literacy'. *Harvard Educational Review*, 58 (2), pp. 195–212.

Griswold, Charles L. (2008). 'Reading and Writing Plato'. *Philosophy and Literature*, 32 (1), pp. 205–216.

Hamilton, A. et al. (1982 [1788]). *The Federalist Papers*. New York: Bantam.

Hart, H. L. A. (1961). *The Concept of the Law*. Oxford: Oxford University Press.

Hartz, Louis (1969). *The Founding of New Societies: Studies in the History of the United States, Latin America, South Africa, Canada, and Australia*. Harcourt Brace and Co.

Heard, Andrew (1991). *Canadian Constitutional Conventions: The Marriage of Law and Politics*. Toronto: Oxford University Press.

Helmke, Gretchen and Levitsky, Steven (2004). 'Informal Institutions and Comparative Politics: A Research Agenda'. *Perspectives on Politics*, 2 (4), pp. 725–740.

Hirschl, Ran (2004). *Towards Juristocracy*. Cambridge: Harvard University Press.

Hobbes, Thomas (1971 [1681]). *A Dialogue Between a Philosopher and a Student of the Common Laws of England*, ed. and intro. Joseph Cropsey. University of Chicago Press.

Hobbes, Thomas (1978). *Man and Citizen*, ed. and intro. Bernard Gert. Peter Smith.

Hobbes, Thomas (1981 [1651]). *Leviathan*, ed. and intro. C. B. Macpherson. Penguin.

Hyland, Drew A. (1968). 'Why Plato Wrote Dialogues'. *Philosophy & Rhetoric*, 1 (1), pp. 38–50.

Jacobsohn, Gary and Roznai, Yaniv (2020). *Constitutional Revolution*. New Have: Yale University Press.

Jaconelli, Joseph (1999). 'The Nature of Constitutional Convention'. *Legal Studies*, 19 (1), pp. 24–46.

Jaconelli, Joseph (2005). 'Do Constitutional Conventions Bind'. *Cambridge Law Journal*, 64 (1), pp. 149–176.

Jennings, Sir Ivor (1936). *The Law and the Constitution*, 2nd edn. London: University of London Press.

Kelsen, Hans ([1930] 1960). *Pure Theory of Law*. Berkeley: University of California Press.

Kerr, John (1978). *Matters for Judgment: An Autobiography by John Kerr*. London: St. Martin's Press.

MacDonnell, Vanessa and Lagasse, Philippe (2023). *Investigating the Legal and Political Contours of Unwritten Constitutional Principles After City of Toronto*. 110 Supreme Court Law Review (2d) 51, Ottawa Faculty of Law Working Paper No. 2022–13. Available at SSRN: https://ssrn.com/abstract=4203787.

Macfarlane, E. (2022). 'The Place of Constitutional Conventions in the Constitutional Architecture, and in the Courts'. *Canadian Journal of Political Science/Revue Canadienne De Science Politique*, 55 (2), pp. 322–341. doi:10.1017/S0008423922000051.

McHarg, Aileen (2008). 'Reforming the United Kingdom Constitution: Law, Convention, Soft Law'. *Modern Law Review*, 71 (6), pp. 853–877.

Menzies, Jennifer and Tiernan, Anne (2014). *Caretaker Conventions in Australia: Minding the Shop for Government*. Canberra: ANU Press.

Milson, S. F. C. (1969). *Historical Foundations of the Common Law*. London: Butterworth-Heinemann.

Mulherin, Peter E. (2020). 'War-Power Reform in Australia: (Re)considering the Options'. *Australian Journal of Politics and History*, 66 (4), pp. 633–645.

Pangle, Thomas (1988). *The Spirit of Modern Republicanism*. Chicago: University of Chicago Press.
Patapan, Haig (2001). 'Educating Devils: Theoretical Reflections on Ethics and Governance'. In: Fleming, Jenny and Holland, Ian (eds.), *Motivating Ministers to Morality*. Aldershot: Ashgate Publishing, pp. 21–36.
Patapan, Haig (2005). 'The Forgotten Founding: Civics Education, the Common Law and Liberal Constitutionalism in Australia'. *Griffith Law Review*, 14 (1), pp. 91–107.
Patapan, Haig (2023). *Modern Philosopher Kings*. Edinburgh: Edinburgh University Press.
Perry, Adam and Tucker, Adam (2018). 'Top-Down Constitutional Conventions'. *Modern Law Review*, 81 (5), pp. 765–789.
Postema, Gerald J. (2003a). 'Classical Common Law Jurisprudence (Part I)'. *Oxford University Commonwealth Law Journal*, 2 (2), pp. 155–180.
Postema, Gerald J. (2003b). 'Classical Common Law Jurisprudence (Part II)'. *Oxford University Commonwealth Law Journal*, 3 (1), pp. 1–28.
Postema, Gerald J. (2011). *Legal Philosophy in the Twentieth Century: The Common Law World*. Treatise of Legal Philosophy and General Jurisprudence, volume 11. Dordrecht: Springer.
Renan, Daphna (2018). 'Presidential Norms and Article II'. *Harvard Law Review*, 131, pp. 2187–2281.
Schleiter, Petra and Fleming, Thomas G. (2020). 'Parliamentary Prorogation in Comparative Context'. *Political Quarterly*, 91 (3), pp. 641–648.
Schmitt, Carl (1932). *The Concept of the Political*. Trans. George Schwab. Rutgers: Rutgers University Press.
Scott, K. A. (2009). 'Platonic Critique of Codification'. *Journal Jurisprudence*, 3 (1), pp. 159–176.
Siegel, Neil S. (2018). 'Political Norms, Constitutional Conventions, and President Donald Trump'. *Indiana Law Journal*, 93 (1), pp. 177–206.
Siegel, S. A. (1981). 'The Aristotelian Basis of English Law 1450–1800'. *New York University Law Review*, 56 (1), pp. 18–59.
Stoner, James R., Jr. (1992). *Common Law and Liberal Theory: Coke, Hobbes, and the Origins of American Constitutionalism*. University Press of Kansas.
Stoner, James R., Jr. (2003). *Common Law Liberty: Rethinking American Constitutionalism*. University Press of Kansas.
Strong, James (2021). 'Did Theresa May Kill the War Powers Convention? Comparing Parliamentary Debates on UK Intervention in Syria in 2013 and 2018'. *Parliamentary Affairs*, in print, pp. 1–20.
Whitlam, Gough (1979). *The Truth of the Matter*. Melbourne: Melbourne University Press.
Whittington, Keith E. (2013). 'The Status of Unwritten Constitutional Conventions'. *University of Illinois Law Review*, 5, pp. 1847–1870.
Young, A. L., Birkinshaw, P., Mitsilegas, V. and Christou, T. A. (2019). 'Europe's Gift to the United Kingdom's Unwritten Constitution – Juridification'. In: Albi, A. and Bardutzky, S. (eds.), *National Constitutions in European and Global Governance: Democracy, Rights, the Rule of Law*. The Hague: T.M.C. Asser Press.
Zuckert, Michael (1998). *Natural Rights and the New Republicanism*. Princeton: Princeton University Press.

Chapter 3

Morality Versus Strategy

Constitutional Conventions Through the Lens of Political Motivation

Zim Nwokora

Constitutional conventions are the "social rules which govern the relations between political parties or the institutions of government" (Jaconelli 1999: 24). They are a specialized kind of rule, both because of the (constitutional) domain they regulate and how they do so – that is, through guidance that is generally unwritten (or written differently) and not court-enforced. Conventions operate at different levels in a democratic system. Some are intricate rules that regulate institutional processes, while others capture broader expectations of political conduct.

The practical significance of conventions is often most apparent when these rules are breached. For instance, in the United States (U.S.), the refusal in 2020 of President Donald Trump to accept the outcome of a free and fair election – which might be regarded as a meta-convention applying to democratic leaders – set in train events that led to the storming of the Capitol Building in Washington, D.C. on 6 January 2021 (Pfiffner 2021). Likewise, conventions featured prominently in the United Kingdom (UK) following the 2016 Brexit referendum, in which the British public voted to leave the European Union (EU). While the referendum's outcome was clear enough, the question of who should get to interpret the meaning of the referendum outcome – the executive or parliament – was not obvious and ended up being structured by conventions, some of which were hotly disputed (Schleiter and Fleming 2020). As these episodes suggest, conventions can both shape and become the subject of major political disputes – yet their significance can easily be overlooked in traditional institutional analyses that focus on written constitutions and the formal structures they create. A country's conventions may therefore seem "hidden," combining as an "invisible constitution" (Dixon and Stone 2018) that is no less fundamental to governance than the visible constitution.

The prominence given to conventions, and the functions they are understood to perform, varies across scholarly research agendas. For example, in research on U.S. politics, the U.S. Constitution has traditionally been read as a self-contained mapping of institutions, powers and rights, with conventions considered absent from (or at least external to) this framework

DOI: 10.4324/9781003506577-3

(e.g., Vermeule 2015; Whittington 2013). In studies of Westminster-style democracies such as the UK and Australia, by contrast, it has long been recognized that conventions are a crucial part of the governance framework. These countries have relatively "thin" formal constitutions, and conventions fill gaps in the mapping of power relations (e.g., Marshall 1984; Jaconelli 1999). In comparative politics research, analysts have shown a particular interest in how conventions emerge and stabilize in a new democracy, motivated by the belief that a political elite's adherence to conventions shows its commitment to democracy (e.g., Helmke and Levitsky 2004; Tushnet and Bugaric 2021).

Although important insights have come from investigation of these themes, the study of conventions is not a unified field, comparable to, say, the study of constitutional law or the study of formal institutions such as legislatures, parties or executives. The approaches to this subject matter come from different disciplines (i.e., law, political science, sociology and economics), applying contrasting approaches, informed by different country experiences. Little has been done to compare and integrate their themes. However, I argue that two concepts of political motivation – *morality* and *strategy* – can be detected across this diverse body of work, and thus political motivation can provide a lens for integration and productive interdisciplinary analysis of conventions. The morality view highlights politicians' beliefs about constitutional propriety when they consider what to do in situations that are defined by conventions, while the strategic view casts politicians as utility maximizers who act conditional on expectations of their opponents' behaviour. These conceptions are ideal types. They can be combined in various ways and may be more or less present, both in practice and in scholarly accounts, but they have not previously been extracted and compared in the manner attempted here.

This exercise can, in turn, shed new light on conventions and the work they do. For instance, I show that morality and strategy inform, among other things, scholarly accounts of why conventions are followed, how convention violations (and violators) should be viewed and what should be regarded as the best way to remedy or pre-empt such breaches. I develop these arguments through an examination of conventions in American politics, Westminster politics, and the politics of democratic transition. In recent times, several controversies involving conventions have played out in the settings these literatures focus on, making them crucial sites in the contemporary scholarly debate about conventions.

The chapter proceeds as follows. In the first section, I summarize the treatment of conventions in research on American politics, Westminster politics and democratic transition. It is from this scholarship that I draw out the moralistic and strategic approaches to conventions, which present fundamentally different views of political behaviour in relation to conventions. The chapter's second and third sections flesh out the two approaches in greater detail, drawing on and synthesizing seminal theoretical contributions to each school of thought. Morality and strategy are directly compared, contrasted and combined in the chapter's fourth section. In the conclusion, I suggest that the morality/strategy dichotomy may have potential as a framework for interdisciplinary research on constitutional conventions.

Constitutional Conventions in Three Research Agendas

This section summarizes the treatment of conventions in research on American politics, Westminster democracies (such as the UK) and democratic transition. It aims to show that this empirical research assumes, more or less explicitly, moralistic or strategic assumptions about political motivation, even though it has been rare for these assumptions to be uncovered and analyzed.

Conventions in American Politics

American politics and governance, it is usually assumed, are organized through the rules of the country's formal constitution (and implications derived from it) (e.g., Vermeule 2015; Whittington 2013). Furthermore, the founding fathers wrote a constitution they expected would be operated by rational politicians, seeking power and prestige. "They assumed," explains Jon Elster (1995: 2400), "roughly speaking, that motives are always and everywhere self-interested." When this constitutional system is working smoothly, its unwritten rules remain in the background. Indeed, the idea that there may be a separate body of rules that cannot be tightly linked back to this text might seem in conflict with the country's political traditions, and a point of contrast with Westminster-style democracies. In fact, as Adrian Vermeule (2015: 283) observes, conventions are periodically rediscovered in American politics, particularly when they have been challenged or implicated in a crisis. What follows is often "shock, incomprehension, and utter confusion," due to the shadowy existence of conventions in standard accounts of how the system works (Foley 2013: 72).

During these rediscoveries, the conventions that draw attention include the filibuster in the Senate, which empowers individual senators to interrupt the lawmaking process; the convention against court-packing, which prevents the majority party in Congress from expanding the number of Supreme Court justices; and the "faithful electors" convention, requiring members of the Electoral College to vote their state's preference rather than their own. All of these are longstanding conventions that continue to operate today (though sometimes under strain). Going back in time, the re-election convention – limiting presidents to no more than two terms in office – was as an important convention until it was formalized as the Twenty-Second Amendment in 1951. As these examples suggest, the United States has prominent rules that are well described as conventions, even if this class of rule has not always been seen as fundamental to the country's constitutional architecture. In this respect, there are parallels between the American system of government and that of the Westminster democracies where conventions are widely acknowledged as central to law and politics.

However, there are also features of the American context which, in addition to a totemic constitution, might help to explain the lower salience of conventions. The scope of activities they cover seems to be narrower than in the Westminster democracies. For example, the process of government formation and the relationships between ministers and public servants are governed by conventions in Westminster democracies but are more likely to be regulated by formal laws in the United States. When governing processes are regulated by conventions in the United States, there seems to be less respect for the mooted benefits of "flexibility" and "adaptability," which are lauded by some scholars of Westminster systems. This distrust of informal rules in the United States is reflected in the descriptions of them "omissions" from the original constitutional text (e.g., Willis and Willis 1952: 469), and in the frequent efforts to codify conventions as soon as they are recognized as being valuable.

In recent years, debates about conventions in American politics have been triggered by the challenge to them during Donald Trump's presidency (e.g., Chafetz and Pozen 2018; Pfiffner 2021; Renan 2018). Trump showed disdain towards the conventions that structure governmental processes, such as the faithful electors convention and the Senate filibuster, but also – and perhaps even more flagrantly – the conventions surrounding the behaviour of democratic leaders. Though he flouted such expectations during his presidential campaign in 2016, the critique of Trump's "unpresidential" behaviour really took shape during his tenure in the White House. This critique emphasized Trump's willingness to tell lies which, as James Pfiffner (2021) explains, went far beyond the usual criticisms of candidates and presidents for being loose with the truth. Trump was unapologetic when, as with his claims to have won the 2020 election, his pronouncements were shown to be complete falsehoods, and he endorsed and promoted conspiracy theories that attacked his political rivals (e.g., the "Pizzagate" charge against Hillary Clinton) as well as governing institutions and officials (e.g., the "Deep State" conspiracy theory) (Muirhead and Rosenblum 2019).

While the Trump presidency revealed conventions that had been hiding in plain sight, because they had been so consistently followed in the past, it also showed the system's resilience when faced with violations of its unwritten rules. Key to this was the ability of the actors who did feel bound by conventions to push back against breaches (Chafetz and Pozen 2018: 1452). As Daphna Renan (2018: 2205) explains, "the President depends on others to implement his decisions and *they* experience the norm as a constraint on their conduct."

Conventions in Westminster Politics

Conventions are fundamental to the British constitutional system, and that of other Westminster-style democracies (e.g., Australia, Canada). Indeed, their democratic character depends on the smooth operation of conventions structuring the crown–cabinet–parliament relationship, which as Dicey (1915) explained, ensures that the formal powers vested in the Crown are, in practice, exercised by cabinet ministers who remain responsible to a popularly elected parliament. Since the importance of conventions is widely acknowledged, following them is obligatory and regarded as nothing less than a responsibility of office and a demonstration of fidelity to the constitutional order, "which transcends the sectional interest of political party" (Jaconelli 1999: 35). For sure, conventions have been challenged at times. However, these debates have usually been about the relevance and priority that should be given to different, competing conventions, and the ensuing tensions have in fact been a driver of the constitution's evolution (Barry et al. 2019).

Since the mid-1990s, the rules of British governance have been transforming, incrementally but significantly, in a process described by Vernon Bogdanor (2009) as the creation of a new constitution. The framework is still emerging, and its final shape remains uncertain. But the changes that have already occurred mean that classic accounts of British constitutionalism, as a system rooted in conventions and parliamentary sovereignty, no longer provide a complete description of the country's governance framework. For example, the new constitution includes formal elements such as the Human Rights Act. The authority of the Westminster parliament (if not its de jure sovereignty) has been diminished as a result of devolution and the creation of elected mayors in London and regional centres. Also notable has been the increasing use and significance of referenda to decide contentious matters, including, in June 2016, whether Britain should remain a member of the EU.

In that referendum, the British public expressed its narrow support for "leave." This outcome had significant political and constitutional ramifications (Schleiter and Fleming 2020; Sumption 2020). Politically, it immediately resulted in the resignation of Prime Minister David Cameron, who had led the "remain" campaign. His successor, Theresa May, took charge of the withdrawal negotiations and presented to parliament a proposal that struggled to gain the support of a majority of parliamentarians. She duly called an election, which did not deliver the supportive parliament she had hoped for. Unable to progress a revised withdrawal agreement through the new parliament, May resigned in May 2019. Her successor, Boris Johnson, confronting the same problem of how to secure Brexit in the face of significant parliamentary opposition, proposed a lengthy and controversial prorogation (i.e., suspension) of parliament for five weeks (from September 9 until October 14), which would limit the time that parliament had to debate, amend and oppose the government's EU withdrawal plan.

Prorogation is a common practice, typically employed in April or May each year in the transition from one annual session of parliament to the next. However, in this case, it seemed that prorogation was being used "to disable Parliament while the government prepared to deliver its preferred form of Brexit on 31 October" (Schleiter and Fleming 2020: 643). The charge, in other words, was that the government was extracting the convention out of the domain of constitutional morality for its use as a strategic tool to advance an ideological goal.

The executive's plan was challenged in the courts. After inconsistent judgments in the lower courts, the matter was heard by the UK Supreme Court in September 2019, which in the Miller/Cherry case determined that the question of whether the prorogation was excessive was justiciable (i.e., not beyond the scope of the courts). It also judged that the government's proposal was unlawful because it would frustrate parliament's ability to carry out its constitutional duties. The court was seen to have supported the conventions of parliamentary sovereignty and separation of powers, or at least the convention of short prorogations (Sumption 2020), though the decision's opponents saw a court that had made an unwarranted foray into politics. The government, in response, called an election that gave it a parliamentary majority and thus a clear mandate to proceed with Brexit on its preferred terms by passing the European Union (Withdrawal Agreement) Act 2020.

One observation that emerged clearly from the various interpretations of this dispute is that conventions had become tools of political strategy during this contentious time. By contrast, the moralistic arguments which suggest that political actors follow conventions out of obligation (see in what follows), seemed much less useful for understanding the prorogation dispute. Indeed, this dispute has led to calls for prorogation to be statutorily defined, perhaps as part of a broader embrace of written constitutionalism in Britain (Schleiter and Fleming 2020).

Conventions in New Democracies

There has been a longstanding belief among political scientists that democratization – that is, the transition to and consolidation of democratic institutions – depends on conventions (more often called "norms" in this work). In one influential model of the process, stable democracy depends on the emergence of a "large consensus" including the major groups in a society, in support of the conventions undergirding democratic institutions (Morlino 2012; see also Levitsky and Ziblatt 2018). The relevant conventions include a willingness to accept election outcomes and the legitimacy of political opposition. Furthermore, political leaders must show respect towards other constitutional actors (e.g., courts and parliaments) by allowing them to perform their constitutional roles. The consensus on these principles does not need to be comprehensive, but it does need to be large enough so that those who oppose the democratic constitutional order deem its transformation to be too costly (Hardin 1999). The stabilization of an emergent democracy, in this perspective, is thus anchored in the strategic behaviour of rational political elites who calculate that pursuing their goals through democratic processes (especially free and fair elections) will generate a higher payoff, especially in the long run, than the attempt to achieve such goals via non-democratic means such as by rigging elections (for a governing party) or by attempting to violently overthrow the government (for opposition leaders).

The significance of conventions in the context of new democracies has been a prominent theme in debates about democratic backsliding around the world since the early 2000s. In their study of this latest wave of "autocratization," which has affected up to 30 countries, Anna Lührmann and Staffan I. Lindberg (2019) show it has mostly occurred through the subversion of conventions – a process they term "democratic erosion." More fully, this arises when "incumbents legally access power and then gradually, but substantially, undermine democratic norms without abolishing key democratic institutions" (Lührmann and Lindberg 2019: 1105). These actions have often been at the initiative of populist leaders. Populist politics, whether right- or left-leaning, is centred on charismatic personalities, which makes populists instinctively sceptical of formal and informal rules that can constrain their leader. There are exceptions and the consequences of a populist leader for conventions are contingent, depending both on the leader's goals and even more so on the democracy's character (Tushnet and Bugaric 2021). However, the general trend is clear. As the cross-national analysis of Jordan Kyle and Yascha Mounk (2018) confirms, the presence of a populist government is associated with a decrease in a country's overall democratic quality.

The accounts from individual countries speak to the ways that populist leaders have stretched and broken conventions, and thereby eroded democracy, in their quest to remake their societies (e.g., Landau 2020). In Hungary and Venezuela, for example, populists attacked the notion of checks and balances, enabling their programmes of constitutional replacement and revision. Courts have been a target of convention-breaking in Poland and Turkey, where the ruling party has violated conventions restricting manipulation of the judiciary by expanding the number of justices, removing life tenure and abusing judicial impeachment powers. The legislature has been challenged in other countries. For instance, the convention that the government should have the backing of a parliamentary majority was broken in the Czech Republic in 2013, when President Milos Zeman appointed a cabinet of "technocrats," led by his protégé Jiri Rusnok, facing down the opposition of all the parties in parliament. That cabinet lasted only six months, but the use of this tactic has set a dangerous precedent in a context in which conventions are still emerging (Brunclík and Kubat 2021: 10).

As the preceding vignettes suggest, conventions have featured prominently, though also rather differently, in the scholarships on American politics,

Westminster politics and the politics of democratic transition. I argue, however, that underlying these discussions are two distinct approaches to conventions, grounded in ideas about morality and strategy. The two traditions have developed in parallel, largely independently of each other, despite their focus on common subject matter. Seminal theoretical contributions flesh out the core ideas of each approach, which empirical studies of conventions build on, more or less explicitly. Typically, this applied work is rooted in either a moralistic or strategic frame, but it is also possible for these approaches to be integrated within an account of conventions in practice, which in turn reflects the reality that morality and strategy may vie with each other for dominance. The subsequent sections describe and compare these two traditions in the study of conventions.

The Morality Tradition on Constitutional Conventions

One influential tradition presents conventions as moral rules. Its seminal contributions include A.V. Dicey's *Introduction to the Law of the Constitution* (Dicey 1915) and Geoffrey Marshall's inquiry into *Constitutional Conventions* (Marshall 1984), as well as numerous more recent studies that develop and refine ideas presented in these books. According to this school of thought, conventions should be understood as prescriptions (or proscriptions) that stipulate what constitutional actors ought to do (or not to do) in the circumstances to which a convention pertains. Conventions therefore act as an action-guiding code, clarifying what counts as proper conduct according to the requirements of good governance. Those who follow the conventions of a given situation "characteristically do it because of their belief that they are obligatory" (Marshall 1984: 6). In this sense, the conventions have normative force and the system of conventions, as a whole, expresses "governmental morality" (Marshall 1984: 7).

Of course, conventions are not always obeyed. How is such non-observance to be understood in moralistic terms? Those who disregard conventions may do so for opportunistic reasons, which suggests that the violator lacks the character or virtue upon which the constitutional system depends. Or, alternatively, they may lack the requisite judgement if their violation is due to an incorrect appraisal of the situation in which they find themselves. As Marshall (1984: 12) confirms, conventions have binding force on actors only "if they have considered the precedents and reasons correctly."

Crucially, though, these are not the only conclusions that might be reached whenever we encounter situations of non-compliance to a convention, because the actor who disobeys such a rule may in fact be seeking to change the convention. Another possibility is that the rule may be ambiguous, making it debatable as to whether a breach has occurred (Postema 2022). Given one of these latter scenarios, a politician who does not follow a convention (or who is accused of this) would not be compromising morality for expedience – indeed, their challenge to the convention may be personally costlier than following it. More generally, this point suggests that the alleged violation of a convention may not always be a matter of moral slackness – it can also reflect differences in the interpretation of what governmental morality requires.

Central to the moralistic perspective is the connection of conventions with the core principles of a constitutional democracy, including values such as accountability, representation and the separation of powers (Jennings 1952). Conventions are instruments to advance these principles. As Anne Twomey (2018: 23) explains, conventions "guide the practical operation of the Constitution so that it accords with constitutional principles" (see also Jaconelli 2005). Thus, a convention's purpose must be derived from the constitutional principles it seeks to advance. Principles are crucial in determining which conventions are relevant in a specific situation, and more generally, for settling disputes about conventions since the principles help to clarify what is at stake in the dispute and often suggest to relevant actors the best way to resolve it.

The counterpoint to "conventions" in studies in this tradition are "laws" that emanate from a written constitution, statutes or judicial decisions. Like conventions, legal rules should seek to advance fundamental democratic principles, but they are codified and enforced by courts. Neither of these properties holds, in general, for conventions. As a result, conventions can be interpreted with much greater flexibility. This property has been praised by some scholars working within the moralistic tradition, as it enables constitutional innovation and adaptability (e.g., Heard 2012). However, the flexibility of conventions has just as often been viewed with suspicion in the morality perspective because of the risks that it poses to the rule of law, another constitutional and democratic principle, which demands predictability, consistency and reliable enforcement (e.g., Bingham 2011). Conventions are relatively weak in these respects.

Nonetheless, it is also accepted by scholars working within the moralistic approach that legal rules may be insufficient, on their own, to support a constitutional value, giving conventions a role in helping actors navigate situations in a manner that is consistent with that principle. Sometimes, "[a] rule that might in general appear to be in accordance with a particular constitutional principle may in practice clash with it" (Twomey 2018: 23). In such cases, conventions can help to align the application of law with deeper principles. Moreover, the system of legal rules may be "silent" on major questions of governance (Loughlin 2018), and conventions interpose to provide the necessary guidance. Indeed, in medieval times, conventions were the only way to constrain Britain's legally sovereign monarch. The British monarch (or their representative in other Westminster democracies) retains many of their historic "prerogative powers" which control, amongst other things, the appointment of the prime minister, proroguing of parliament and giving and refusal of assent to bills (which is necessary to turn bills into laws).

The conventions relating to the exercise of the Crown's prerogatives were especially prominent in Dicey's (1915) account, which stressed the purpose of these conventions in ensuring that the Crown's discretionary powers were used in accordance with the principles of responsible and representative government. Building on Dicey's treatment, Marshall (1984) identified a wider range of constitutional relationships that were governed by conventions, including the relations between the prime minister and cabinet, between ministers and the civil service, between governments and the judiciary, and between the UK and other Commonwealth countries. More recently, scholars developing this research agenda have explored the properties of different types of conventions (e.g., Heard 2012; Jaconelli 1999; Twomey 2018), as well as the dynamics of convention change (e.g., Barry et al. 2019). Courts, which traditionally have adopted a hands-off approach to conventions, have been shown to be increasingly interested in the potential of conventions to resolve legal disputes (Ahmed et al. 2019). The conventions identified by Dicey and Marshall were "bottom-up" practices that emerged organically, but in recent times, constitutional actors – especially executives – have attempted to use practical guidebooks such as ministerial codes and cabinet manuals to articulate and thereby shape conventions (Perry and Tucker 2018).

Furthermore, although the moralistic tradition has been closely associated with the collection of Westminster democracies, its influence has spread beyond this group of countries. For example, as I noted earlier, scholars of American politics have drawn on moralistic ideas and arguments in their accounts of norm breaking during the Trump presidency (Ahmed 2022). Even before this period, scholars such as Keith Whittington (2013) took inspiration from the moralistic tradition to map conventions in the American context, presenting them as the "maxims, beliefs and principles that guide officials in how they exercise political discretion" (Whittington 2013: 114). In a different context, András Jakab (2016: 200) sees Westminster-style conventions as a way to improve democracy in the EU. In particular, he argues that a new convention by which each nominee for the European Commission, the EU's executive arm, would need the backing of a majority of the European Parliament (and not just the support of a sponsoring nation state) would improve participation in EU elections and help to generate "a shared system of values."

The Strategic Tradition on Constitutional Conventions

Conventions have also been analyzed with a strategic perspective in empirical studies. This view, which presents conventions as a device and outcome of interparty competition, prevails in U.S. politics and comparative politics scholarships. Indeed, Steven Levitsky and Daniel Ziblatt (2018) draw lessons from comparative research on democracy to interpret the erosion of conventions in the United States. A coup or revolution is not needed for "democratic breakdown," they warn – "it can be the result of a sequence of unanticipated events – an escalating tit-for-tat between a demagogic, norm-breaking leader and a threatened political establishment" (Levitsky and Ziblatt 2018: 75). As such, their account stresses the strategic foundations of the conventions that support democracy across various contexts.

The "constitutional conventions" I have been discussing in this chapter, following the terminology used by studies of Westminster conventions, are more often described as "norms" in strategically oriented studies. This contrast is more than semantic, as it points to a difference in the treatment of conventions/norms between these traditions. While moralistic studies focus on a specialized constitutional domain, strategic accounts more often interpret conventions/norms within a wider lens of *informal social control* that spans collective behaviour in general (see e.g., Bicchieri 2006). The constitutional domain is the focus for some empirical studies that draw on strategic arguments (e.g., Whittington 2013; Tushnet 2004), and some theoretical contributions do present the governmental arena as distinctive (e.g., Elster 2014). But, generally, the differentiation of the constitutional domain is weaker in this tradition.

To consider how conventions/norms are construed in the strategic tradition, a useful point of departure is the theoretical discussion by Elster (2014), which sets out a strategic account of norms with an unusual (for this perspective) focus on constitutional matters. Elster presents conventions as devices that enable mutually beneficial reciprocation. Interactions over conventions bear the properties of *cooperation* in general, but especially as depicted in game theory whereby the players can gain collectively by working together, but each player can exceed the collective payoff – at least in the short run – by reneging on cooperation. While there are many potential cooperative game setups, Elster identifies the well-known Prisoner's Dilemma (PD) as the appropriate model. He does not flesh out this model as it applies to conventions, but some elaboration along these lines can help to clarify what conditions promote stable conventions and what can destabilize them.[1]

As the foundation of this sketch, let us suppose that two players (or parties), L and R, dominate a country's politics and take turns to form the government. The parties' interactions are structured by constitutional laws and conventions. The laws, we assume, are "exogenous" (i.e., fixed) and thus not part of the immediate game. But conventions are "endogenous," and there is a game to determine which set of conventions, among a wide variety, is activated. These conventions will influence, among other things, lawmaking procedures, judicial independence, opposition privileges and modes of public

1 It is also worth mentioning that there are limitations with PD representations that can be more precisely explained with the aid of a simple model.

communication. The parties, especially their leaders, must take positions on the conventions that relate to these areas.

For the sake of simplicity, we can assume that their decision-making follows one of two broad strategies. First, a party leader may show "restraint," abiding by conventions that limit the power of a political majority. Second, a party leader may show "ambition," and in this case they want to make the most out of their time in government by implementing their preferred policy manifesto as completely and swiftly as possible. This might be because the leader believes that they face a time constraint during which they must prove their credibility, as Tushnet and Bugaric (2021) argue to explain the motivation of populist leaders. Policy maximization by an ambitious leader can lead to tensions with the set of conventions, and when clashes arise the party will prioritize its policy agenda over fidelity to convention.

The game begins with an election, which both parties stand a similar chance of winning. Once in power, the winning party must decide whether to adopt a posture of restraint or ambition vis-à-vis the system of conventions. Table 2.1 shows one plausible set of payoffs for the parties. The payoff to Party L, the initial party of government, is greatest when it adopts an ambitious posture while Party R shows restraint (L's payoff equals 4 and R's equals –2). Conversely, the payoff to Party R would be greatest if it were to show ambition while Party L shows restraint (R's payoff equals 3 and L's equals 0).[2] However, if Party L is ambitious, Party R's optimal response is in fact to match that approach by also adopting an ambitious posture (and in this scenario, L's payoff equals 3 and R's equals –1). For example, the opposition party might take steps to magnify and publicize the government's convention transgressions and use, to the extent possible, institutional opportunities to frustrate the government. In short, the dominant strategy (i.e., the most profitable play) for both players is "ambition," with Party L earning a payoff of 3 and Party R a payoff of –1. The expected (Nash) outcome from their play is therefore that they both play that strategy. As depicted in the table, the payoffs that follow are not symmetrical. Capturing what seems like an empirically plausible conjecture, the governing party will gain more than the opposition party, which nonetheless will still be better off playing an aggressive strategy than a more passive, accommodative one.

The simple PD representation suggests that sustaining conventions – in other words, both parties adopting a "restraint" posture and thereby sharing the maximum collective payoff (2 for each party) – will generally be deeply challenging. So, how and why, in strategic terms, have some systems overcome this dilemma? The key is the combination of iteration and punishment. While cooperation is not sustainable in any single round of the game, the

2 The opposition party might gain from playing an ambitious strategy by forcing concessions on the governing party or by enhancing its visibility or credibility with potential supporters.

Table 2.1 Convention Politics as a Prisoner's Dilemma

Party L \ *Party R*	*Restraint*	*Ambition*
Restraint	2, 2	0, 3
Ambition	4, −2	3, −1

extension of the game in time makes cooperation possible because now the returns from long-term cooperative behaviour may exceed the gains from a one-time defection. This will be the case if the game is ongoing (i.e., there is no definite endpoint) and each player is prepared to impose a "punishment" in response to any defection from cooperation by the other player. As Elster (2014: 55) confirms: "Each side would, when in power, prefer to be able to renege on the promise given by its predecessor, were it not for the fact that 'the same could then later be done to us.'"

Several implications follow from the PD representation of conventions. Most fundamentally, anything that has the effect of shortening the time horizons of constitutional actors, or their capacity to punish/reward, may destabilize the system of conventions. This is an observation with practical significance. For instance, it suggests that conventions may be destabilized by turbulence in party politics, including, for instance, change in the electoral competitiveness of parties or regular leadership instability, both of which may have the effect of reducing the time horizons of the players whose interactions are structured by conventions.

While Elster argues that a system of conventions can be fully represented as a PD, other research in the strategic tradition suggests that the game structure *may change as it is played over time* (Bicchieri 2006). A limitation with Elster's representation, then, is that it is static. It assumes that the same game, a PD, continues to play out. In fact, argues Christina Bicchieri (2006), games of conventions/norms can, over time, assume the characteristics of *coordination*. As she explains, "[w]hen a norm of cooperation is obeyed, a game like the PD . . . is transformed into a coordination game" (Bicchieri 2006: 26). This transition can be practically important because a key difference between the PD and a game of coordination is that the incentive to renege is ever present in the former but recedes in the latter. In a coordination game, players disagree about the best solution, but they all prefer to cooperate in some form. The classic example is the problem of deciding which side of the road to drive on – some drivers may prefer the left side and others may prefer the right side, but all prefer a coordinated convention (even on their less preferred side) than a free-for-all.

This contrast between cooperation (in the terms of the PD) and coordination can help to explain the rather different political interactions around conventions in new democracies as compared with established democracies. To be more precise, the PD model seems to be the more relevant one for understanding the politics of conventions in new democracies, while interactions in established democracies more typically resemble those of a coordination game. In other words, it is easier for elites in established democracies to follow conventions than it is for elites in emerging democracies, where the temptation to be constitutionally "ambitious" remains strong given doubts about the motivations and commitments of other players. Unfortunately, the transformation of the game structure takes time. It involves the PD game being played over many rounds – in practice, this might be thought of as electoral cycles – sufficient for expectations to form. The fulfilment of these beliefs constitutes an equilibrium that becomes more entrenched and stable over time. At this point, we can say that conventions have taken root (though this represents an equilibrium that can also unravel). The formalization of rules as law might be a shortcut to this end, as Richard H. McAdams (2008: 4) suggests, and therefore potentially more advantageous (or necessary) for new democracies than for established ones.[3]

Comparing the Two Traditions

Having now fleshed out the traditions, this section aims to compare them. The goal of this exercise is not to criticize one approach from the vantage point of the other. As I see it, both perspectives provide powerful ways to think about conventions. Its purpose, then, is to gain a deeper understanding of how the perspectives differ, and to stimulate questions and ideas that lie at the intersection of these traditions.

I compare the moralistic and strategic perspectives according to seven criteria. Three deal with substantive features of conventions: (1) how they are defined and conceptualized in each approach; (2) how adherence to conventions is explained; and (3) how the emergence of conventions and their change over time is depicted. A further three criteria deal with context. One considers (4) whether – and if so, the extent to which – constitutional conventions are portrayed as distinctive in comparison to other kinds of informal rules; we can call this "constitutional distinctiveness" or "exceptionalism." The other contextual considerations are: (5) what geographical settings are salient in the accounts of conventions in each tradition; and (6) within these settings, what institutions and relationships are brought into focus by the approach to conventions. Finally (7), I compare the methodologies that are

3 Indeed, Russell Hardin (1999: 134) explains the value of written constitutions in these terms, that is, as a means "to hasten the establishment of relevant conventions and to direct them in certain ways . . . rather than bumbling through to a result, a result that might [be] the rise of a tyrant by force."

Table 2.2 Comparing the Two Traditions

	Moralistic Perspective	*Strategic Perspective*
Defining and identifying conventions	Precedents supported by reasons	Equilibrium of expectations
Explaining adherence to conventions	Praise, shame, censure	Rationality over substantive preferences
Explaining convention emergence, change and collapse	Due to changing norms and functional requirements	Due to changing expectations among game players
Constitutional distinctiveness	High	Low
Countries/contexts in focus	Westminster democracies	United States; new democracies
Institutions/ relationships in focus	Crown, cabinet and parliament	Political parties
Analytical approach	Legal institutionalism	Rational-choice institutionalism

associated with each approach. Table 2.2 provides a head-to-head summary of the traditions in terms of these criteria. Following this, I flesh out the criteria in subsections on "substantive features of conventions" (criteria 1–3) and "context and methodology" (criteria 4–7), before suggesting some ways to integrate morality and strategy.

Substantive Features of Conventions

In defining conventions, the two perspectives resemble each other insofar as they both identify a behavioural pattern alongside the absence of a formal rule. However, lying beneath this common ground are two different accounts of when we know that a convention exists. In the morality perspective, the touchstone for this task remains the three-pronged test devised by Ivor Jennings (1952: 136), which proposes that a convention exists when there are applicable precedents, in which the actors involved believed they were bound by a rule, and there is a reason (i.e., a constitutional purpose) for that rule. For contributions in the strategic perspective, the existence of a convention depends on a convergence of expectations about the rule and the strategies (e.g., punishment) that support it. Elster (2014: 52, emphasis in original) argues that "unwritten norms cannot have causal efficacy unless one believes that other relevant actors believe in them and will act on them. If violating a norm causes no reaction, *it may never have existed in the first place.*" Put simply, then, conventions are "bundles of self-fulfilling expectations" (Bicchieri 2006: 23). While there is some overlap between this view and the first and second limbs of Jennings' test, the reason condition that forms the third part of that test – and which is central to the moralistic lens – is downplayed in strategic accounts.

The accounts of why actors follow conventions build on these foundations. In the moralistic tradition, the costs of violation may be internal (i.e., personal shame) or external (i.e., social opprobrium). Either way, consequences flow from the acknowledgment among constitutional actors that they are obliged to uphold rules that serve a social purpose. These actors follow a logic of *homo constitutionalus* (Congleton 2018), according to which they understand the world through rules. In the strategic perspective, by contrast, the motivations are primarily tactical. Political parties, which are often the main actors in these accounts, are motivated by substance (i.e., policy) more than procedure (e.g., whether their actions abide by convention). They are rational in the sense of *homo economicus*. Ultimately, they realize that violation of conventions will make their substantive goals harder to achieve in the long term because this will cause their opponents to play "hardball" tactics, as well (Tushnet 2004).

To account for the dynamics of conventions (i.e., their emergence and change over time), studies in the moralistic tradition extrapolate from the idea that conventions serve the function of expressing a society's deep values. This approach is aligned with accounts of constitutions that see them as representations of a community in a never-ending process of formation and reformation – that is, the term "constitution" operates as a verb (Pitkin 1987). In such an organic view, we should expect that conventions will change, mostly slowly (though not always), as a society's values evolve. For instance, as Scott Stephenson (2021: 15) suggests, the rising prominence of equality and diversity norms may lead to "demands that judges come from a diverse set of backgrounds . . . [and] cause the destruction of [traditional] constitutional conventions relating to the process for the nomination and appointment of judges."

In the strategic perspective, convention dynamics are bound up with political competition, and especially the conditions that shape the governing and opposition parties' expectations and strategies. So, while the moralistic approach to conventions complements an organic approach to constitutions, the strategic approach to conventions can be seen as an outgrowth of a broader strategic approach to constitutions, in which constitutions are viewed in light of the political "bargains" and "contracts" underlying them (e.g., Cooter 2000). As noted earlier, this perspective leads to the expectation that conventions can emerge and stabilize under conditions of repetition, of actors and competitive situations. Accordingly, fundamental changes to a party system – including, for instance, a shift in the parties' standing in the electorate – may exert pressure on conventions. Elster moves toward this observation in his description of the pairing convention in Britain, Australia and Canada, in which a politician who will be absent for a vote is paired with one from the opposing party, who abstains. Though well established, this convention, notes Elster (2014: 56), might break down if elections become less competitive and "the governing party firmly expects to be reelected."

Context and Methodology

The moralistic tradition has been developed primarily by scholars of the Westminster democracies, and within this setting, the relationships among the monarch, executive and legislature has been a major focus. The strategic perspective has been more influential in the United States, particularly in accounts of judicial independence, but also in descriptions of conventions within institutions (e.g., Senate filibuster), certain inter-institutional practices (e.g., periodic raising of the debt ceiling), and politicians' orientations towards their opponents (Azari and Smith 2012; Levitsky and Ziblatt 2018; Weingast 1979). The strategic tradition can also be detected in accounts of democratization and democratic backsliding, in descriptions of the expectations that are necessary for a constitution to take root and endure (e.g., Levitsky and Ziblatt 2018; Morlino 2012). The differences between these settings suggests that the relevance of the two perspectives may be related to a constitution's formal characteristics. As noted earlier, the brevity (or absence) of written constitutions in the Westminster democracies has been cited as a key reason why the morality perspective has been dominant in these countries. Attention to this contrast prompts questions and conjectures about, for instance, how the increasing written-ness of British constitutional arrangements or the difficulty of amending the formal U.S. constitution have shaped the development of conventions – and their moral and strategic bases – in those countries. The controversies in these contexts that I referred to earlier have also provoked unusual debates in which, in the United States, Donald Trump has been criticized on moral grounds and strategic considerations loomed large in the British conventions dispute.

Courts occupy an interesting position in the two perspectives. On one level, they might be regarded as peripheral to both accounts. In moralistic accounts, conventions mainly regulate the actions of and relations among the sovereign, ministers, parliamentarians and public servants – and although there are important conventions relating to the judiciary, which aim to insulate it from political pressures, the enforcement of conventions is often described as being beyond the scope of the courts. The strategic perspective is rooted in party competition but, once again, courts are not protagonists in the story of how and why conventions bind these actors. In some circumstances, both traditions acknowledge, courts can become involved in the management of conventions. This point was noted earlier with respect to the moralistic tradition (see Ahmed et al. 2019), and in the strategic tradition scholars recognize courts' potential (though largely unrealized) role as convention enforcers. For instance, Tushnet (2004: 526) observes that when Democrats in the Senate broke convention by filibustering judicial nominees during the presidency of George W. Bush, Republicans responded by threatening litigation even though "Senators typically have been quite jealous about refraining from submitting intra-house disputes to judicial supervision."

Another contrast between the traditions, which I alluded to earlier, concerns the differentiation of the constitutional domain. Contributions to the morality tradition treat that domain as a specialized one, whereas strategic studies tend to identify mechanisms that operate across social domains in general, including in constitutional affairs. There are exceptions to this claim in both traditions. For instance, in the strategic tradition, Elster (2014) points to distinctive features of the norms of elite-level politics. On the other hand, in the moralistic tradition, Graeme Orr's (2015) study of elections as meaningful rituals teases out connections between this democratic practice and other social rituals.

Finally, the two perspectives can be contrasted in terms of their methodological orientation. Descriptions of methodology in the social sciences often classify studies according to their form of "institutionalism" (see especially Hall and Taylor 1996). The strategic tradition can be placed within the "rational-choice institutionalism" (RCI) paradigm, which uses tools from microeconomics, depicts actors as instrumental rationalists and emphasizes strategic interaction and collective dilemmas. The moralistic tradition is not fully captured by any of the three variants of institutionalism identified by Hall and Taylor in their seminal article. However, Hall and Taylor do not give attention to what others have called "legal institutionalism." This might be regarded as another strand of institutionalism, and it seems to capture more precisely the methodology of the moralistic tradition on conventions. As articulated by Neil MacCormick (2007: 20), legal institutionalism focuses on rules that may be more or less formal, but which in all cases create normative order – that is, "common or overlapping conceptions of what one ought to do in various recurring situations."

Integrating Morality and Strategy

My analysis thus far has kept separate the morality and strategy perspectives, so their claims and implications could be unpacked and compared. But scholarly applications of these models often bring more nuance to the discussion than these "pure" models would suggest. For example, discussions of the prorogation crisis in Britain bring strategic considerations to the fore, even though the context is one in which adherence to conventions is more often understood through the moralistic lens. Likewise, in the United States, where conventions have typically been interpreted with a strategic lens, some commentators have invoked morality to inform their arguments (e.g., Ahmed 2022) which, to the extent that morality-based arguments are viewed as being more compelling or urgent than strategic arguments, may bolster the case that Trump's convention-breaking was (and remains) a threat to democracy.

While analyzing the two models separately can help us to understand each of them better, it also provides a surer footing to consider how they might be usefully integrated. Elster (2014) suggests one possible integration, arguing that strategy applies more to political elites while citizens are likely to adopt a moral view of conventions.[4] This difference can help to sustain conventions insofar as moral citizens are willing to "punish" representatives who violate conventions for strategic purposes. Second, another integration might present morality as a description of coordination dynamics once the PD game has been transformed into a game of coordination. A third kind of integration might progress through exploration of the ways in which the models relate in a specific context. As I have argued, in general, the morality frame seems to be more prominent in studies of Westminster politics, while strategic arguments are more common in research on American and comparative politics. Yet, as the Trump and prorogation examples suggest, the interpretation of convention politics in these contexts can go against the grain. Indeed, these kinds of situations – when a convention (or set of conventions) is rationalized on different grounds than it had been in the past – may be worth exploring as signs of potentially fundamental change to the system of conventions.

It might be argued, of course, that politicians often fuse moralistic and strategic considerations when they deal with conventions – for example, a politician might attempt to present a moralistic justification of what might actually be a strategic move. Indeed, the incentive for elites to describe what they do in anything less than moral terms is likely to be very weak. In these circumstances, what judgments can an analyst reach about the motivations underlying the convention? This problem suggests another important line of inquiry, concerned with mapping the discourse associated with the two perspectives. Analyses along these lines would provide the basis for empirical studies of the pattern of communication around a convention, including the balance between its moralistic and strategic content.

Conclusion

This chapter has drawn out and compared two approaches to constitutional conventions, one rooted in moralistic assumptions and the other in strategic assumptions. In so doing, my aim has been to show the potential for political motivation to generate new insights into conventions. Centring political motivation in the analysis of conventions provides a means to integrate the diverse literatures in which conventions are discussed. The chapter demonstrated this point by interpreting three empirical research agendas through the morality/strategy prism. Thus, I explained that conventions feature in different ways

4 This argument echoes Machiavelli's (1996) depiction of elites as ambitious, cunning and prideful, and the masses as decent and honourable (see Patapan 2018).

in the literatures on American politics, Westminster politics and the politics of democratic transition. However, morality and strategy can help us to make sense of these treatments, bringing coherence to our understanding of how conventions are defined across this work, why actors follow them, and what issues we should consider after observing the breach of a convention. Beyond its value in elucidating the study of conventions, the morality/strategy lens can also stimulate interesting and practical new lines of inquiry, including into questions about how morality and strategy interact in different settings and how these motivations can be detected in political behaviour and communication. To engage these questions, and more generally, to work with the morality/strategy dichotomy, analysts will need to apply and develop interdisciplinary analyses, and this should be considered another payoff from seeing conventions through the lens of political motivation.

References

Ahmed, Ashraf. 2022. A Theory of Constitutional Norms. *Michigan Law Review* 120(7), 1361–1418.

Ahmed, Farrah, Richard Albert and Adam Perry. 2019. Enforcing Constitutional Conventions. *International Journal of Constitutional Law* 17(4), 1146–1165.

Azari, Julia R. and Jennifer K. Smith. 2012. Unwritten Rules: Informal Institutions in Established Democracies. *Perspectives on Politics* 10(1), 37–55.

Barry, Nicholas, Narelle Miragliotta and Zim Nwokora. 2019. The Dynamics of Constitutional Conventions in Westminster Democracies. *Parliamentary Affairs* 72(3), 664–683.

Bicchieri, Cristina. 2006. *The Grammar of Society: The Nature and Dynamics of Social Norms*. Cambridge: Cambridge University Press.

Bingham, Tom. 2011. *The Rule of Law*. Penguin.

Bogdanor, Vernon. 2009. *The New British Constitution*. Oxford: Hart Publishing.

Brunclík, Milos and Michal Kubat. 2021. Constitutions Conventions in Central Europe: Presidents in Government Formation Process. *Problems of Post-Communism* 70(1), 42–54.

Chafetz, Josh and David E. Pozen. 2018. How Constitutional Norms Break Down. *UCLA Law Review* 65(6), 1430–1459.

Congleton, Roger. 2018. *Towards a Rule-Based Model of Human Choice: On the Nature of Homo Constitutionalus*. West Virginia University, Department of Economics, Working Paper Series 2.

Cooter, Robert. 2000. *The Strategic Constitution*. Princeton, NJ: Princeton University Press.

Dicey, A.V. 1915. *Introduction to the Study of the Law of the Constitution* (8th edition). London: Macmillan.

Dixon, Rosalind and Adrienne Stone. 2018. *The Invisible Constitution in Comparative Perspective*. Cambridge: Cambridge University Press.

Elster, Jon. 1995. Strategic Uses of Argument. In Kenneth Arrow, Robert H. Mnookin, Lee Ross, Amos Tversky and Robert Wilson (eds.), Barriers to Conflict Resolution. New York: W.W. Norton, pp. 236–257.

Elster, Jon. 2014. Political Norms. *Iyyun: The Jerusalem Philosophical Quarterly* 63(January), 47–59.

Foley, Michael. 2013. *The Silence of Constitutions: Gaps, 'Abeyances' and Political Temperament in the Maintenance of Government*. Abingdon: Routledge.

Hall, Peter A. and Rosemary C.R. Taylor. 1996. Political Science and the Three New Institutionalisms. *Political Studies* 44(5), 936–957.

Hardin, Russell. 1999. *Liberalism, Constitutionalism and Democracy*. Oxford: Oxford University Press.

Heard, Andrew. 2012. Constitutional Conventions: The Heart of the Living Constitution. *Journal of Parliamentary and Political Law* 6, 319–338.

Helmke, Gretchen and Steven Levitsky. 2004. Informal Institutions and Comparative Politics: A Research Agenda. *Perspectives on Politics* 2(4), 725–740.

Jaconelli, Joseph. 1999. The Nature of Constitutional Convention. *Legal Studies* 19(1), 24–46.

Jaconelli, Joseph. 2005. Do Constitutional Conventions Bind? *Cambridge Law Journal* 64(1), 149–176.

Jakab, András. 2016. *European Constitutional Language*. Cambridge: Cambridge University Press.

Jennings, Ivor. 1952. *The Law and the Constitution* (4th edition). London: University of London Press.

Kyle, Jordan and Yascha Mounk. 2018. *The Populist Harm to Democracy: An Empirical Assessment*. Tony Blair Institute for Global Change. https://institute.global/sites/default/files/articles/The-Populist-Harm-to-Democracy-An-Empirical-Assessment.pdf

Landau, David. 2020. Personalism and the Trajectories of Populist Constitutions. *Annual Review of Law and Social Science* 16, 293–309.

Levitsky, Steven and Daniel Ziblatt. 2018. *How Democracies Die: What History Reveals About Our Future*. London: Penguin.

Loughlin, Martin. 2018. The Silences of Constitutions. *International Journal of Constitutional Law* 16(3), 922–935.

Lührmann, Anna and Staffan I. Lindberg. 2019. A Third Wave of Autocratization Is Here: What Is New About It? *Democratization* 26(7), 1095–1113.

MacCormick, Neil. 2007. *Institutions of Law: An Essay in Legal Theory*. Oxford: Oxford University Press.

Machiavelli, Niccolo. 1996. *The Prince*, Trans. H.C. Mansfield Jr. Chicago: University of Chicago Press.

Marshall, Geoffrey. 1984. *Constitutional Conventions: The Rules and Forms of Political Accountability*. Oxford: Oxford University Press.

McAdams, Richard H. 2008. *Beyond the Prisoner's Dilemma: Coordination, Game Theory and the Law*. John M. Olin Program in Law and Economics Working Paper No. 437.

Morlino, Leonardo. 2012. *Changes for Democracy*. Oxford: Oxford University Press.

Muirhead, Russell and Nancy L. Rosenblum. 2019. *A Lot of People are Saying: The New Conspiracism and the Assault on Democracy*. Princeton, NJ: Princeton University Press.

Orr, Graeme. 2015. *Ritual and Rhythm in Electoral Systems: A Comparative Legal Account*. London: Routledge.

Patapan, Haig. 2018. The Politics of Modern Honor. *Contemporary Political Theory* 17(4), 459–477.

Perry, Adam and Adam Tucker. 2018. Top-Down Constitutional Conventions. *The Modern Law Review* 81(5), 765–789.

Pfiffner, James P. 2021. Donald Trump and the Norms of the Presidency. *Presidential Studies Quarterly* 51(1), 96–124.

Pitkin, Hanna Fenichel. 1987. The Idea of a Constitution. *Journal of Legal Education* 37(2), 167–169.
Postema, Gerald J. 2022. Constitutional Norms – Erosion, Sabotage, and Response. *Ratio Juris* 35(2), 99–122.
Renan, Daphna. 2018. Presidential Norms and Article II. *Harvard Law Review* 131, 2187–2282.
Schleiter, Petra and Thomas G. Fleming. 2020. Parliamentary Prorogation in Comparative Context. *The Political Quarterly* 91(3), 641–648.
Stephenson, Scott. 2021. Constitutional Conventions and the Judiciary. *Oxford Journal of Legal Studies*. doi:10.1093/ojls/gqaa047.
Sumption, Jonathan. 2020. Brexit and the British Constitution: Reflections on the Last Three Years and the Next Fifty. *The Political Quarterly* 91(1), 107–115.
Tushnet, Mark V. 2004. Constitutional Hardball. *John Marshall Law Review* 37, 523.
Tushnet, Mark V. and Bojan Bugaric. 2021. *Power to the People: Constitutionalism in the Age of Populism*. New York: Oxford University Press.
Twomey, Anne. 2018. *The Veiled Sceptre: Reserve Powers of Heads of State in Westminster Systems*. Cambridge: Cambridge University Press.
Vermeule, Adrian. 2015. Conventions in Court. *Dublin University Law Journal* 38(2), 283–310.
Weingast, Barry R. 1979. A Rational Choice Perspective on Congressional Norms. *American Journal of Political Science* 23(2), 245–262.
Willis, Paul G. and George L. Willis. 1952. The Politics of the Twenty-Second Amendment. *Political Research Quarterly* 5(3), 469–482.
Whittington, Keith E. 2013. The Status of Unwritten Constitutional Conventions in the United States. *University of Illinois Law Review* 5, 1847–1870.

Chapter 4

Conventions All the Way Down

The Emergence of Parliamentary Conventions Over MP Qualifications

Graeme Orr

Introduction

This chapter is a close and novel study of the evolution of conventions within a bespoke, yet politically charged, area. The area boils down to this question: Who decides – and how – whether an MP (Member of Parliament) is qualified to sit in Parliament? It focuses on the question within the Australian legal and parliamentary system.

The chapter takes this focus not for the sake of the answer itself, but to uncover how conventions evolve within even relatively narrow issues and even at a high level of detail. This is in contrast to the older paradigm of thinking about conventions, where they are typically seen as fundamental, yet fuzzy, concepts. Conventions thus exist not just on an exalted level, as high principles structuring foundational questions; they permeate constitutionalism, all the way down.

Constitutionalism, here, means the frameworks that govern public governance. Constitutionalism in Westminster-derived systems, of course, is notoriously porous. Even in countries with an entrenched constitution, such as Australia, the boundary between 'constitutional law' and 'administration' can be a matter of Borgesian librarianship as much as Mosaic decree. Framework can blur into mere lower-level practices, but such boundary concerns can be put aside here. The domain of this chapter – parliamentary law and practice – is a rich source of conventions. Parliamentary law and practice straddles formal constitutional law and parliamentary norms, and so goes beyond mere administrative practices (Nethercote 2015).

Conventions, as classically understood, are demarked by two factors. They emerge through the conduct revealed in historic or notable episodes. Second, they are enforceable via norms of adherence rather than litigation. The tendency to only study foundational conventions of often fuzzy application has meant an obsession with two yin/yang qualities: stickiness and plasticity. As Jennings (1959, p. 136) put it, conventions are revealed through 'precedents', to which 'the actors . . . believe[d] that they were bound' (Jennings then added, as a lawyer would, that conventions should be grounded in principle, revealing a 'reason for the rule').

DOI: 10.4324/9781003506577-4

Each of these factors and qualities is a matter of degree. The absence of judicial enforcement should not be understood pejoratively, to imply that conventions are lesser than law.[1] Conventions are more than mere habits or rituals of governance.[2] Conventions need not be invariably followed to be considered alive. Their 'stickiness' speaks to their compelling character.

Conventions may evolve. But that does not mean they must be or remain fuzzy. As we shall see, they can end up highly particularised, even partly codified – and hence, less than plastic. Conventions around the handling of MP qualification disputes emerged over a long but staccato process, solidifying recently. Let us turn now to framing this case study.

The Problem of Handling MP Qualification Disputes

The substantive factors that ought disqualify someone from being an Australian MP have been on the reform agenda for over 40 years (House of Representatives Standing Committee on Legal and Constitutional Affairs 1997; Joint Standing Committee on Electoral Matters 2018; Senate Standing Committee on Constitutional and Legal Affairs 1981).[3] Concern with the inflexibility of these underlying rules – e.g., barriers to dual citizens or public servants – erupted in 2016–2018, when there was a slew of parliamentary referrals and court cases, leading to many MPs being disqualified. Despite this protracted hullabaloo, limited attention has been given to the *procedures* for handling or determining disputes about whether an individual is qualified to sit in Parliament. The bulk of this chapter fills that space. In particular, the conventions we will uncover here:

- Emerged through a staccato or punctuated evolution, with competing principles playing out across different precedents.
- Solidified quickly after a welter of problems erupted in 2016–2018, so as to be relatively sticky.
- Reflect the ultimate principle of depoliticising a power, whose guiding principle had once been seen as an intimate aspect of the autonomy of the (political) branch that is Parliament.

1 When push comes to shove, courts occasionally enforce some conventions (e.g., *R (Miller) v. The Prime Minister* [2019] UKSC 19, where executive prerogative to prorogue the House of Commons collided with parliamentary supremacy).

2 This can include symbolics, like the Crown opening parliament, but it does not extend to every important aspect of public life. Australia's Parliament was built with grass on top, so the public could walk over it. Until security fears led to that being curtailed, it was a conventional practice symbolising accountability – but not a 'constitutional' convention.

3 The earlier reports ignore procedure; the latest one touches on it in passing.

- Have been particularised, in detailed, subsidiary conventions that are less foundational principles than 'conventional' – in the sense of non-arbitrary – commitments.[4]
- Not subject to court superintendence, yet intimately related to court jurisdiction.[5]

The overarching convention – that any serious, publicly known allegation about an MP's qualifications is now to be determined by the High Court, not the Parliament – represents the triumph of two principles. One is that parliaments are too politicised to determine such questions. The other is that their makeup should be stabilised as soon as possible. These principles have come to trump a single, older principle that each house of a parliament should have sole autonomy over its members. This triumph may seem obvious to contemporary eyes, yet it is not necessarily the case that a question of democratic moment such as 'can X be seated in Parliament?' should be despatched for resolution by generalist judges rather than reflected upon by the parliamentary body itself. So, how we reached this point is a story in itself.

A Short History of the Power to Determine an MP's Right to Sit

The question of MP qualifications is vexed and long (Carney 2000, chs 2–4; Morris 2012, chs 3–6) For our purposes, a potted history will suffice. Until Stuart times, the right to sit in the British Parliament could be challenged in Chancery. The Commons wrested this power from the Crown in the 17th century. For centuries, it was then clasped close to the parliamentary breast: an 'extremely special' power, 'jealously maintained and guarded' (*Strickland v Grima* [1930] AC 285, p. 296). The standard method for challenging someone's right to sit came to be via petitioning Parliament over the result of an election, if the qualification issue were known beforehand. Or, it could arise by the house itself raising and determining the issue on its own motion, especially if the alleged disqualification was incurred during an MP's term. Either way, the putative MP's peers were to judge the matter. By 1770, a dedicated committee was established to determine claims (Parliamentary Elections Act 1770 [UK], a.k.a. Grenville's Act). This removed hearings from the floor of

4 Admittedly, this is not a strict dichotomy. A foundational question – like who gets to call an election – could be answered crisply (e.g., 'the Prime Minister, at any time'), since it is in narrow compass. Or it may be hard to particularise (e.g., 'usually at the Prime Minister's direction, but subject to a reserve power to delay or refuse in exceptional cases').

5 Since they concern when parliaments should refer such questions to the courts. That courts do not meddle in the liminal decision over whether to refer matters to them puts them beneath judicial 'cognisance', due to the deeper principle that courts do not rule on the exercise of internal parliamentary affairs.

Parliament, for efficiency and better deliberation over a potentially heated question. Such committees, through their reports, could also build up explicit precedents of their own.

Partiality was inevitable, however, and so in 1868, the Commons surrendered the most fraught element of this power – disputed elections – to the judiciary (Parliamentary Elections Act 1868 (UK)). The courts initially saw this as a hot potato, fearing being caught up in partisanship (Seymour 1915, p. 423). That concern was partly addressed by a judicial 'rota' to share this contentious work around the bench. Whilst Australian colonies soon followed the UK model of vesting power over contested elections in the judiciary, other models were suggested. For example, for 30 years in Queensland, disputed elections were heard by a tribunal with a judge presiding over two MPs, drawn from a panel, acting as 'assessors' of fact or jurors (Elections Tribunals Act 1886 (Qld), ss. 11–13).

Election petitions must be brought before the courts expeditiously. Any elector may use this process to challenge the *election* of an unqualified candidate. In practice, this is rare, for two reasons. One hurdle is gathering evidence, including sometimes hidden personal facts (e.g., about a candidate's citizenships), within a strict 40-day time period to bring an election petition (Commonwealth Electoral Act 1918 (Cwlth), s. 355(e)). In addition, there is the risk of bearing two sets of legal costs if the petition is lost.

Judging the qualifications of an existing MP, during the life of a parliament, is different from challenging an election, in several ways. A disqualification allegation may arise long after an election, either because the disqualification comes to light late or because it did not arise until well into the MP's term (e.g., falling into bankruptcy). In addition, disqualification cases tend to be narrower than challenging an election due to alleged maladministration or campaign chicanery.

As a result, the power to determine if a *sitting* MP has a right to sit has never been automatically or exclusively assigned to the courts, unlike the power to challenge a recent election (cf. Commonwealth Electoral Act, s. 356). Instead, it has been retained by most parliaments. Thus, during the 1890s Australian federation debates, a distinction was drawn between disputed elections, where the 'rights of electors' are foremost a 'matter . . . for the courts', and disqualifying an MP, which concerns the 'internal discipline . . . of Parliament itself' (Mr Wise, delegate, quoted in Australasian Federation Conference 1897a). In 1901, then, it was expected the new Australian Parliament would continue the British approach vesting electoral disputes in the courts (Mssrs Lewis, Brown and Barton, but cf. Sir W.A. Zeal, delegates quoted in Australasian Federation Conference 1897a). Yet each house would remain free to decide if an MP was disqualified, as part of its ancient privileges. The Constitution left it up to each house to exercise power itself *or* for the Parliament to legislate to share the power with some other body (Australian Constitution 1900 (Cwth), s. 47).[6] This politesse reflected the principles within the historical struggle over the power.

The new Australian Parliament quickly divested itself of any role in election disputes, rendering petitions to the High Court as the sole avenue for such claims (Commonwealth Electoral Act, s. 353). Initially, each house retained sole power to rule on existing MPs' qualifications. But, by 1907, it legislated to vest jurisdiction in the High Court to allow either chamber to refer qualification matters affecting any of its members to that Court (Disputed Elections and Disqualifications Act 1907 (Cwlth)).[7] One lesson and three issues arise from this. The lesson is that the power involved is inherently politically sensitive, but not insuperably so.

The first issue was whether referral amounted to the Parliament abandoning its power to rule on MP qualifications. In the second half of the 20th century, Senators Murphy and Barwick (each an Attorney-General at the time, before becoming a High Court Justice) argued it had. But that is now clearly not accepted (Carney 2000, p. 148; Senate Standing Committee on Constitutional and Legal Affairs 1981, pp. 93–94).[8] A second issue, persisting to this day, is the risk of a citizen filing an election petition to argue a winning candidate was disqualified. This could create embarrassment, if the High Court were hearing that petition whilst the relevant house issued its own ruling on the question.[9] The third issue – to be explored now – is *what conventions would evolve* over when and how Parliament would decide an MP's qualifications or refer it to the Court.

The Emergence of the Contemporary Conventions

The core disqualifications for Australian MPs – unusually for a Constitution that is otherwise thin on basic democratic issues and does not even mention

6 The 1891 draft left all questions of qualifications or vacancies to the house concerned (Quick and Garran 1901, p. 495). The 1897 draft continued to distinguish between 'qualification of a member or vacancy' – whereby the default rule was each house would decide – and a 'disputed election' – whereby the default was that a federal court decides (Australasian Federation Conference 1897b). But the Constitution could not immediately vest power over elections in a federal court, because for the very first election, there was as yet no federal judiciary.

7 This was not motivated by concern about houses ruling on qualifications. It was merely a response to complexities about when a 'vacancy' arose: see the long litigation involving the contested 1904 Senate election between Vardon and O'Loghlin and Barton CJ's suggestion that Parliament should clarify that particular sub-issue (Blackshield 2016).

8 See also examples from the 1990s and 2000s, discussed later in this chapter, of each house ruling on a matter rather than referring it.

9 Such a clash can no longer occur outside an election petition, as the route for a 'common informer' petition' via Constitution s 46 is now staunched by *Alley v Gillespie* (2018) 326 CLR 328.

the right to vote – were set in stone in 1900 (Australian Constitution, ss 43–45). They are based in 19th-century values, leading to angst for those wanting flexibility in the area; but that is another matter. Section 44 lists five disqualifications. These fall into two categories: (1) moral taint, through existing criminal conviction or bankruptcy; and (2) conflicts of interest and duty, through foreign citizenship or allegiance, working for the Crown, or pecuniary interests in agreements with the public service. Besides such disqualifications, positive qualifications for election are set by legislation. These are unproblematic in application as they are invariably bright-line rules, like minimum age (Orr 2022, pp. 318–319).[10]

For much of the 20th century, there was little litigation or parliamentary consideration of disqualifications. It is unlikely that earlier generations of candidates and MPs were perfectly self-policing. One explanation for the dearth of consideration is that the governing class ignored the issue.[11] They (and the media) were less interested in strictly enforcing disqualifications, and more concerned about pragmatics and honour. On top of that, information about the backgrounds of candidates and MPs was less widely available than it is in today's social media age. Finally, in the case of dual citizenships, immigration until the late 1940s was mostly from parts of the 'Empire' that were until recently not considered 'foreign' (*Sue v. Hill* (1999) 199 CLR 462). Those disqualification matters that were aired were sometimes cranky. An example is mid-20th century sectarian petitions trying to argue that Roman Catholic MPs owed allegiance to the Vatican.[12]

On rare occasions prior to 1975, each house considered alleged disqualifications, raised ad hoc by one MP against another, without resorting to a court referral. Instead, the houses ruled directly on the claims. In 1924, a Labor MHR moved a motion to have two rural MPs from the governing parties, Mr A.G. Manning and Mr W.W. Killen, declared disqualified. Each had been appointed to a depression-era Meat Council, funded by the government. The claim was not that the appointments were offices under the Crown, but that since each was a signatory to the account for distributing the fund, they had a pecuniary interest with the public service (Mr West in House of Representatives 1924, pp. 1350–1351). The argument reads like bush-lawyering, suggesting that West had not sought formal legal advice.

10 On imprecision, see Orr 2022, pp. 318–319.

11 I am indebted to Anne Twomey for this insight.

12 *Crittenden v Anderson* (unreported, High Court of Australia, Justice Fullagar, 23 August 1950, pp. 4–5) dismissing petition as 'vexatious and oppressive' and contrary to the Catholic Relief Act 1829 (UK). Before that came *Sarina v O'Connor* (petition withdrawn, High Court of Australia, 10 December 1946). In each instance, the MP was a Labor MHR (Member of the House of Representatives) and the petitioner an unsuccessful independent candidate. In neither case did the parliamentary Liberal Party support the claim, nor did the House do more than formally note it.

The Attorney-General rebutted the argument. After noting the House had disbanded its 'Elections and Qualifications Committee' in 1907, he described the procedure of asking the house to rule as 'unprecedented'. This obvious overstatement was less a statement of historical truth than a way to avoid the house investigating let alone debating something embarrassing to his side of politics:

> the qualifications of an honorable member depends upon the sifting of facts as well as upon the interpretation of the law; yet the honorable member has asked the House to pass judgment upon the facts as he has presented them. He invites the House to express an opinion. The question for consideration . . . is one to be determined in a proper legal way, in accordance with the procedure laid down in the Electoral Act, and only after the facts have been sifted in a proper atmosphere.
>
> (Sir L Groom in House of Representatives 1924, p. 1353.)

Yet the Attorney-General did not seek to refer the allegations to the Court. On the contrary, he gave his legal opinion that there was no 'agreement' to taint the MPs personally (Groom in House of Representatives 1924, p. 1356). Others debated the facts and law, before the motion was rejected by the House. The Attorney-General seems to have been asserting a kind of legal demurrer: knocking down a claim as misguided on its face. Labor MPs, for their part, lamented that it 'would be a sorry day for Parliament if the time ever arrived when it could no longer be entrusted with the reputation of its members' (Mr West in House of Representatives 1924, p. 1362) and 'I cannot . . . regard the High Court – which is the creature of this Parliament – as a tribunal superior to and controlling this Parliament. . . . Parliament is the guardian of its own honour' (Mr Brennan in House of Representatives 1924, p. 1360).

In 1974, the Senate considered the high-profile 'Gair Affair'. Senator Vince Gair had led the crossbench Democratic Labor Party. He accepted the Ambassadorship to the Holy See, offered by then Labor government to free up a strategic extra vacancy in a pending half-Senate election. Conservative figures, however, waylaid Gair, so his resignation was not submitted before the election writ was hastily issued, a tactic designed to prevent his seat being filled by election. Gair then wrote to the Senate President, asserting that accepting the Ambassadorship automatically disqualified him from the Senate.

Miffed by the conservative counter-ruse, Attorney-General Lionel Murphy moved that the Senate refer the question of *when* Gair had become disqualified to the High Court (Senate 1974b, p. 681). In doing so, he adduced Solicitor-General and General Counsel opinions (Senate 1974b, p. 682, 1974a, p. 639). Echoing Groom from 1924, whilst quoting a conservative Attorney-General's remarks from 1971, Senator Murphy claimed it would be an 'unreal situation if . . . any one House of the Parliament were to decide whether or not a senator' retained their qualifications (Senate 1974a, p. 681). Curiously, Senate Standing Orders retained a notional standing committee on 'Disputed Elections and Qualifications', although it had long been moribund. Less curiously, in opposition in 1971 Murphy had suggested revitalising that committee to consider the constitutionality of MPs holding newly created assistant ministerships (Senate 1971, pp. 280, 283).

In the Gair Affair, senators briefly debated what, if any, procedure to adopt, before breaking into rancour over the proprieties of the appointment itself.[13] Whilst the disqualification was legally obvious, the government lacked the numbers in the Senate to have it referred to the Court. In the end, the legal and strategic niceties were washed away when the entire Senate was dissolved in a double dissolution. Nonetheless, and unlike the 1924 precedent, here the party in control of the house was *avoiding* a referral, despite advice that there was a serious legal point requiring determination. A lesson from these two imbroglios is that, when the goose becomes the gander, political dexterity tends to shape principle in the absence of any clear rule or accepted convention.

The First Court Referrals (1975 and 1988)

It took until 1975 for the first referral from Parliament to the High Court to occur. That involved a pecuniary interest in the supply of timber, by Country Party Senator James Webster's family company to the Commonwealth public service (*Re Webster* (1975) 132 CLR 270). The matter was first raised, by a citizen and a journalist, before the Joint Committee on Pecuniary Interests of Members of Parliament. That committee referred it to the Senate as a whole. The Senate *unanimously* resolved to refer the matter to the Court and to grant Webster leave. It was left to Webster to decide if it felt 'improper for him to take part in [parliamentary] deliberations while the court decision is pending' (Senator Withers in Senate 1975a, p. 1139). Webster did take leave and was granted a pair so the tight party balance of that Senate was not affected.

Chief Justice Barwick took the case for himself and ruled in favour of the Webster. That Barwick had himself been an MP and Minister might explain his pragmatic approach; his reasoning on the substantive question has recently been overruled as unduly narrow (*Re Day (No. 2)* (2017) 343

13 E.g., Senator Wright in Senate (1974b, p. 700):

> It is suggested that this chamber should abdicate its function to decide on its own Constitution . . . when an assault has been made upon its integrity by the Prime Minister . . . offering an office of profit . . . to one of our members, keeping it secret until the appropriate time . . . and then purporting to trundle it out before the public at a time when the advantage would be unassailable.

ALR 181). At the time, it was feared that a broader ruling could create chaos in the affairs of MPs with business interests or even those who just wished to keep alive a professional qualification.

The Webster referral is instructive, as it occurred *despite* multi-party sympathy for the MP.[14] The Labor Leader in the Senate pointed to the 'technical and involved matters of law' as reason for the house not to determine the question itself. Another Labor Senator stated that, regardless of sympathy, as the question was serious 'there [ought] never have been any thought [of the Senate] adjudging' the matter, lest the public assume MPs would show 'leniency or sympathy to one of their own' (Senator Milliner in Senate 1975c, pp. 1199–1200). Liberal Senator Reg Wright went as far as to (wrongly) claim that the 1907 legislation permitting Parliament to refer matters to the courts all but extinguished the ability of the House to resolve the matter. He also appealed to the optics of impartiality. But his concern was not with MPs favouring their collective interest. Rather, he voiced concern about 'political pressures and interests' that would face even a multi-party committee tasked to hear the matter (Wright in Senate 1975b, p. 1202).

Whilst the referral was unanimous, this did not prevent the Senate engaging in over three hours of discussion, over a week of sittings, around Webster's and other MPs' affairs. An informal precedent was also set, with this first court referral, that the impugned MP should have the cost of their legal representation borne by the Commonwealth (Prime Minister Whitlam in House of Representatives 1975, p. 2013). One can see how MPs of any stripe might rationalise that as a cost of their service, to be publicly met. Despite an appeal by the Senate Opposition Leader for the government to publish any legal opinion (e.g., from the Australian Government Solicitor) it had on Webster (Withers in Senate 1975a, p. 1141), there was no such release. To this day, the government makes ad hoc decisions about making such advice public.

The year 1975 was, above all, one of Senate-induced constitutional crisis. Had Webster been disqualified, a conservative majority in the Victorian Parliament ensured no risk to his side's numbers in the Senate (thanks to a constitutional rule that the state parliament fills the vacancy). Later in that tumultuous year, another Senate qualification imbroglio arose, over Senator Albert Field. Field was the pick of a conservative Queensland Premier to replace a dead Labor senator, breaching a convention that the nominee of the affected political party should fill the vacancy.[15]

14 Such sympathy led to the fast-tracking a law limiting penalties if a 'common informer' (a.k.a. bystander) sued over the MP continuing to sit. It passed in a day, with multi-party approval (*Common Informers (Parliamentary Disqualifications) Act 1975* (Cwlth)).

15 A convention later put in constitutional stone by a 1977 referendum.

Field was, however, arguably disqualified from the Senate, due to his employment with Queensland railways and membership of a government board at the date of his appointment. Labor fought back, with Senator Murphy moving to refer Field to a revitalised Committee of Elections and Qualifications, for investigation and report (Senate 1975c, p. 603). The (Labor) President of the Senate agreed, commenting that 'in a matter such as this the Senate is the master of its own affairs' (Senator O'Byrne in Senate 1975c, p. 604). The opposition had the numbers to block the motion and let Field be sworn in (Senate 1975c, p. 605). But even the opposition soon accepted that Field was under such a cloud that he needed to be granted leave of absence (Senate 1975d, p. 823). Labor was however, still down one voting member compared to before the death. In the end, the dismissal of the Whitlam government and dissolution of both houses rendered the debate moot.[16] Once again, positions were taken as much on political manoeuvrings as on principle.

The second-ever referral occurred 13 years later, also from the Senate. Senator Robert Wood had been elected as a Nuclear Disarmament Party MP in August 1987. In January 1988, the Immigration Department advised the Senate that Wood was taking out Australian citizenship. Wood was clearly not qualified to be elected or sit.[17] Despite that clarity, the Minister for Home Affairs said that whilst 'the Senate may have a residual power on this particular matter, it is clearly more desirable to send the matter to the High Court'. This was not a case of the major parties ganging up on a poorly-advised minor party MP. Rather, there was 'speculation as to what the consequences would be' of the disqualification (Senator Ray in Senate 1988, pp. 3, 5). The Court helped clarify this technical question, holding that a Senate vacancy should be filled by a recount of the votes cast by the electorate – not a fresh election – to preserve the proportional representation system in the Senate (*Re Wood* (1988) 167 CLR 145.)

The upshot of the decisions of the Senate in 1975 and 1988 can be summarised as a nascent cluster of conventions. At that point, it seemed that the house in question should err on the side of referring any seriously contested disqualification to the High Court (including if there were some secondary legal question about the consequence of a vacancy). If the disqualification were blatant, it could alternatively rule on the matter. In doing this, MPs

16 At that point, a common informer's and a High Court petition by a Labor Party figure were in train (Orr 2018, p. 18). Parliamentary consideration of a British dual-citizen, Senator-elect Heather Hill, was also overtaken by private court action (Senate 1998, p. 616, 1999, p. 4984).

17 He was less culpable than might seem. Citizenship was only required of MPs in 1981 and Wood had been unaware of his citizenship status when he was nominated for election. He also survived a poorly framed election petition, in which a conservative MP's wife threw a kitchen sink of allegations against him, including that he owed allegiance to a foreign power – not via the UK, but his socialism (*Nile v. Wood* (1988) 167 CLR 133).

under a cloud were not to be thrown to the legal wolves, but to have their legal costs covered. However, the government did not have to publish any legal opinion it had sought on the matters involved.

Counter-Examples – Refusals to Refer MPs (1990s–2010s)

Three instances of Parliament explicitly *not* referring allegations – in effect deciding in favour of the MP – are noteworthy. All involved thorny 'pecuniary interests' of government MPs and ministers. Two involved members of the House of Representatives, where a government normally has a majority and can thus feel confident of controlling the outcome of House motions.

In 1999, the Labor opposition sought to refer Mr Warren Entsch (an MHR and assistant minister) to the High Court (House of Representatives 1999b, p. 6638). A company of which he was a director had supplied concrete to the Department of Defence. Entsch had claimed he was unaware of the contract until after it was awarded, a moral rather than legal defence (House of Representatives 1999b, p. 6710).[18] The House considered the matter and, on the government's numbers, declared Entsch was not disqualified (House of Representatives 1999b, p. 6724).[19] The government tabled advice from the Acting Solicitor-General, which reasoned that the contract was unobjectionable under the *Webster* precedent (House of Representatives 1999b, pp. 6722, 6730). The opposition cited its legal advice that the matter was 'unclear' and that there was a 'substantial prospect' that the Court would not follow *Webster's* case anyway (House of Representatives 1999b, p. 6722). In short, unlike with Webster, bipartisanship was absent. The opposition even sought to censure the Attorney-General for 'usurping the role of the High Court' (House of Representatives 1999b, p. 6734). Clearly, any convention that all contested disqualification matters were to be referred to the judiciary was susceptible to a government relying on its own legal advice – at the risk of appearing partisan and raising the political temperature over the issue.

Then, in the early 2000s, Senator Nigel Scullion (Country-Liberal Party) was under doubt. For some years, his family company supplied significant services to departments and to a fisheries authority. After Scullion himself raised the matter, the Senate authorised its President to brief a senior barrister to advise, but not before 16 months had elapsed. This forestalled a motion by The Greens to have the matter referred to the High Court. Greens' leader, Senator Bob Brown, argued that 'the best legal advice – the determinative,

18 He also argued he had not derived dividends or remuneration but was only formally involved in the company 'to help a mate' (House of Representatives 1999a, p. 6496).

19 Whilst debate was limited, the Opposition Leader asked questions about the matter and sought to censure the Prime Minister for not dismissing Entsch under the Ministerial Code of Conduct (House of Representatives 1999a, p. 6481).

definitive and historical source of legal advice – has been the High Court' (Senate 2003, p. 15533). On this occasion, the opposition agreed with the government to have the matter handled by seeking advice from the private bar (Senate 2003, pp. 15533–15534). Perhaps the opposition's rationale was that the advice would appear more independent than advice given by, or via, the Attorney-General (a government figure).

The advice that was tendered doubted the fishery authority was part of the 'public service'. In relation to supplies to core government departments, it followed *Re Webster's* precedent. The advice also went beyond *Re Webster* to consider whether Scullion displayed 'any intention to allow the Crown to influence him' as an MP. This ungainly wording seems designed to capture a broader approach to the disqualification than in *Re Webster*, as well as the parliamentary principle that it is contempt for an MP to accept favours to influence their role. Without giving reasoning, on this point the advice was also negative (Holland 2004).

As in Entsch's matter, a referral may have led to *Re Webster's* narrow precedent being revised much sooner. On the other hand, the handling of this matter was notable for co-operation between government and opposition. As a senior opposition Senator put it, in the spirit of Pilate:

> An allegation of disqualification] presents us . . . with a problem. . . . What *normally* happens in these circumstances is that . . . senior senators who have dealt with these matters before . . . try to work out a course of action. . . . [O]ne thing we do not like to do is judge our peers and colleagues. How can we do that objectively? How can we in fact put aside political partisanship? . . . On this occasion it was decided to seek the advice of a senior QC [Queen's Counsel] as to the appropriate level of action, because *ultimately* these matters are determined not by the Senate but by the High Court . . . *But the real question is: should this chamber refer the matter for decision there? Are there or were there substantial grounds to refer this matter to the Court . . .* ?
>
> I think the process was right this time: *refer it outside the chamber, get an advice and agree basically in advance that, whichever way the chips fall, we will cop the advice.*
>
> (Senator Robert Ray in Senate 2004, p. 19569, emphasis added.)

A third notable decision not to refer involved Mr Peter Dutton, an MHR and Minister for Immigration, in 2018. This occurred in the middle of the slew of referrals, discussed in what follows, and after *Webster*'s precedent had been expanded to catch more pecuniary interests. Dutton had an interest in childcare centres. Welfare law defrayed childcare costs for parents, via a subsidy claimed directly by childcare centres. In Dutton's matter, the Prime Minister – himself in a rivalrous relationship with Dutton – instigated urgent Solicitor-General's advice. The advice said the 'better view' was that

Dutton was not disqualified (Donahue 2018, para. 4). It reasoned, cogently, that Dutton had a general pecuniary interest to register but not a conflict of interest at the constitutional level. His position was little different to an MP who, for example, remains an occasional doctor and claims health rebates on behalf of patients (Orr 2019, p. 591).

There was, however, some doubt in the advice's tail. First the advice hedged that, given the complexity of the law, 'it is impossible to state the position with certainty' (Donahue 2018, para. 9). Second, the childcare centres had also applied for grants to enhance services to disabled children. Whilst the families concerned were still the real benefit of that money, in legal terms, a grant is like a contract, subject to leverage if not haggling, and not merely a formulaic welfare subsidy. Third, the Labor opposition presented its own QC's advice that the issues were so arguable that Dutton should be referred to the Court. In the event, the House voted along party lines, by a margin of just one, to not refer the matter (House of Representatives 2018, p. 8261). The episode was thus settled in a matter of days, at a time when the government's numbers were paper-thin. This was in sharp contrast to say Senator Scullion's matter, which proceeded as slowly as Bleak House, yet with bipartisanship.

The choice of Parliament to 'refer', or to rule on the qualification itself, is not a true binary. Besides referral to a court, Parliament can rule on the qualification, leading to a third and fourth option – that is, to uphold the MP's position or to unseat them. There is even a fifth possibility – namely, to ignore the matter by kicking it into the long grass. That would often have a similar effect to upholding the MP's position.

There is even a sixth intermediate position: vote to refer but delay the referral to give the MP time to renounce any conflict, with a view to resigning and seeking re-appointment or re-election. That occurred in the case of Senator-elect Jeannie Ferris in 1996. Ferris's matter was considered over no fewer than nine days, including documentary evidence and legal arguments (e.g., Senate 1996, pp. 1253–1255, cf. 1250–1251; Laing 2016, ch 6). Rosemary Laing, as Clerk of the Senate, advised that Ferris was 'almost certainly' disqualified due to a public role she had accepted. Having renounced that conflicting role and then resigned, Ferris was re-appointed by the South Australian Parliament to fill her own Senate vacancy. In legal theory, an MP cannot truly resign if their election was void, as a void office was never filled in the first place. But in practice, they can if neither the Parliament nor the Court ever rules against them. Similar workarounds occurred during the 2016–2018 citizenship debacle (discussed in what follows).

The cluster of non-referrals just discussed reminds us that although a nascent convention had appeared in favour of referring any seriously contested qualification issue to the Court, a governing majority in a house could fall back on apparently cogent legal advice to avoid a referral. Or it could lean on the member to resign, to expedite the filling of the vacancy. When non-referral raises a perception of partisan protection of the MP concerned, however, an unseemly partisan squabble was risked. This would be most obvious if the initial (even official) legal advice were not absolute and a rival QC's report were produced.

A Circus of Referrals Over Dual Citizenships (2016–2018)

The story of Parliament's 'citizenship crisis' – in truth, a circus – has been well told elsewhere (Hobbs et al. 2018; Twomey 2017b). It began with realisations, in mid-2017, affecting two Greens senators. One, Senator Scott Ludlam, had been born in New Zealand but not naturalised when his family immigrated when he was young. The other, Senator Larissa Waters, had been born during a short parental stay in Canada, but naturalised. Waters had mistakenly assumed that her Australian naturalisation had cancelled her birthright Canadian citizenship.[20] Each resigned, honourably but precipitously, since a court order for a recount was needed to fill the Senate vacancy. (A resignation from the House of Representatives precipitates a by-election, equivalent to a court ordered vacancy ordering a fresh election.)

These two discoveries quickly snowballed into a slew of revelations, affecting more than a dozen members across both chambers, mostly related to inherited dual citizenships. In some, the law was relatively routine (at least once foreign citizenship law was consulted), but some were downright obscure and contestable.

As it happened, this renewed focus and even zealousness over parliamentary qualifications was preceded, in late 2016, by the referrals of two minor party senators over problems – not relating to citizenship – that obviously required legal adjudication. Senator Bob Day was held to be disqualified for holding an indirect pecuniary interest in the lease of his electorate office (*Re Day (No 2)* (2017) 343 ALR 181). Senator Rod Culleton was referred over a criminal conviction at the time of his nomination, but which had been rescinded by a court after his election (*Re Culleton (No. 2)* (2017) 263 CLR 176). Neither survived their referral.

Besides the slew of (mostly) dual citizenship referrals, which proved a burden on the High Court's hearing schedules, as noted earlier other potential referrals were forestalled when members of the House of Representatives fell on their swords. For instance, Mr John Alexander MHR resigned and renounced his dual citizenship within time to (successfully) contest the ensuing by-election. Electors seemed to be much more forgiving than the

20 A reasonable misapprehension given the reverse would have been true: for a long time, Australian birth citizenship would be lost if the person concerned later took out another citizenship.

Constitution. A few MPs who were referred to the High Court also survived the subsequent ruling. Notable amongst these were Senators Matt Canavan (Liberal National Party) and Nick Xenophon (minor party), who were given the benefit of doubt over obscure, decades-old facts and Italian and UK citizenship law, respectively (*Re Canavan* (2017) 263 CLR 284). In a few matters, there was even secondary litigation, when senators chosen on recounts to fill vacancies of disqualified elected senators were themselves subject to qualifications questions (*Re Day* [2017] HCATrans 86; *Re Lambie* (2018) 263 CLR 601; *Re Nash (No. 2)* (2018) 263 CLR 443).

Analysis of the fracas has focused on impracticalities and undemocratic effects in the substance of the Section 44 disqualifications. A parliamentary committee even produced a nearly 200-page report, whose title 'Excluded' telegraphed its concerns about the substantive effects of inflexible disqualification rules (Joint Standing Committee on Electoral Matters 2018). A radical but pragmatic solution would have been for Parliament to eschew referring its members. It might have instead undertaken a full audit of its members and assisted members with advice via the Clerks' offices. As part of this, as a carrot-and-stick approach, it could have chosen to refer only intransigent members or those who could not renounce or undo their disqualification, to the Court. But once the first referrals were made – and it is notable that these initially affected minor party MPs – the die was set for the solidification of a convention strongly in favour of referring disqualification issues to the judiciary.

Thus, the 2016–2018 'circus' involved an embarrassed parliamentary class outsourcing the job of ruling on disqualifications to the High Court. That said, it would be an overstatement to suggest that these events generated a simple, singular convention that each house would refer each and every non-trivial allegation to the High Court. In 1924, as we saw, the House of Representatives had accepted the Attorney-General's legal argument that two MPs did not have a case to answer. In 1974–1975, the Senate made one referral unanimously (*Webster*) but avoided referring or deciding two other contentious matters. In 2018, despite referrals being routinely made, the House avoided discussing sensitive allegations that the Treasurer, Mr Josh Frydenberg, held dual citizenship. The sensitivity was moral, since the allegations related to Frydenberg's Jewish mother and events after the Holocaust.[21] The sensitivity was echoed across partisan divides: the Prime Minister called them 'offensive', the Deputy Opposition Leader 'a bridge too far' and members generally feared descent into a 'witch hunt' (Morgan 2017). On an election petition after the subsequent election, the Federal Court decided that

21 Frydenberg's mother believed herself stateless, despite having acquired Hungarian nationality for a few years in the 1940s in between Austro-Hungarian, Nazi and Soviet occupations, before seeking refuge in Australia.

the allegations were arguable, but unprovable either way in part due to the impenetrability and age of the foreign law concerned (*Staindl v. Frydenberg* (2020) 276 FCR 301).

Another aspect of relevance to the emergence of the conventions, which had begun to emerge as early as the Entsch matter in 1999, is that legal advice was not a panacea. Matters could be arguable to one QC but less so to another. Even the Solicitor-General might hedge otherwise cogent advice. Thus, by 2018, there was a clear presumption that any reasonably arguable point should lead to a referral to the Court, rather than a ruling by parliamentary debate and vote. The principles behind this were that parliaments were too partisan (and legally inexpert) to trust themselves to decide. Yet even the best government and private lawyers were not 100% reliable, either: their opinions might be hedged, if not fudged by being shopped around. Only the High Court was seen as both independent and determinative.

Conventions Emerged, Then Solidified

After 120 years of evolving practice as to how the Parliament should deal with qualifications questions, where do we sit? A set of nested conventions has emerged. The overall rule is for each house to refer any credible allegation raising sufficient doubt about one of its members to the High Court. Beneath that overall rule, there are more particular sub-conventions guiding the process and parliamentary practice.

As was noted at the outset of this chapter, the most commonly studied constitutional conventions (e.g., about responsible government) are understood at a high level of generality. This renders them flexibility, at the expense of being disputed in some of their concrete applications. This is not the case here. It is not that the power to disqualify an MP is trivial. Rather the processes – and proprieties – which were up for grabs during the occasional matters that arose across the 20th century solidified quickly from the lava of the eruption of allegations in 2016–2018.

To adapt Kipling, the conventions that have emerged concern the what, the who, the when and the how. To meet Jennings' concern for underlying principles, we can also try to state the why. I lay them out in what follows: those in italics are clear conventions; those not in italics are suggestive or contextual.

What: *All matters when an MP's qualification is seriously arguable should be referred to the High Court for determination (especially if the law or facts are contestable). In other cases, the relevant house can rule the MP is qualified or dismiss a motion to refer.* Except in irrefutable cases, Parliament should not declare one of its own MPs to be disqualified. In such cases, the MP should in any event resign. (Even then, if it involves a Senator whose disqualification existed at the time of their election, a referral is needed so the electoral commission receives a court order to fill the vacancy via a recount.)

Who: *Each house considers its own member's qualifications. As part of this, it should refer the matter to a privileges committee first, for investigation and report. It is now customary for the Solicitor-General to provide legal advice, but the government is not bound to release that to the house or presiding officer. Conversely, it is not now conventional for the Attorney-General or their department to give such advice.* Such advice is not definitive, but persuasive. Non-government parties or individual members may commission and present legal opinions, but they merely feed into debate. *The MP concerned is entitled to continue sitting until declared disqualified by their house or the Court.* That said, there are precedents for MPs concerned being given leave or pairs.

When: Debate and consideration should take place expeditiously once the essential facts are known. *A house should not refer to its privileges committee allegations that are obviously trivial or vexatious.* Conversely, if a private citizen has mounted an electoral petition that alleges disqualification, the Parliament should treat the matter as sub-judice and refrain from considering it.

How: *Referral (or formal debate alleging disqualification) is by way of a motion directing the presiding officer to state a legal question or questions, to the High Court, about a named MP and particular disqualifying provisions. The legal costs of an MP referred to the Court are borne by the Commonwealth.*

Why: *These conventions reflect Parliament recognising its own limitations in a complex area of law, where ruling on facts and outcomes will often appear politicised. Disqualification questions are not now purely aspects of the internal discipline of an autonomous, dignified Parliament, as was thought in centuries past. However that older principle remains in remnant form, in that Parliament acts like a grand jury, filtering referrals.*

The preceding is my statement of the position, based on the evolution of the practices discussed across this chapter. Parliament itself also acted explicitly, in two ways, just before the 2019 national election. The first action was to amend electoral law, to require all candidates to complete a checklist disclosing what they know about their qualifications. The electoral commission is not to query or act on those disclosures, but to publish them to allow rivals to scrutinise them and electors to petition a winning candidate (Commonwealth Electoral Act, ss. 181A–C and Form DB).

Second, each house adopted a motion partly codifying the conventions previously described (Senate 2019, pp. 849–851; House of Representatives 2019, pp. 1936–1939).[22] In doing so, they added one roadblock. The Register of Member's Interests (otherwise a pecuniary register) is to contain MP's

22 These were influenced by JSCEM (2018, p. 103) listing 'strategies to mitigate the impact of section 44'.

checklist disclosures and to be attested to and updated by MPs once sworn in. In that way, false or hidden material becomes contempt of Parliament. If an MP raises a disqualification issue about another (or themselves), the presiding officer informs the chamber and it can be referred to the privileges committee. That committee is to hear from the impugned member and seek expert opinion on foreign citizenship law (if relevant). If there is sufficient doubt about a Member's qualifications, the committee may recommend referral by the house to the High Court.

The roadblock is this: the committee is only to recommend referral if the facts were not disclosed by MP via the candidate checklist. The onus thus falls on electors (or rival parties) to petition the Court of Disputed Returns – to challenge the election of an MP if the facts were public at the time of the election – or to forever hold their peace (e.g., House of Representatives 2019, p. 1937). The Parliament has, in effect, imposed a duty on candidates and MPs to be open about facts affecting their qualifications – but balancing the principle favouring referrals to the judiciary, another traditional principle has come into play. This is the principle that the makeup of Parliament should be stabilised expeditiously.[23] Hence, as long as MPs disclose potential disqualifications known at the time of their election, they ought not be subject to a kind of double jeopardy by being challengeable, before a judge, in both an election petition and a later parliamentary referral.

These conventions may yet continue to evolve. They are not yet deeply entrenched by time. Exceptional political pressures could always see back-tracking on them.[24] Formally, a parliamentary motion is not as enduring as either legislation or a court decision interpreting the written Constitution. Finally, a question yet to be answered by a clear convention is the propriety – if not legality – of a Minister continuing in that executive office whilst under a referral cloud (Twomey 2017a, cf. Orr 2018, pp. 20–21).

Conventions All the Way Down: Politics, Principle, Precedent and Particularity

What sparked bipartisanship in the referral of Senator Webster in 1975, and again in the citizenship circus of 2016–2018, was a realisation that MPs on all sides were potentially affected. In 2016–2018, Parliament could have clammed up and protected its own or, conversely, descended into political partisanship and resolved matters by brute numbers in each house. Instead, the pall of the flood of disqualification questions led parties, Ministers and

23 A principle established in electoral law over 150 years ago (*Théberge v. Laudry* (1870) 2 App. Cas. 102).

24 Political pressures are not always partisan: there may be occasions when rivals *within* a party wish to see a fellow MP squirm (as in the Turnbull-Dutton example).

MPs alike to adopt practices embodying conventions erring on the side of outsourcing matters to the judiciary. This was in contrast with isolated cases in the intervening decades (such as involved Mr Entsch and Senator-elect Ferris).

Thus, after a long and punctuated process of evolution, an intense period of development led to the solidification of a nested set of conventions, partly codified. Partial codification (as opposed to being stated exhaustively) via a motion (not locked into legislation or a written constitution) does not in itself break the evolutionary chain.

Nethercote (2015, p. 137) reasoned that parliamentary conventions should be seen 'not so much as rules or obligatory precepts or maxims, but . . . instead as precedents . . . guiding rather than prescribing conduct and behaviour'. We should be careful here. 'Precedent' misleads if it is read straight from the legal lexicon, as meaning prior rulings binding on adjudicators. Constitutional conventions, especially parliamentary ones, rest on an internalised force, akin to what Hart (1961, pp. 56–57) dubbed 'the internal aspect of rules'. A convention's stickiness is partly a product of its congruence with some higher principle. Here, avoiding partisanship but also, such principles or deeper rationales help ensure that people within institutions adhere to conventions (as Jennings suggests). However, conventions may also have a 'conventional' aspect. That is, they may involve somewhat arbitrary commitments to a stable *modus operandi*. That is certainly the case with the more particular sub-conventions described here (such as the guarantee of legal costs or the involvement of privileges committees).

Principles ideally and ordinarily inform the emergence of core conventions, but not in a predictable or linear way. An almost inevitable feature of principles is that they form rationales at a high level of generality and can point in different directions and require accommodation. The overarching convention uncovered here – that any serious allegation about an MP's qualifications should be determined by the High Court, not the Parliament – represents the triumph of two modern principles (that parliaments are too politicised to determine such questions, and that their makeup should be stabilised as soon as possible) over one old principle (that parliaments have sole autonomy over their members).

Whilst not binding like judicial precedents, conventions have some analogy and common ground with the general common law developed by judges. The age of a convention, like a judicial precedent, may make it more compelling. Conventions, like common law precedents, can nevertheless evolve to adapt to unforeseen challenges and exigencies. A precedent, and hence a convention, may reveal plasticity when it faces entirely new circumstances.

As with judicial precedents, the more foundational the convention, the greater its gravitational pull. Yet the more general its formulation, the greater the wriggle room, especially when distinct conventions are in tension. An example of this arose during the COVID19 pandemic in 2020–2022.

Australian Prime Minister Scott Morrison had himself secretly appointed to be a co-minister of five portfolios. In this, he relied on the convention that the Governor-General follows prime ministerial direction in ministerial appointments, but his appointments also contradicted the convention of responsible government, since a parliament can hardly question a minister whose identity is not known (Bell 2022).

In contrast, the more particularistic a convention, the more likely it can be stated in a clear rule; yet the less grave may be any avoidance of the convention. The conventions around responsible government or the reserve powers of a Governor-General are notoriously difficult to list as a set of positive rules or even a flow chart, but allegations of their breach are usually matters of high anxiety. In contrast, as we have seen in this chapter, many of the processes around handling MP qualification disputes are now detailed and particularised, but of less moment than, say, disputes about the application of conventions surrounding responsible government or reserve powers.

Judges, by training, are steeped in respect for precedent. They swear to do 'justice according to law' and are usually subject to an appeals hierarchy that reinforces the binding nature of judicial precedent. Political actors have no such training or oath. Their roles are wider and less constrainable. As a result, the internal commitment to a 'convention' within the political branches rests on more diffuse forces: the weight or age of the convention, the rule utility of maintaining the convention versus any act utility in bucking it, and social sanctions such as political blow-back for acting in an unorthodox way.

How parliaments (not just in Australia, but anywhere) deal with MP qualification disputes offers an intriguing case study in the evolution of conventions. At no point in the fairly episodic history described here did any one committee or expert inquiry assay the question in any explicit – let alone holistic – way. Another lesson from this case study is that conventions need not evolve slowly. They can emerge suddenly through a major imbroglio like the 2016–2018 qualifications circus in the Australian Parliament. An analogy with punctuated equilibrium, in natural evolution, is apt.

Such episodic evolution is a common enough feature of much law-making. It is just that conventions are emergent properties arising out of semi-reflective practices within politics and government. In contrast, harder sources of law like statutes are drafted purposively and debated directly, whilst court precedents require explicit, reasoned judgments. This is not to say, however, that the evolution of conventions is blind. Indeed, one point of studying and reflecting on them (and of books such as this) is to draw attention to their existence, nature and justification.

Nor, as this case study has demonstrated, is there some lofty divide between highly principled conventions and grubbier political practices and norms. They evolve in tandem. Conventions are neither some expression of some unguided genius (or 'cosmos') of anglophonic governance. Nor are they brittle rules, tottering like the pieces in a game of pick up sticks such that a single mishandling will upset the edifice of governance.

This illustrates the point, made at the outset, that conventions need not be grand or sweeping. The study of constitutional conventions, understandably, has focused on broad or fundamental principles, such as those concerning responsible and cabinet government or the reserve powers of the titular Crown – power rather than mere procedure; basic assumptions filling constitutional lacunae. But no constitution can be codified fully. Codification at most reduces the space for less consciously evolved conventions. There will always be room not just for interpretive wriggle-room, but for conventions to lubricate and fill gaps. Conventions, in a sense, are inescapable. Not in the sense that they pre-exist, immanent within a constitutional structure, but that they will emerge as required and at surprisingly detailed level. To adapt the saying about turtles and hierarchical regression, 'it's conventions all the way down'.

References

Australasian Federation Conference 1897a, *Proceedings*, 13 September.

Australasian Federation Conference 1897b, *Proceedings*, 21 September.

Bell, V 2022, *Report of the Inquiry into the Appointment of the Former Prime Minister to Administer Multiple Departments*, Commonwealth of Australia, Canberra, 25 November, viewed 29 February 2024, <https://web.archive.org.au/awa/20230921070016mp_/https://www.ministriesinquiry.gov.au/system/files/2022-11/ministries-inquiry-report.pdf>.

Blackshield, AR 2016, 'Void or Vacant: The Vibes of Vardon', *AUSPUBLAW*, 26 August, viewed 29 February 2024, <https://www.auspublaw.org/blog/2016/08/void-or-vacant-the-vibes-of-vardon>.

Carney, G 2000, *Members of Parliament: Law and Ethics*, Prospect, Sydney.

Donahue, S 2018, *In the Matter of the Eligibility of Mr Dutton Pursuant to Section 44(v) of the Constitution*, Solicitor-General's Office, SG No. 21 of 2018, 24 August.

Hart, HLA 1961, *The Concept of Law*, Clarendon Press, Oxford.

Hobbs, H, Pillai, S and Williams, G 2018, 'The Disqualification of Dual Citizens from Parliament: Three Problems and a Solution', *Alternative Law Journal*, vol. 43, no. 2, pp. 73–80.

Holland, I 2004, 'Section 44 of the Constitution', Australian Parliamentary Library, E-Brief, March, archived on *ParlInfo* database, viewed 29 February 2024.

House of Representatives 1924, *Hansard*, 18 June.

House of Representatives 1975, *Hansard*, 23 April.

House of Representatives 1999a, *Hansard*, 9 June.

House of Representatives 1999b, *Hansard*, 10 June.

House of Representatives 2018, *Hansard*, 23 August.

House of Representatives 2019, *Hansard*, 4 April.

House of Representatives Standing Committee on Legal and Constitutional Affairs 1997, *Aspects of Section 44 of the Australian Constitution: Sub-Sections 44(i) and (iv)*, Parliament of Australia, Canberra.

Jennings, I 1959, *The Law and the Constitution*, 5th edn, University of London Press, London.

Joint Standing Committee on Electoral Matters (JSCEM) 2018, *Excluded: The Impact of Section 44 on Australian Democracy*, Parliament of Australia, Canberra.
Laing, R (ed) 2016, *Odger's Australian Senate Practice*, 14th edn, Department of the Senate, Canberra.
Morgan, M 2017, 'Labor Backs Frydenberg, Says Citizenship Speculation Getting "Disturbing"', *SBS News*, 3 November, viewed 16 October 2024, https://www.sbs.com.au/news/article/labor-backs-frydenberg-says-citizenship-speculation-getting-disturbing/joah72012.
Morris, C 2012, *Parliamentary Elections, Representation and the Law*, Hart Publishing, Oxford.
Nethercote, JR 2015, 'Parliament', in Galligan, B and Brenton, S (eds), *Constitutional Conventions in Westminster Systems: Controversies, Changes and Challenges*, Cambridge University Press, Cambridge, pp. 137–156.
Orr, G 2018, 'Fertilising a Thicket: Section 44, MPs' Qualifications and the High Court', *Public Law Review*, vol. 29, no. 1, pp. 17–23.
Orr, G 2019, 'Parliamentary Disqualification for Financial Conflicts', *Federal Law Review*, vol. 47, no. 4, pp. 583–605.
Orr, G 2022, 'Qualifications to Be an Elected Representative', in Gardner, JA (ed), *Comparative Election Law*, Edward Elgar, Cheltenham, pp. 304–320.
Quick, J and Garran, RR 1901, *The Annotated Constitution of the Commonwealth of Australia*, Angus and Robertson, Sydney.
Senate 1971, *Hansard*, 24 August.
Senate 1974a, *Hansard*, 3 April.
Senate 1974b, *Hansard*, 4 April.
Senate 1975a, *Hansard*, 21 April.
Senate 1975b, *Hansard*, 22 April.
Senate 1975c, *Hansard*, 9 September.
Senate 1975d, *Hansard*, 1 October.
Senate 1988, *Hansard*, 16 February.
Senate 1996, *Hansard*, 29 May.
Senate 1998, *Hansard*, 25 November.
Senate 2003, *Hansard*, 18 September.
Senate 2004, *Hansard*, 10 February.
Senate 2019, *Hansard*, 3 April.
Senate Standing Committee on Constitutional and Legal Affairs 1981, *The Constitutional Qualifications of Members of Parliament*, AGPS, Canberra.
Seymour, C 1915, *Electoral Reform in England and Wales: The Development and Operation of the Parliamentary Franchise 1832–1885*, Yale University Press, New Haven.
Twomey, A 2017a, 'If High Court Decides Against Ministers with Dual Citizenship, Could Their Decisions in Office Be Challenged', *The Conversation*, 18 August, viewed 29 February 2024, <https://theconversation.com/if-high-court-decides-against-ministers-with-dual-citizenship-could-their-decisions-in-office-be-challenged-82688>.
Twomey, A 2017b, 'Section 44 of the Constitution – What Have We Learnt and What Problems Do We Still Face?', *Australasian Parliamentary Review*, vol. 32, no. 2, pp. 5–20 (published 2018).

Legal Authorities

Alley v. Gillespie (2018) 264 CLR 328.
Crittenden v. Anderson (Unreported, High Court of Australia, Fullagar J, 23 August 1950).

Nile v. Wood (1988) 167 CLR 133.
R (Miller) v. The Prime Minister [2019] UKSC 19.
Re Culleton (No. 2) (2017) 263 CLR 176.
Re Day [2017] HCATrans 86.
Re Day (No. 2) (2017) 343 ALR 181.
Re Lambie (2018) 263 CLR 601.
Re Nash (No. 2) (2018) 263 CLR 443.
Re Webster (1975) 132 CLR 270.
Sarina v. O'Connor (Petition Withdrawn, High Court of Australia, 10 December 1946).
Staindl v. Frydenberg (2020) 276 FCR 301.
Strickland v. Grima [1930] AC 285.
Sue v. Hill (1999) 199 CLR 462.
Théberge v. Laudry (1870) 2 App. Cas. 102.

Chapter 5

How Constitutional Actors Resist Conventions Without Breaking Them

The Case of UK's Salisbury Convention

Narelle Miragliotta and Frank Algra-Maschio

Introduction

In established democracies, constitutional conventions are considered useful and desirable rules that regulate actors, institutions and processes sometimes in the absence of, and other times in contravention of, formal rules. What makes conventions such remarkable properties of constitutional systems is that they are neither codified nor generally justiciable – and yet, at least in established democracies, they are rarely explicitly abrogated by constitutional actors.

While constitutional actors are often reluctant to deny outright the existence of a convention, they are much more willing to claim that a convention is, in some way, not applicable to a particular circumstance in which it might ordinarily apply. This raises the question of how constitutional actors justify resisting the obligation to adhere to a convention without necessarily denying the legitimacy of the convention.

This chapter traces one particular constitutional convention since its modern inception in order to better understand how actors negotiate acts of resistance to a convention rule, and the effects of such actions on the developmental profile of that convention. This is done by tracing the evolution of the Salisbury–Addison convention (hereafter the Salisbury convention), a convention rule of the UK House of Lords that prescribes that government manifesto bills should enjoy a second reading by the chamber.

The Salisbury convention is instructive in that it is a well-established convention, having managed to survive several high-profile instances of resistance by opposition Lords since its declaration in 1945. Although some constitutional scholars have ventured that the convention ceased to apply after 1999 (e.g., Brazier 2006; Shell 2006), the convention has been affirmed by several parliamentary committees (Royal Commission on Reform of the House of Lords 2000; Joint Committee on Conventions 2006; Lords Select Committee on the Constitution 2014), is often invoked by name by members of the Lords, and it is also mentioned in *Erskine May's Treatise* (Natzler and Hutton 2019), the UK's parliamentary bible.

DOI: 10.4324/9781003506577-5

This chapter examines claims made by opposition actors when seeking to resist the Salisbury convention by denying, or threatening to deny, a government manifesto bill a second or third reading. The central question we pose is: How do constitutional actors resist a convention without necessarily threatening the rule itself? The arguments presented by opposition peers to justify resistance are reviewed, with the material sourced primarily from parliamentary debates.[1]

The findings suggest that constitutional actors typically frame a challenge to the convention in ways that are broadly resonant with (or sympathetic to) the *raison d'etre* of the convention and the values which it expresses. Actors resist observance by challenging some aspect of the scope of the rule, typically by claiming some form of qualification to the rule and not the rule or the constitutional values it expresses. Sometimes these qualifications are incorporated into the content of the convention, gently redrawing its operating parameters.

This chapter is organized into three sections. The first section sketches three familiar challenges to conventions that constitutional actors might mount. The second section contextualizes the Salisbury convention. The third section reviews the claims advanced by different constitutional actors to justify resistance to the Salisbury convention in the period between 1945 and 2021.

Conventions and Non-Adherence

Conventions are unwritten or informal rules that typically manifest as social practices (Jaconelli 1999). They are, however, constitutional, informing positive law, but they are not justiciable in most jurisdictions.[2] They are generally considered to be stable constitutional rules that supplement while, at other times, alter the meaning of the formal constitutional text.

Despite their tendency to stability, conventions are not always strictly or faithfully observed by constitutional actors.[3] At its most extreme,

1 To the extent possible, we have privileged the respective leaders of the parties in the Lords, who have capacity to influence the actions of partisan legislators. Party leaders generally have greater capacity to whip the numbers on the floor of the Lords and are therefore better able to succeed in pressing their interpretation of the convention among their partisan counterparts should they so choose.

2 See Ahmed et al. (2019) on this point.

3 It is not entirely clear why conventions tend towards stability. Ahmed (2021) summarises three familiar explanations found in the scholarship. One type of explanation understands observance as path dependence. Conventions are observed because they have always been observed (precedence). A second explanation regards the stability of conventions as a function of the benefits that the rule yields, specifically coordinating elite action. A third common type of explanation perceives the stability of conventions as an outgrowth of the desire of constitutional actors to avoid potential or actual deleterious political consequences occasioned by non-observance (self-interest).

Table 5.1 Common Types of Non-Observance

Abrogation	Denial of the normal precedence or rules or law which is not usual. Abrogation is deliberate, often unjustified, and typically motivated by undemocratic goals or aims.
Departure	A claim to a variation in some way from the normal precedence of the convention. Does not reject the convention but claims some kind of exception.
Abandonment	A convention that has fallen into disuse, generally by agreement.

non-observance takes the form of abrogation, which involves the violation of normal precedence, rules or law (see Table 5.1). For our purposes, abrogation is a purposeful and provocative act intended to deal a "deathblow" to a convention rule (Postema 2022: 111).[4] Abrogation is more than just the act of denying a convention but involves the denial of the very constitutional value that it purports. Those who engage in such actions evoke Gerald Postema's notion of a "norm saboteur". Norm saboteurs are often exercised by anti-democratic ends and will often "deploy the rhetoric of democracy or the rule of law, but their behavior reveals that they have no deep commitment to them" (Postema 2022: 113). In the context of stable constitutional democracies, abrogations receive greater attention because these events are rare, dramatic and may foreshadow an anti-democratic turn (Hinterleitner and Sager 2023; Tushnet 2004).

At the other end of the spectrum are conventions that have fallen into disuse. The abandonment of a convention occurs quietly, although not necessarily by accident.[5] Abandonment is marked by broad consensus among constitutional actors that the convention is no longer relevant or necessary and, as a result, its abeyance is generally uncontroversial. In these cases, non-observance signifies the death of a convention that has outlived its purpose (Barry et al. 2019). The demise of the convention under these conditions does not necessarily entail the rejection of some deeper constitutional principle or value that gave rise to that convention.

4 Postema (2022: 15–16) refers to three types of norm deviators: norm infringers (unintentional), norm entrepreneurs (those seeking reform to the rule) and norm saboteurs (those deliberately seeking to destroy the rule).

5 See, for example, the UK convention that the full Cabinet had the power to advise the monarch to dissolve the Parliament. However, from 1918 (when Prime Minister Lloyd George departed from this convention) up until the passage of the Fixed-terms Parliament Act 2011, the convention has been that this power is exercised by the Prime Minister (Jaconelli 2013: 128–129).

In between abrogation and disuse are *departures*.[6] In these cases, constitutional actors might claim that a convention does not strictly apply to the circumstances or events that are in contention. Unlike the case of abrogation, constitutional actors acknowledge the relevance of the convention but cite (what are generally situational) exceptions in light of the particular nature of events that bring the convention to attention. Departures can be controversial,[7] but what distinguishes them from abrogation is that the legitimacy of a convention is not under direct challenge. Rather, disagreement abounds over the extent to which a convention must be fully observed and/or which constitutional rule takes precedence given the particularities of the triggering event.

While each type of non-observance has the potential to be disruptive to a greater or lesser extent, scholars do not regard every infraction as leading inevitably to the demise of a convention. Leading scholars have long accepted that conventions can and do survive non-observance. Ivor Jennings (1959), for example, draws a distinction between obligatory conventions and those he characterizes as usages, with the former being prescriptive (must observe) and the later, descriptive (should observe) (see also Brazier 1992).[8] Colin Munro (1975) tends to the view that not every convention has to be strictly observed. He reasons that whether a convention must be observed depends on the precision of its framing. Similarly, Andrew Heard (1989 distinguishes between conventions that bind and those which are less binding. Heard (1989: 68) suggests that the extent to which the obligation to adhere is binding depends on the importance of the principle which lies behind the rule, the *degree* and *level* of consensus about the rule, the extent to which the body of the rule elides with its content and whether the rule is supported by precedents.

A shared implication arising from these different formulations is that only some conventions must be faithfully observed and that, by extension,

6 We adopt Postema's use of the word departure, which he defines as a "conscientious action, as when the actor plausibly argues that the action does not violate the norm if properly understood" (2022: 111).

7 Chafetz and Pozen (2018) describe the effects of norm decomposition as a situation whereby "the preexisting pattern of behavior is incrementally and imperceptibly tweaked until, at some point far down the line, the aggregation of all those tweaks yields a new normative pattern, one that informed observers would agree is a departure from the status quo ante" (2018: 1436). They regard norm decomposition as a more frequent occurrence but also significantly more dangerous because it involves a "subtle", largely imperceptible chipping away at the integrity of the norm.

8 Rodney Brazier contends that a convention can be breached without it being cast asunder. He writes (1992: 268):

> Does an unambiguous breach of such a clear convention call into question its very existence? Of course it does not, any more than the millions of breaches each year of the Theft Acts can be said to prove that no laws exist to protect the ownership and possession of property.

most do not cease to exist if they are not observed.[9] Even conventions that might be regarded as vital can survive violation. Gerald Postema contends that a convention may endure violation if the assailed convention expresses "reasonably robust social norms". In some cases, conventions might emerge even "stronger" when the "responses of the norm community challenge the deviations and hold the violator to account for deviating" (Postema 2022: 107; see also Chafetz and Pozen 2018). In a similar vein, Stephenson (2015: 448) argues that refusals "can create a discursive moment, presenting constitutional actors, including the public, with a rare opportunity to discuss a neglected constitutional issue or to reframe a constitutional issue". In a stable liberal constitutional polity, a convention can survive infraction and may even be strengthened through clarification as a result (Barry and Miragliotta 2015; Stephenson 2015).[10]

Finally, there may be legitimate grounds for actors to not observe a convention because to do so would prove constitutionally unsafe. Take the case of the Australian reserve powers for the Governor General. These are discretionary powers awarded to the Crown and exercised by the Governor General. Such powers are exercisable by the head of state according to his or her discretion but generally are not. As Anne Twomey (2018) explains, reserve powers are "not only necessary for the operation of government, but also provide the last line of defense against governmental actions in breach of fundamental constitutional principles". Hence, *in extremis*, where breaches of convention are directed toward protecting the constitutional order, a departure is necessary to protect against anti-democratic conduct.

Scholars agree that conventions are natural sites of negotiation, challenge and change, even more so than their formal counterparts. This is because conventions "can be dynamically interpreted in a more or less restrictive manner, and at higher or lower levels of generality" (Chafetz and Pozen 2018: 1434; see also Barry et al. 2019). Three properties imbue conventions with this quality. The first is related to the uncertain provenance of some conventions, especially older conventions. Unlike formal rules which are "created through official channels (such as executives and legislatures) and communicated and

9 For example, the British monarch retains the legal power to refuse royal assent to a bill passed by Parliament. However, the monarch may no longer refuse their assent if they disagree on personal grounds but if advised by a minister or where the bill has not been passed correctly (Brazier 1992: 269).

10 Stephenson (2015: 451) makes this case particularly in relation to the democratic constitutional systems prone to an excess of stability. He reasons that they:

> can induce complacency where a country fails to critically reflect on its system of government and consider options for improvement. It will typically be easier for government actors to make do with what they have, begrudgingly accepting any problems or developing patchwork solutions to them, than to spend the considerable political capital it would take to initiate, persist with and ultimately achieve major reform.

enforced by state agencies (such as the police and courts), informal rules are created, communicated, and enforced outside of public channels, and usually outside of the public eye" (Helmke and Levitsky 2004: 731). Their *sometimes* mysterious origin story may further mean that it is not entirely clear who, when and why the convention was created, which in turn can invite different interpretations about when and how the convention should apply.

A second property of conventions that can invite actors to strain against them is the manner of their construction. Some conventions have a fixed formulation; for example, the prime minister chairs the cabinet. Other conventions, however, are framed in sufficiently broad terms to create sufficient ambiguity that good faith, rival interpretations might occur over what the convention demands depending on the circumstances (Marshall 1984: Chapter 1). The (lack of) materiality of conventions compounds this problem. Their uncodified nature means there are no formal barriers that would otherwise prevent actors from succeeding in expressing some kind of alternative interpretation of a convention if a majority of those who are essential to its enforcement agree.[11] Nor is there any formal action or event that necessarily marks a convention's birth or its demise, as occurs with the passage or the repeal of law. While conventions are sometimes "declared",[12] they most often evolve into existence.

A third attribute of conventions that be the source of disagreement among elites derives from their system-dependent nature. A convention rule, much like positive rules, does not operate in a vacuum, even if the rule it expresses is particular. Conventions have, in fact, been described as "internally connected – . . . hunt[ing] in packs – and their meaning or content and their normative force depend on the relationships that exist among conventions" (Postema 2022: 108). Hence, the application of any particular convention is sensitive to the conditions in play, and any other rules that may have been broken (Aroney 2015; Barry and Miragliotta 2015). That is, the context or situation that activates a convention has to reckon with any other rules – formal or informal – that have also been triggered, and which may make different demands on constitutional actors. This can give rise to contestation over which rule should assume precedence when responding to challenges.

The next section examines the claims advanced by constitutional actors to justify resistance toward the Salisbury convention.

11 Ahmed (2021: 1367) argues that one of the defining characteristics of conventions is their "contingent" nature, with the emergence and survival of a convention depending on a variety of historical forces.

12 Robert Hazel, for example, writes about how the UK's Sewel Convention was created when Lord Sewel, a government minister, stood in parliament and announced that he "would expect a convention to be established" that Westminster would not legislate on devolved matters pertinent to the Scottish Parliament (2015: 174–175). See Perry and Tucker's (2018) efforts to elucidate the differences between bottom up and top-down conventions.

The Salisbury Convention

To the extent that one can say that any one event or utterance marks the emergence of a convention, the Salisbury convention began as an agreement – or understanding reached – between the Labour and Conservative party leaders in the Lords, Lord Addison (Labour peer) and Viscount Cranborne (later Lord Salisbury, Conservative peer), over the approach for dealing with the passage of government bills though the Lords (Dymond and Deadman 2006).

The particular circumstances that gave rise to the convention was Labour's victory at the 1945 election. Labour had secured a commanding majority in the Commons but was confronted by a Conservative-dominated Lords[13] which had the power to delay bills passed by the Commons for two years. The Salisbury convention sought to affirm the legislative supremacy of the elected House of Commons in relation to those matters that the government had expressly taken to the people at election and that were contained within the winning party's election manifesto.

The Salisbury convention built upon an earlier constitutional principle that recognized the supremacy of the elected House of Commons over a non-elected House of Lords. This principle had its origins in the doctrine of the mandate expounded by the third marquess of Salisbury in 1863 (Dymond and Deadman 2006: 1). This doctrine held that when the will of the people and the Commons conflict, the Lords has an obligation to reject such bills, in order that the matter be referred to the people for their consideration (Joint Committee on Conventions 2006: 24).

The Salisbury convention, and the doctrine of mandate which preceded it, were a response to changing political ideas and values that challenged the desirability of a non-elected House being able to frustrate the will of a democratically elected government in the "other place". The convention also emerged against the specter of a Labour government keen to further constrain the legislative power of the Lords. To this extent, the continuation of the convention is a pragmatic response by the chamber to "perpetuate the influence of the House in an age of widening suffrage" on account of its unelected status (Dymond and Deadman 2006: 1).

The convention was articulated by the then Viscount Cranborne (Salisbury, hereafter) on the floor of the Lords in the context of the opposition's reply to the King's speech in 1945:

> Whatever our personal views, we should frankly recognize that these proposals were put before the country at the recent General Election and

13 In the Lords at that time, there were 16 Labour peers out of a total of 831 voting peers (HM Government 2007: 10).

> that the people of this country, with full knowledge of these proposals, returned the Labour Party to power. The government may, therefore, I think, fairly claim that they have a mandate to introduce these proposals. I believe that it would be constitutionally wrong, when the country has so recently expressed its view, for this House to oppose proposals which have been definitely put before the electorate.
>
> (Cranborne [Conservative], Lords 1945)

Salisbury's declaration received a grateful reception from Lord Addison, Labour Leader of the Lords, who credited his opposite with "render[ing] a public service in exhorting this House and the country, now that the verdict of the Election has been declared, to give the Government in power a trial, and not to be unduly obstructive" (Addison [Labour], Lords 1945).

The declaration was also tacitly endorsed by Viscount Samuel, Liberal Leader in the Lords, who acknowledged that:

> if the outcome were to be nothing better than futility, if the policy which they have advanced, and which has been approved by the people, were to be dissipated in the swamps and shallows of Parliamentary procedure, that would be not only an injury to the Labour Party but a blow to the whole system of democratic government and an injury to the country, for that reason, and to the whole Commonwealth.
>
> (Samuel [Liberal] Lords 1945)[14]

Yet even during the initial articulation of the convention in the Lords, its parameters and its obligations were challenged. Viscount Samuel, for example, while sympathetic to the disparities between Labour's commanding majority in the Commons and the government's meager representation in the Lords, warned that:

> there might easily arise situations of great delicacy, difficulty and indeed danger. We on these Benches recognize that occasions might arise where any second Chamber, no matter how constituted, would be bound to

14 In this parliamentary period, Labour held 329 seats in the 640-member Common. In the Lords, by contrast, the Conservative Party dominated the benches. This was described by Viscount Samuel (1945) in the following terms:

> We have in this Parliament one Chamber of 640 members in which the Labour Party has a majority of roughly two to one over all other Parties, while we have a second Chamber here with a membership of about 800 in which the Conservative Party has, on paper at all events, a majority of not less than four to one against all others.

> intervene, as for instance if some new and unforeseen and rash measures were proposed.
>
> (Samuel, [Liberal] Lords 1945)

Members of the Lords questioned the absolute obligation on the part of the chamber to simply accede to the government in Commons on proposed legislation within the manifesto.

Over the years, the convention has been reviewed in some form by several parliamentary inquiries. Such inquires have generally resolved that the convention has changed from its original formulation. For example, the 2006 Joint Select Committee of Conventions concluded that the Salisbury convention has altered in two respects: (1) it applies to a manifesto bill introduced in the House of Lords, as well as one introduced in the House of Commons; and (2) it is now recognized by the whole House and not just the two major parties (Joint Committee on Conventions 2006: 32, see also Lords Select Committee on the Constitution 2014, 2017).[15]

However, aspects of the convention are not as settled as several parliamentary inquiries purport. Table 5.2 compares the written statements furnished to the Lords Constitutional Committee by the four leaders from the Conservatives, Labour, Liberal Democrats and the crossbench in 2017. A tick mark indicates agreement, a cross signifies disagreement and an exclamation point represents partial agreement. As Table 5.2 shows, there is divergence of understanding about the broad dimensions of the convention. Labour, the Conservatives, and Convenor of the Crossbench share a broad view about what the convention entails: that the Lords must not reject, unnecessarily delay or advance "wrecking" amendments in relation to any government bill which seeks to give effect to those policies set out in its election manifesto. Only the leader of the Liberal Democrats breaks with their counterparts by asserting that the convention is "redundant". Even outside of broad areas of agreement held by three of leaders of the Lords, they do not entirely agree over what constitutes a manifesto bill and how observance is affected by the composition of government in the Commons.

Discourses of Convention Rule Exemptions

In this section, we examine the arguments leveled by constitutional actors to justify departing in some way from the convention. There are two matters that must be noted. The first is to acknowledge the particular *nature* of this

15 David Beamish (2018) has observed that the Salisbury convention has likely influenced the evolution of party manifesto commitments, proposing that it has encouraged the parties to assemble more detailed election manifestos in order that they could appeal to the convention.

Table 5.2 Party Leaders Interpretation of the Salisbury Convention, 2017

	Leader of the House of Lords, Baroness Evans of Bowes Park (Conservatives)	*Shadow Leader of the House of Lords, Baroness Smith of Basildon (Labour)*	*Leader of the Liberal Democrats, Lord Newby*	*Convenor of the Crossbench Peers, Lord Hope of Craighead*
What the convention entails	√ In the House of Lords, a manifesto bill: is accorded a second reading; is not subject to "wrecking amendments" which change the government's manifesto intention as proposed in the bill; and is passed and sent (or returned) to the House of Commons, so that they have the opportunity, in reasonable time, to consider the bill or any amendments which the House of Lords may wish to propose.	√ In the House of Lords, a manifesto bill: is accorded a second reading; is not subject to "wrecking amendments" which change the government's manifesto intention as proposed in the bill; and is passed and sent (or returned) to the House of Commons, so that they have the opportunity, in reasonable time, to consider the bill or any amendments the Lords may wish to propose.	X an agreement between the leaders of the Conservative and Labour parties in the House of Lords in 1945. The convention is now largely redundant. The context in which the agreement was made in 1945 was therefore very different than the circumstances of today.	√ bills implementing a manifesto commitment by the government are not blocked by the House of Lords at second reading; are not subjected to wrecking amendments; and are passed and sent or returned to the House of Commons in reasonable time to consider any amendments that the House of Lords may propose.

(Continued)

Table 5.2 (Continued)

	Leader of the House of Lords, Baroness Evans of Bowes Park (Conservatives)	*Shadow Leader of the House of Lords, Baroness Smith of Basildon (Labour)*	*Leader of the Liberal Democrats, Lord Newby*	*Convenor of the Crossbench Peers, Lord Hope of Craighead*
Definition of a manifesto bill	! policies which have been put before the electorate and voted on directly; it is clear in most cases from the subject matter of the bill and the debate in Parliament which legislation stems from manifesto commitments.	! when it is unambiguous and clear; and the elected government has a Commons majority, then it is clear that will be respected by the House of Lords.	X It is our belief that legislation now cannot easily be identified – either positively or negatively – as a direct transposition from a manifesto. Manifestos have changed out of all recognition since the Salisbury–Addison convention's inception in 1945.	! A precise match between the wording of a manifesto and the wording of a bill is not to be expected. A broad statement of intention which is sufficient to indicate the policy objective will do. Where a bill covers multiple policy areas, the position is unlikely to be clear-cut.
Second readings	! The Lords does not reject a second reading, but not related to the Salisbury–Addison convention.	! Lords normally gives a Second Reading to any government bill, whether based on the manifesto or not.	X Agree with the view that they must not *regularly* reject bills at second reading, as this would be inconsistent with the Lords' role as the revising chamber". Lords is entitled to propose amendments to any legislation, and to insist on those amendments, in particular where there are constitutional issues at stake.	X That the Lords should not reject a second reading is a "*general presumption*" and carries less weight than the convention.

(Continued)

Table 5.2 (Continued)

	Leader of the House of Lords, Baroness Evans of Bowes Park (Conservatives)	*Shadow Leader of the House of Lords, Baroness Smith of Basildon (Labour)*	*Leader of the Liberal Democrats, Lord Newby*	*Convenor of the Crossbench Peers, Lord Hope of Craighead*
Coalition/ minority	! Applies to the manifesto commitments of the government, whether that is a majority government, coalition or minority government. It does not apply to the manifesto commitments of a party providing confidence and supply to the government.	! It is far from clear that the Salisbury–Addison convention was ever intended to apply to minority governments, but a confidence and supply arrangement, such as the current one between the Conservative Party and the Democratic Unionist Party (DUP), does not materially change the convention, as again the convention is clear that primacy lies with the Commons in Parliament, not the government or the executive.	X We believe that a minority government does not have the right to expect that the House of Lords will abide by the Salisbury–Addison convention. In these circumstances we would need to look at how the minority government managed to get its manifesto legislation through the House of Commons.	! It would seem that the practice which has evolved of the Lords not blocking government bills to which the presumption gives effect should apply to minority governments as well as those which have a majority. A confidence and supply agreement is a cross-party arrangement, which does not differ in principle from a coalition as to whether the Salisbury Convention applies.

Source: Author constructed table using material sourced from the Lords Select Committee on the Constitution (2017)

convention, which is that it is a rule of self-denial imposed by the Lords on their statutory power. Under the Parliament Act 1949, the Lords can only delay a bill passed by the Commons for a period of 12 months. The Salisbury convention requires the Lords to pass bills that the government had pledged in their election manifesto, without delay or seeking amendment (Joint Committee on House of Lords Reform 2002: 9).

The second matter to note is that the Lords has rarely openly defied the convention, as understood as refusing a second or third reading of a government manifesto bill. The 2006 report of the Joint Committee on Conventions found that between 1971 and 2005, there were "13 attempts to defeat a government bill at Second Reading in the last 25 years, five of them successful". The report concluded that: "[i]t is evidently uncommon for a government Bill to be assailed at second reading in the Lords, and very uncommon for such an attack to succeed" (Joint Committee on Conventions 2006: 31).

Nevertheless, opposition peers have occasionally resisted the convention, largely by pressing their right to improve a bill. We organize claims advanced by opposition peers according to Chafetz and Pozen's (2018: 1436) *axes of instability* framework. While Chafetz and Pozen's (2018) framework is intended to explain the breakdown of norms, it is useful for parsing the various internal features of conventions. Chafetz and Pozen propose that the "multiple dimensions" of conventions give rise to *axes of instability* (2018: 1436) which create opportunities for elite contestation in relation to: (1) "what" actions or responses the convention permits constitutional agents to pursue; (2) "whom" precisely, or which set of constitutional agents, the convention attaches; and (3) "when" the convention must be observed. Elites might challenge a convention along one or more of these axes simultaneously.

"What" the Convention Requires

Opposition peers have occasionally sought to justify departing from the Salisbury convention by (re)conceptualizing the range of actions that the convention permits and the obligations that the convention entails upon their actions. In general, disagreements over *what* the convention requires often involves the claim that the Lords must allow a second reading of a bill but the chamber retains the right to propose an amendment to any bill. In these instances, the opposition might assert that an amendment to the government's manifesto bill is permissible so long as the proposed amendment is not a "wrecking amendment" in that it does not substantially affect the spirit or intent of the bill.

An illustrative example of such a claim was articulated in relation to the Trade Union and Labour Relations amendment bill, 1975. The opposition in the Lords pressed for an amendment on the grounds that while it was a "bad bill", it was "capable of improvement" (Mansfield [Conservative]

Lords 1975). The leader of the opposition, Lord Carrington, justified sending the bill to a third reading on the following grounds.

> In our system we have hitherto taken the view that the will of the elected House must in the end prevail, but that there should be a second House which has the opportunity – in rare cases, perhaps – to enforce a delay in which there can be a reassessment by government, by Parties and by the people of this country of the rights or wrongs of an issue. If now we decide to use that very limited power, we are not thwarting the will of the people for, in so far as it is represented by the House of Commons, it will and must prevail in a comparatively short time. We shall be using those powers for the purpose for which they were given to us – *that is, as an* opportunity for further consultation, for second thoughts before this legislation inevitably reaches the Statute Book and because we did not want the Second Chamber to be associated with what the Government are doing.
>
> (Carrington [Conservative], Lords 1975)

"Whom" the Convention Attaches

Another type of exemption claim articulated by some opposition peers is that they are not specifically bound by the convention. This has involved claims by the minor party peers that they are not subject to the convention on the grounds that they were not party to the convention. This position has been advanced most frequently by minor parties and the crossbench on the grounds that the convention attaches only to Labour and Conservative peers, the architects of the convention.[16] Even then, non-major party peers have typically observed the convention, as noted by Lord Williamson:

> Like the Liberal Democrats, the Cross-Bench Peers were not parties to the original convention, which was created by the Labour and Conservative Front Benches, but, with the passage of time, they have gone along with it.
>
> (Williamson [Cross-bench], Lords 2007)

Beginning in the 1990s, some opposition peers began to assert that the Lords was no longer subject to the Salisbury convention because it had been rendered obsolete. Such declarations were pressed following the reform to the method of selection of, and consequent changes to the composition of the

16 For illustrative purposes, see *Queen's Speech debate* (June 2015); *Conventions: Joint Committee Report debate* (2007); *House of Lords Reform debate* (January 2005).

Lords in 1999.[17] Claims about the convention's redundancy are captured by the following:

> There is an argument that the Salisbury convention has served the House and the Parliament well, so let us leave it alone. The noble and learned Lord might think that that is a good old Conservative argument. But I am beginning to think that there is a greater argument; namely, that times have changed, conditions have changed, the composition of the House has changed, and the time has come for that particular convention to change too.
>
> (Ferrers [Conservative], Lords 2001)

> It did not seem to me that a convention which had been arrived at 60 years ago between the Labour and Conservative parties alone, and was about how government business should be treated in a wholly hereditary House with a large built-in Conservative majority, could apply in the new circumstances of a partially reformed House where no party had an overall majority
>
> (McNally [Liberal Democrats] Lords 2007)[18]

Declarations of the convention's obsolescence is based on the view that the circumstances that had necessitated the rule – a Lords with a permanent Conservative majority – no longer operate.[19] That is, the reason for the convention no longer existed – and therefore, neither did the convention.

This discourse of exemption based on the convention's redundancy have amounted to weak, mostly performative challenges. Nevertheless, such

17 The House of Lords Act 1999 altered the composition of the chamber, removing the right to a hereditary peerage (although 92 continued on an interim basis) and reduced the numerical size of the chamber (sources). The alteration in composition removed the Conservative control of the Lords, increasing the power of the crossbench and the Liberal Democrats (Russell 2003; Russell and Sciara 2007).

18 See also, Lord Desai, who argued that reform to the Lords had meant that the convention was nothing more than "a further restriction" in relation to government bills "which it perfectly legitimately" for the chamber to do. He went on to say (Desai [Labour] Lords 2001):

> Either this House has powers that it exercises and is taken seriously, or we have no powers. At present, our powers are limited by one or other *convention*, or some bullying, and we may as well not bother . . . We should have slightly more edge in our debates.

19 Rodney Brazier also supports this position. In a statement he supplied to the 2005 Joint Committee on Conventions, he wrote (quoted in the Joint Committee on Conventions 2005: 30–31) that the:

> well-known view that the Salisbury-Addison convention ceased to exist when most of the hereditary peers were excluded from membership of the House of Lords in 1999. This view is accepted in Conservative, Liberal Democrat, and other circles, although I understand that it is not the view of the Government.

claims – when they assert the Lord's right to reject a bill that otherwise enshrines a government's manifesto commitment, could be construed as a challenge to the principle of the legislative supremacy of the Commons that underlies the convention.

"When" the Convention Is Triggered

Most of the challenges to the convention over the decades have involved some claim about whether the convention has been rightfully triggered. Opposition peers have sometimes argued that the particular conditions that would otherwise warrant observance of the convention are not satisfied. Such claims generally fall into two camps: (1) that a bill is not a government manifesto commitment; and (2) that a bill, even though it reflects the incumbent governments manifesto commitment, violates an important "wider" constitutional principle.

Challenges to a Bill's Bona Fides as a Government Manifesto Commitment

The Lords opposition has occasionally claimed that they are not bound by the convention because the measures contained within a bill is not enshrined in the government's election manifesto.

An example of this is the 1949 debate on the Iron and Steel Bill, which provided for the nationalization of major firms engaged in the iron and steel industry and their subsidiary companies, and for the licensing of smaller firms. Having passed the Commons, it was debated on second reading in the House of Lords on 24 May 1949. However, both the leader of the Liberals, in addition to some of the Conservative Lords, argued that the bill was not protected by the convention:

> this Bill bears no resemblance to anything in the Election programme, or even to the Government's intentions as expressed in the Motion submitted in another place in 1946, to which the noble Viscount referred, which was to transfer to the ownership of the nation appropriate sections of the iron and steel industry. No one could imagine that we should see a Bill which, while leaving large parts of the so-called appropriate sections of iron and steel making outside, embraces huge engineering enterprises which are not steel-making at all. Indeed, whatever claim the Government could advance for a mandate to nationalize iron and steel, they have no authority whatever for this particular Bill.
>
> (Swinton [Conservative], Lords 1949)

A variation on this claim challenges whether the government's manifesto commitment has sufficient popular support to warrant being considered a manifesto commitment. Arguments of this kind have turned on either the size of the government's vote share *or* seat share in the Commons following an election. Opposition party leaders might accept that the measures contained within the bill reflect the government's manifesto commitment but claim that the government's slim majority (the indeterminacy of popular support for the government in "the other place") releases peers from the obligation to observe the convention.

Conservative peers pressed this argument in the periods following the narrow election victories of Labour under Harold Wilson (1964–1970),[20] but also at the 1950 UK general election when Labour was returned with a reduced majority. Such claims continue to be leveled to justify non-observance. Referring to the Conservatives slim victory at the 2015 elections, Lord Greaves, during the Queen's Speech debate, reasoned that:

> but they [Conservative party] did so on 37% of the vote, which means that nearly two out of three people who voted against the present government. Indeed, only 25% of eligible voters voted for them. So the idea that they have an overwhelming commitment by the people of this country to all the things in their manifesto is a slightly dodgy argument.
>
> (Greaves [Liberal Democrats], Lords 2015)[21]

The break with the certainty of single party government formation in the Commons since 2010 has extended the grounds on which the opposition has been able to challenge the inevitability of the convention's observance. The crux of the constitutional dilemma was outlined in the Lords Select Committee on the Constitution (2014: 30) thus:

> It cannot be said that any one party's manifesto has been given a mandate through that party getting a majority. Nor is it axiomatic that the coalition agreement can be considered a substitute for a manifesto in considering whether the convention should apply to any particular measure: in the words of Viscount Cranborne in 1945, the understanding applied to those measures which have been "definitely put before the electorate".

20 See, for example, the debates that transpired in the House of Lords on 4 November 1964 (vol. 261).

21 (Stoddart [Labour], Lords 2004):

> The Government may claim a majority of 163 in the House of Commons, but that is based on their gaining only 42 per cent of the vote on a 59 per cent turnout at the last election. That does not give them the right to ride roughshod over our constitution on one sunny afternoon in June by way of a throwaway line in a government reshuffle.

A third variation is for the opposition to contend that the government's bill fails to reflect its own election manifesto pledge. Here, the opposition has argued that the government's failure to honor its manifesto commitment effectively releases the Lords from the obligation to obey the convention and, in fact, it would be improper for the chamber to observe the convention under these conditions.

An example of such a claim surfaced in debates over the implementation of the recommendations arising from the inquiry into the Grenfell Tower tragedy,[22] and which were enshrined in the government's manifesto commitments. In pressing amendments to the proposed bill moved by the Liberal Democrats, Lord Adonis stated:

> The Government's commitment at the election was to sort out this issue; it was *not not* to sort out this issue. If we take that reading of the role of this House, we will actually be implementing the Salisbury convention this evening if we pass the amendment of the noble Baroness, Lady Pinnock. We are seeking to hold the Government to their manifesto commitments to the people, not going against them . . . it is manifestly not the case that we are breaking the Salisbury convention, it is manifestly not the case that we are going against the commitments that the Government themselves have given, and it is manifestly not the case that we would be the cause of the Bill falling. The Government would be the cause of the Bill falling, because they were not prepared to accept the amendment.
>
> (Adonis, [Labour] Lords 2021)

A fourth type of argument advanced to justify non-observance relies on opposition peers reading of the conditions set down in the government's manifesto commitment. Labour's 2001 manifesto, for example, included a pledge to ban fox hunting as a free vote. This commitment included the following dispensation in the manifesto text:

> [s]uch issues are rightly a matter for a free vote and we will give the new House of Commons an early opportunity to express its view.

The subsequent *free vote*[23] in the Commons produced a bill that proposed a total ban on hunting, a proposal which the Lords had rejected several times previously. Labour invoked the convention during several debates in the Lords, to which peers responded that the manifesto promised a free vote and

22 Other examples of the convention working in reverse include *Fire Safety Bill* (2021); *United Kingdom Internal Market Bill* (2020); *Health and Social Care Bill* (2011); *Sexual Offences (Amendment) Bill* (2000); *Freedom of Information Bill (2000)*.

23 See, for example, debates in relation to the *Hunting Bill* (2003) and *Hunting Bill* (2004).

for the Parliament to reach a conclusion. Here the Conservatives argued that the pledge for a free vote effectively released the Lords from convention. As a result, the Conservative Lords asserted that the convention did not apply, forcing the government to invoke the Parliament Act to pass the legislation in the Lords (see also, Plumb and Marsh 2013).

Manifesto Bill Violates a Constitutional Principle

Opposition peers have also justified departing from the convention on the grounds that the government's bill includes provisions which violate an important constitutional principle (or procedure). The opposition accepts that the bill reflects the government's manifesto commitment but that other features of the bill, as it is constructed, are constitutionally suspect and therefore should not advance.

This argument has been invoked by the opposition in the Lords on several occasions,[24] including in relation to Labour's 1997 manifesto pledge to remove hereditary peers from the Lords.[25] More recently, this argument was advanced by opposition peers to block the passage of Part 5 of bill that would have the effect of breaching the European Union withdrawal agreement.[26] The Labour opposition made clear that their opposition to the bill was "not about Brexit" but rather:

> it is about destroying one of the foundational values of our country. Without a government committed to obeying the law, everything is at risk. The law is the ultimate protector. We will invite this House, at the appropriate time, to remove Part 5 of the Bill neck and crop. I hope thereafter that this House will do everything it legitimately can to ensure that it does not return.
>
> (Falconer [Labour], Lords 2020)

While opposition peers have, over the years, made claims to some kind of exemption to the convention, these challenges have typically evoked the constitutionality of the convention. Moreover, few of these claims have been pressed by opposition peers. As noted earlier, it is only very occasionally that the Lords has insisted on voting down a bill down on a division in the second reading. Often, they have used the opportunity to trigger ping-pong[27]

24 See, for example: *United Kingdom Internal Market Bill* (2020); *Queen's Speech debate* (2015); *Government of Wales Bill* (2006); *Reform of the House of Lords debate* (2000).

25 See, for example the following debates: *House of Lords Bill* (1999); *House of Lords Reform* (1998); *Welsh Devolution Government of Wales Bill* (2006).

26 See the debate in the Lords on the *United Kingdom Internal Market Bill* (2020).

27 Ping-pong is defined by the UK Parliament's glossary (UK Parliament, n.d.) as the "to and fro of amendments to Bills between the House of Commons and the House of Lords".

to secure modest amendments to a bill. In even fewer cases, and in order to express displeasure with a government bill, the Lords opposition has turned to even gentler tactics of resistance, such as approving the bill but inserting a vesting date that would delay its implementation until after the next election or seeking to add a statement to a bill expressing discontent with its contents and the actions of the government.

Conclusion

This study on the Salisbury convention reveals that while this rule is entrenched, constitutional actors have intermittently challenged one or more elements of the convention. Opposition peers have done so by claiming a situational exemption that releases them from strict observance of the convention. These exemptions, however, rarely – if ever – strain against the broader principle contained within the convention. If anything, opposition peers have mostly been assiduous in affirming the relevance of convention even while seeking to temporarily vary it in some way. Such challenges have led, over time, to minor adjustments to the convention – the most well-known of these being that the Lords may press for amendments to government manifesto bills so long as they are not wrecking amendments.

There are powerful forces which create strong incentives for the members of the Lords to observe the Salisbury convention. The Conservatives have dominated both chambers for extended periods of time, which has meant that the party in government and the party that controls the Lords have often been the same. Quite apart from this, there is also a powerful driver for the chamber to observe the convention owing to lingering questions about the desirability of a non-elected legislative body. This aside, this study has sought to better understand how actors navigate departures from the convention when it suits their interests without compromising the integral core of the convention. The tentative lesson from this study of the Salisbury convention is that constitutional actors balance resistance and adherence by claiming a situational exemption along one or more dimensions of the rule. In some cases, such exemptions are imprinted on the convention, thereby facilitating its evolution.

References

Addison, Christopher (1945) *House of Lords*, 25 May, Volume 162.

Adonis, Andrew (2021) *House of Lords*, 9 February, Volume 811.

Ahmed, Ashraf (2021) 'A Theory of Constitutional Norms', *Michigan Law Review*, 120: 1361–1418.

Ahmed, Farah, Albert, Richard and Perry, Adam (2019) 'Judging Constitutional Conventions', *International Journal of Constitutional Law*, 17(3): 787–806.

Aroney, Nicholas (2015) 'On the Distinction Between Law and Convention', in Brian Galligan and Scott Brenton (eds) *Constitutional Conventions in Westminster*

Systems Controversies, Changes and Challenges, Cambridge University Press (Melbourne), pp. 24–51.

Barry, Nicholas and Miragliotta, Narelle (2015) 'Australia', in Brian Galligan and Scott Brenton (eds) *Constitutional Conventions in Westminster Systems Controversies, Changes and Challenges*, Cambridge University Press (Melbourne), pp. 204–216.

Barry, Nicholas, Miragliotta, Narelle and Nwokora, Zim (2019) 'The Dynamics of Constitutional Conventions in Westminster Democracies', *Parliamentary Affairs*, 72(3): 664–683.

Beamish, David (2018) *What Is the Salisbury Convention and Have the Lords Broken It Over Brexit?* UCL, The Constitution Unit Blog. URL: https://constitution-unit.com/2018/06/12/what-is-the-salisbury-convention-and-have-the-lords-broken-it-over-brexit/#more-6746

Brazier, Rodney (1992) 'The Non-Legal Constitution: Thoughts on Convention, Practice and Principle', *Northern Ireland Legal Quarterly*, 43(3): 262–287.

Brazier, Rodney (2006) *Memorandum by Professor Rodney Brazier to the Joint Select Committee on Conventions*, UK Parliament. URL: https://publications.parliament.uk/pa/jt200506/jtselect/jtconv/265/265we03.htm

Carrington, Peter (1975) *House of Lords*, 11 November, Volume 365.

Chafetz, Josh and Pozen, David (2018) 'How Constitutional Norms Break Down', *UCLA Law Review*, 65: 1430–1459.

Constitution Committee (2017) *The Salisbury-Addison Convention*, 5th Report of Session, HL28, UK Parliament.

Cranborne, Robert (1945) *House of Lords*, 16 August, Volume 137.

Desai, Meghnad (2001) *House of Lords*, 24 January, Volume 621.

Dymond, Glenn and Deadman, Hugo (2006) *The Salisbury Doctrine*, Library Notes, House of Lords, LLN, pp. 1–87.

Falconer, Charles (2020) *House of Lords*, 19 October, Volume 806.

Ferrers, Robert (2001) *House of Lords*, 24 January, Volume 621.

Greaves, Tony (2015) *House of Lords*, 2 June, Volume 762.

Hazel, Robert (2015) 'The United Kingdom', in Brian Galligan and Scott Brenton (eds) *Constitutional Conventions in Westminster Systems Controversies, Changes and Challenges*, Cambridge University Press (Melbourne), pp. 173–188.

Heard, Andrew (1989) 'Recognizing the Variety Among Constitutional Conventions', *Canadian Journal of Political Science*, XXII(1): 63–82.

Helmke, Gretchen and Levitsky, Steven (2004) 'Informal Institutions and Comparative Politics: A Research Agenda', *Perspectives on Politics*, 2(4): 725–740.

Hinterleitner, Markus and Sager, Fritz (2023) 'Political Challengers and Norm Erosion in Advanced Democracies', *European Journal of Political Research*, 62(4): 1301–1319.

HM Government (2007) *The House of Lords: Reform*, Cm7027, February.

House of Lords (1998) *House of Lords Reform Debate*, 15 October, Volume 593.

House of Lords (1999) *House of Lords Bill*, 27 April, Volume 600.

House of Lords (2000) *Reform of the House of Lords Debate*, 7 March, Volume 610.

House of Lords (2000) *Sexual Offences (Amendment) Bill Debate*, 11 April, Volume 612.

House of Lords (2000) *Freedom of Information Bill Debate*, November, Volume 619.

House of Lords (2003) *Hunting Bill Debate*, 16 September, Volume 652.

House of Lords (2004) *Hunting Bill Debate*, 12 October, Volume 665.

House of Lords (2005) *Lords Reform Debate*, January, Volume 668.

House of Lords (2006) *Welsh Devolution Government of Wales Bill Debate*, 24 July, Volume 684.

House of Lords (2007) *Conventions, Joint Committee Report Debate*, January 2007, Volume 688.
House of Lords (2011) *Health and Social Care Bill Debate*, December, Volume 733.
House of Lords (2015a) *Queen's Speech Debate*, 1 June, Volume 762.
House of Lords (2015b) *Queen's Speech Debate*, June, Volume 762.
House of Lords (2020) *Lords on the United Kingdom Internal Market Bill Debate*, 19 October, Volume 806.
House of Lords (2021) *Fire Safety Bill Debate*, 28 April, Volume 811.
Jaconelli, Joseph (1999) 'The Nature of Constitutional Convention', *Legal Studies*, 19(1): 24–46.
Jaconelli, Joseph (2013) 'Continuity and Change in Constitutional Conventions', in David Butler and Martin Qvortrup (eds) *The British Constitution: Continuity and Change*, Hart Publishing (Oxford), pp. 121–139.
Jennings, Ivor (1959) *The Law and the Constitution*, 5th edition, University of London Press (London).
Joint Committee on Conventions (2006) *Conventions of the UK Parliament*, Volume 1 (HL Paper 265-1. HC 1212-1).
Joint Committee on House of Lords Reform (2002) *House of Lords Reform: First Report* (HL Paper 17; HC 171).
Lords Select Committee on the Constitution (2014) *Constitutional Implications of Coalition Government* (5th Report, HL Paper 130).
Lords Select Committee on the Constitution (2017) *The Salisbury-Addison Convention* (5th Report, HL Paper 28).
Mansfield, William (1975) *House of Lords*, 10 March, Volume 358.
Marshall, Geoffrey (1984) *Constitutional Conventions: The Rules and Forms of Political Accountability*, Clarendon (Oxford).
McNally, Tom (2007) *House of Lords*, 16 January, Volume 688.
Munro, Colin (1975) 'Laws and Conventions Distinguished', *Law Quarterly Review*, 91: 218–235.
Natzler, David and Hutton, Mark (2019) *Erskine May's Treatise on the Law, Privileges, Proceedings and Usage of Parliament*, 25th edition, UK Parliament.
Perry, Adam and Tucker, Adam (2018) 'Top-Down Constitutional Conventions', *Modern Law Review*, 81(5): 765–789.
Plumb, Alison and Marsh, David (2013) 'Beyond Party Discipline: UK Parliamentary Voting on Fox Hunting', *British Politics*, 8: 313–332.
Postema, Gerald (2022) 'Constitutional Norms – Erosion, Sabotage and Response', *Ratio Juris*, 35(2): 99–122.
Royal Commission on Reform of the House of Lords [Wakeham Commission] (2000) *A House for the Future*, Cm 4534, January.
Russell, Meg (2003) 'Is the House of Lords Already Reformed?' *The Political Quarterly*, 74(3): 311–318.
Russell, Meg and Sciara, Maria (2007) 'Why Does the Government Get Defeated in the House of Lords? The Lords, the Party System and British Politics', *British Politics*, 2(3): 299–322.
Samuel, Herbert (1945) *House of Lords*, 16 August, Volume 137.
Shell, Donald (2006) *Memorandum by Donald Shell*, University of Bristol to the Joint Select Committee on Conventions, UK Parliament. URL: https://publications.parliament.uk/pa/jt200506/jtselect/jtconv/265/265we05.htm
Stephenson, Scott (2015) 'When Constitutional Conventions Fail', *Dublin University Law Journal*, 38(2): 447–464.
Stoddart, David (2004) *House of Lords*, 8 March, Volume 658.
Swinton (1949) *House of Lords*, 24 May, Volume 162.

Tushnet, Mark (2004) 'Constitutional Hardball', *Marshall Law Review*, 37: 523–553.
Twomey, Anne (2018) *The Veiled Sceptre: Reserve Powers of Heads of State in Westminster Systems*, Cambridge University Press (Cambridge).
UK Labour Party (2001) *2001 Labour Party General Election Manifesto*. URL: http://labourmanifesto.com/2001/2001-labour-manifesto.shtml
UK Parliament (n.d.) *Glossary*. URL: https://www.parliament.uk/site-information/glossary/
Williamson, David (2007) *House of Lords*, 16 January, Volume 688.

Chapter 6

How Do Constitutional Changes Affect Conventions and Constitutional Identity?

A Case Study of a Republic in Australia

*Sarah Murray**

Introduction

Amendments to a nation's constitution and key political and legal institutions will often affect or threaten established constitutional norms and practices. This can cause constitutional soul-searching about how to change institutions without disrupting established conventions. This can be particularly difficult when there are concerns that particular conventions or practices reflect constitutional values that contribute to, or form part of, a nation's constitutional identity or identities. The place of the head of state's reserve powers if Australia were to become a republic presents precisely this predicament.

The British-formed colonies moved to establish Australia, from 1 January 1901, as a federal constitutional monarchy, notwithstanding the many millennia of governance by Aboriginal and Torres Strait Islanders as Australia's First Peoples. Less than 100 years on from federation, the failure of the 1999 Australian Republic referendum came as a surprise to many Australian republicans, with blame falling upon deep divisions over the selected republican model for an Australian presidency.[1] As Paul Kelly (cited in Winterton 2001, p. 1) observed:

> This was not a vote for the Queen; it was not just a vote against the republic on offer, it was, at a deeper level, a vote of distrust in the political class and its agenda.

There are numerous obstacles to Australia in the future becoming a republic and cutting ties with the monarchy. One of the clear challenges is the existence of unfinished constitutional business following the failure of the Aboriginal and Torres Strait Islander Voice to Parliament Referendum in October 2023.

* The author wishes to acknowledge the helpful feedback of the attendees at the Constitutional Conventions workshop held at Deakin University, September 2022.

1 The title of the Head of State in an Australian Republic could well be Governor-General, President or another similar title, but President is used in this chapter for the sake of simplicity.

DOI: 10.4324/9781003506577-6

This resounding failed attempt to amend the Commonwealth Constitution saw Professor Emerita Anne Twomey opine in an interview that 'there is just no point in putting a referendum to the people' in Australia (Morse 2023).

But the challenges do not stop there. Any successful section 128 constitutional amendment in Australia represents a herculean feat of bipartisanship, public education and drafting simplicity (Williams & Hume 2010, Ch 7). For a referendum on Australia becoming a republic, this is compounded by lingering monarchical affection, only strengthened by Queen Elizabeth II's Jubilee celebration and passing followed by King Charles' coronation. As Altman colourfully described, 'My sense is that most Australians feel about the republic rather like the character in *Alice in Wonderland* who wanted jam yesterday and jam tomorrow but never jam today' (Altman 2022).

The republican model itself has also represented an ongoing constitutional headache. While many experts remain convinced that a parliamentary model would be unlikely to succeed over a more popular direct election model, the constitutional dilemmas are stark. If a direct election model is put up, how are the concerns regarding competing governing mandates being claimed by the Prime Minister and the President to be dealt with – 'the car with two steering wheels' quandary? (Winterton 2001, p. 13) And as this chapter examines, what is to be done about the emergency powers of the President – the reserve powers which can be exercised by the head of state in the absence of (and sometimes even in contradiction of) ministerial advice, and that are regulated by constitutional convention rather than formal rules that are legally enforceable?

The focus of this chapter is on the debate over how the reserve powers of the head of state, and the conventions associated with their exercise, are to be treated in a shift to an Australian Republic. To narrow the scope of the chapter, it will focus particularly on the power to appoint and dismiss a Prime Minister, and the power to dissolve – or refuse to dissolve – the Parliament. If the powers are codified to neutralise the concerns about what direct election might do to the President's powers, what difficulties does this pose? Even if agreement can be reached on what to codify, might it detract from the flexibility and dynamic nature of the conventions, as well as their non-justiciability? The concern remains, however, that if they remain loose and uncodified, their exercise might become highly politicised – something particularly concerning in the tense historical moment of a constitutional crisis. It could then be that their inherent adaptability might in fact become their Achilles' heel. The key point is that, as Winterton (1994, pp. 38, 42) explained, our constitutional system is a delicate balance such that as:

> The exercise of reserve powers is governed by constitutional conventions, which evolve and adapt to new situations, the advent of a republic in itself is likely to affect the exercise of reserve powers.

A recent constitutional skirmish over the former Australian Prime Minister secretly holding multiple ministerial portfolios already held by other ministers has highlighted the centrality of constitutional conventions to Australia's constitutional functioning (Donaghue 2022). It has also shed light on the question of whether constitutional mechanics need formal legal or constitutional enshrinement even at the risk of the loss of some of their malleability.

The chapter will use the Republican-reserve power question as a case study of a larger constitutional problem. How do states embark on constitutional change without unwittingly and unintentionally breaking with their engrained constitutional practices and norms, as essential parts of their core constitutional identity? As Jacobsohn (2011, p. 129) identifies, constitutional identity is caught up in constitutional 'experience' and results from a 'dialogica[l]' mix of history, culture and cherished beliefs. Constitutional reform can result in a cleavage from these roots and can make adopting new governmental models incredibly difficult. This is because established patterns of constitutional practice and mores – such as conventions and established principles such as responsible and representative government – do not necessarily operate or align in quite the same way. To leave these behind would represent a great rupture, which often means that the pursuit of change is abandoned because it is regarded as too difficult. The chapter commences with an analysis of Australia's constitutional norms regarding the exercise of reserve powers in the second section. The third section looks at the potential impact of the direct election Republican model on reserve powers. The fourth section then looks at the challenge in codifying reserve powers, while the fifth section teases out possible solutions to the codification dilemma. What is evident is that conventions inevitably get entangled in questions of constitutional change but can also have a disrupting impact on constitutional change progressing. Accordingly, the sixth and final section explores how the Australian Republican endeavour is best conceived as bundled up in questions of Australia's future constitutional identity and what aspects of constitutional functioning, including conventions, should be retained and what should be revisited. The dissent in relation to what Republican model to adopt and which continues to this day is therefore only able to be resolved alongside questions of constitutional identity.

Constitutional Conventions and Reserve Powers

Reserve powers are a tricky phenomenon to pin down. They are rare powers that allow a head of state to act to restore constitutional order in the absence of advice from the government of the day, or sometimes even in contradiction of such advice. These powers are also inherently adaptable and flexible to circumstance. Instead of being subject to judicial review or legal regulation, the constitutional conventions governing their exercise are determined by past practice and established use. On the rare occasions when these powers are used, it can be difficult to determine whether or not it is consistent with convention, a departure from convention or an iterative adjustment to the convention in light of changing circumstances (Commonwealth of Australia 1993).

The most relevant Australian reserve powers for the purposes of this chapter are the power to appoint and dismiss a Prime Minister and the power to dissolve or refuse to dissolve Parliament. Some conventions relating to these powers are quite clear. For example, the convention that the Governor-General should appoint as Prime Minister the leader of the party, who commands the support of the House of Representatives, is well established, as is the convention that the Governor-General should refuse to dissolve Parliament if there is sufficient support on the floor of the lower house for a person to fulfil the role of Prime Minister (Twomey 2018, p. 16).

However, politics is often not as neat as this, and even these relatively clear conventions can sometimes be difficult to apply. For while there may be 'broad consensus regarding the core of such conventions . . . the boundaries are often indistinct' (Winterton 1993, p. 254). For example, when a government is acting or threatening to act illegally, it may be that the Governor-General can use their reserve power to dismiss the Prime Minister; however, precisely what conduct warrants this action – and when dismissal is required – is not always certain (Commonwealth of Australia 1993, pp. 258–259). Even the power to appoint the government can be difficult to apply. For example, it may be that there is a hung Parliament, in which case it is unclear who will be able to command the support of the House of Representatives and it is not clear to whom the crossbench members may guarantee supply.

The Australian 1975 constitutional crisis when a sitting Prime Minister was dismissed for failure to secure supply from the Senate is a prime example of the ambiguity surrounding constitutional conventions. The difficulty for the Governor-General, Sir John Kerr, was the intersection between the Senate's constitutional powers to not pass an appropriation bill (under Chapter I, Part V of the Commonwealth Constitution), with the conventions of responsible government, which only require a government to be able to secure support in the House of Representatives (Commonwealth of Australia 1993, p. 263). For that reason, Sir John Kerr's action – dismissing the Prime Minister to ensure that the capacity to meet the ordinary annual services of government was secured – was unprecedented.

The challenge is that while some constitutional conventions can be suitably sketched out providing a blueprint for governance, others cannot, either because they are ambiguous or because there is some disagreement over their precise form. Ever since November 1975, there has been debate over whether the crisis highlights the need for greater clarity around the reserve powers and the conventions guiding them. However, the debate has stalled because of a lack of agreement over how the crisis ought to have been resolved. The possibility that Australia will become a republic makes answering such questions more pressing, particularly because of the widespread belief that the absence of the monarchy will affect the operation of long-standing conventions.

Direct Election and Reserve Powers

Surveys prior to and since the referendum in 1999 have consistently shown public support for a republican model that involves direct election of the President by the people rather than a parliamentary appointment presidential approach (Winterton 1993, p. 259, 2001, pp. 2–3; Fenna 2010, pp. 134–135; Harris 2019, p. 71; French 2021, p. 17). The 1999 constitutional proposal that was put to the people was a parliamentary-controlled 'minimalist' model rather than a direct election model (Murray 2010). It required a two-thirds majority of the members of the House of Representatives and the Senate to support a presidential appointment and the appointee would be precluded from being a member of the Commonwealth, State or Territory parliaments or a member of a political party. This was seen as more in tune with our parliamentary heritage with concerns that a direct election model would introduce more American-style features into our system of government (or what Winterton [1993, p. 249] colourfully described as 'some hybrid mutant which might well combine the worst features of both systems').

The proposal contemplated that the Commonwealth Constitution would be amended to refer for the first time to the office of Prime Minister and the constitutional conventions by providing in section 59 (emphasis added) that:

> The executive power of the Commonwealth is vested in the President, and extends to the execution and maintenance of this Constitution, and of the laws of the Commonwealth. The President shall be the head of state of the Commonwealth.
>
> There shall be a Federal Executive Council to advise the President in the government of the Commonwealth, and the members of the Council shall be chosen and summoned by the President and sworn as Executive Councillors, and shall hold office during the pleasure of the President.
>
> *The President shall act on the advice of the Federal Executive Council, the Prime Minister or another Minister of State; but the President may exercise a power that was a reserve power of the Governor-General in accordance with the constitutional conventions relating to the exercise of that power.*

There was, however, still great concern that the President might be more inclined to exercise a reserve power than the Governor-General. In fact, Professor Winterton (1993, p. 262), in noting the difficulty of properly regulating a President in this regard, had counselled a prophylactic disincentivising approach whereby a President who adopts a 1975-type approach and exercises the reserve powers would automatically surrender their office.

The proposed Australian Choice Model of the Australian Republican Movement (2022) provides an example of a direct election model. Announced in 2022, it favours state parliaments and the federal Parliament nominating candidates to be put to the Australian people who would be voting for a President to serve for a five-year period. The model also seeks to codify, through a series of drafted provisions, the powers of the head of state including in relation to the appointment and dismissal of the Prime Minister and the instances when Parliament can be dissolved. Controversially, in light of the different perspectives on Sir John Kerr's actions in 1975 when Prime Minister Gough Whitlam was denied supply by the Senate, cl 70A(v) provides that:

> The Head of State shall not terminate the appointment of a Prime Minister who holds the confidence of the House of Representatives.

Clearly, the approach taken to the reserve powers very much depends on the Republican model adopted. In particular, it has often been thought that the reserve powers of a directly elected President would need to be locked in to a greater extent. This stems from a fear that a directly elected President might feel more inclined to exercise their powers, unbridled by monarchical loyalties and emboldened by the backing of having been personally elected by a majority of the Australian population (Winterton 1993, p. 260, 2001, pp. 12, 15, 1994, pp. 38, 43–44; Brennan 2004, p. 9). As Fenna (2010, p. 126) explains, '[t]he chief objection to direct election has long been its potentially destabilising impact'. This is most notably because the Prime Minister is only elected by one electorate currently out of 151 nationally while a directly elected President would face the ballot of all Australian voters.

In light of these concerns, however, the problem of how to regulate reserve powers in a post-monarchical Australia is not an easy one to resolve. This is primarily because it is not clear whether codification can be achieved and, if it can, what is to be codified, especially when so much of Australia's constitutional order is unwritten. For this reason, Fenna (2010, pp. 135, 138) has recommended the lining up of constitutional documents with practice, while noting:

> Both concerns – the concern that codification is necessary if direct-election is to be chosen, and the concern that codification would ask too much of the referendum process – remain valid.

'Locking Them In': Codifying the Reserve Powers?

While there is 'no necessary coincidence between our system of government and retention of the reserve powers', the dominant view is that it would be too drastic a change to depart from them altogether (Commonwealth of Australia 1993, Ch 6). As Winterton (1993, pp. 249, 252) has argued, constitutional crises would be hard to resolve without 'umpires' to steer the nation back on course. However, there has been disagreement over how these reserve powers should be regulated if Australia were to become a republic, with a variety of models being put forward, ranging from minimal adjustments to full codification.

Reserve powers, and the conventions that regulate them, present an interesting example of the tension associated with codification as part of structural change to the Constitution. Whether to formalise 'softer' rules into 'harder' (Barry et al. 2019, pp. 664, 676) rules, ossifying conventions in a particular form in the Constitution presents a range of issues, both constitutional and political.

The Report of the Republic Advisory Committee (Commonwealth of Australia 1993, p. 272) highlighted the complexity of the reserve powers in the Republican debate:

> Any attempt to set out the rules in full would be seen by some as an attempt to change them. It would also be criticised as 'freezing' the conventions in time and reducing their flexibility . . . . Yet there are obviously strong arguments for replacing a system of unwritten rules, fully understood by nobody, with a settled text which tells people what to expect of their rulers and tells the rulers what they are allowed to so. The text could establish practices which are considered desirable, rather than those which have been inherited, and could set out which powers are discretionary (and ensure that they remain non-justiciable) and which are not.

For Malcolm Turnbull (1993, p. 94), former Australian Prime Minister but then Chairman of the Australian Republican Movement, Republican reform should go hand in hand with codification to clear away 'uncertainty and mystery' and the dangers of 'differing interpretation[s]'. He also was keen to emphasise that we should not attribute disagreements over codification to the Republican question but instead to the Australian constitutional framework (p. 113).

Paul Keating, while Prime Minister, preferred a different route, whereby the present powers of the head of state would be carried over to an Australian President without being clearly set out in the text of the Constitution. This is because he believed that doing so would fail to 'find general community acceptance *and* cover every possible contingency'. It may also 'result in fundamental change to our system of government' and in the reserve powers becoming susceptible to judicial scrutiny (Keating 1995, p. 9). Harris (2019, pp. 65, 74–76), on the other hand, has questioned why there is such trepidation surrounding codification of the reserve powers. He argues that the flexibility surrounding the use of these powers is precisely the problem, as the events of 1975 illustrate. The need for flexibility is rebutted by comparative examples of republics that have effectively set out the reserve powers of the President (Ward 1999). Harris (2019, p. 76) also argues that codification provides a real chance to resolve constitutional uncertainty in Australia's system of government by delineating the roles and appointment mechanism for the Prime Minister, as well as the republican head of state (Real Republic Australia 2022).

The 'Australian Choice Model' of the Australian Republican Movement (2022) recommend 'limited' and 'ceremonial' powers for a directly elected head of state who would typically act on advice and lack the power to 'terminate the appointment of a Prime Minister who holds the confidence of the House of Representatives'. The Australian Republican Movement's proposed cl 5 provides:

> The Head of State may, by Proclamation, dissolve the House of Representatives
>
> (a) where the confidence of the House of Representatives is indeterminate for a period of no less than seven consecutive days; or
> (b) [i]n accordance with the procedure for a simultaneous dissolution of both the House of Representatives and the Senate, as provided for in section 57; and not otherwise.

The process of codification requires agreement as to what the powers of the President should be and the circumstances in which those powers should be exercised. The dilemma, of course, is ensuring that all potential circumstances are suitably addressed or that the Constitution guarantees that the President is able to act appropriately in relation to situations that arise.

'Leaving Things Out?': Avoiding the Immobilisation of the Reserve Powers

The answer to the codification dilemma for Professor Winterton (2001, p. 17) lay in codifying the reserve powers, but only to the limited extent that it provided for the ongoing retention of Australia's existing constitutional conventions 'in the interstices of the reserve powers'. He noted (p. 17–8) that:

> The Constitution should provide that after a general election the President should appoint as Prime Minister the person most likely to enjoy the confidence of the House of Representatives. The President should be obliged to refuse a dissolution of Parliament to a Prime Minister who has lost a constructive no-confidence motion; while a motion of no-confidence is pending; and before the House of Representatives has met after a general election, unless the House has proved unable to elect a Speaker.

For Winterton (2001, p. 18), 1975 proved a real sticking point in determining how to treat the reserve power relating to the dismissal of the Prime Minister:

> The power should probably be exercisable only if the Prime Minister refused to comply with an order of the High Court or has contravened a fundamental constitutional provision or, more questionably, a fundamental constitutional principle.

In this way, the reserve powers should be codified in a way that retains suppleness in their exercise and allows them to be subject to ongoing regulation by pre-existing conventions. This ensured that the Republican head of state would be:

> granted only such power as is absolutely necessary to enforce the fundamental constitutional principles of the rule of law, and representative and responsible government
>
> (p. 18).

Winterton (2001, pp. 18–19) also saw benefit in the establishment of a Constitutional Council of up to five 'former Presidents and High Court justices' to advise the head of state in the exercise of reserve powers. It would also be possible to allow the eventual publication of the Council's advice.

A real concern with codification is not only the loss of flexibility, but the potential for the exercise of reserve powers to become justiciable or amenable to judicial consideration (Twomey 2018, p. 39). This would radically alter the High Court's traditional position by throwing inevitable political questions at the Court's feet. Sir Gerard Brennan (2004, p. 14), former Chief Justice of the High Court, also expressed concern that the Court would not be able to act with sufficient speed to resolve potential constitutional crises in time. We see in this the concern that the republican shift might not only alter our Westminster heritage but also threaten the independence and impartiality of Australia's highest court.

Sir Gerard Brennan (2004, p. 15) agreed that the powers could not be entirely locked in and saw the need for what he called a 'Council of State' or 'Constitutional Council' for ensuring that reserve powers are properly exercised in accordance with constitutional principle. Sir Brennan contemplated the Council having the ability to issue a 'certificate' which could shield the head of state from judicial review, but also allow High Court justiciability if the reserve powers were exercised without this certificate. For Sir Brennan (2004, p. 19), the Council would help address a 1975-style crisis if it arose again – allowing 'independent consideration of the circumstances justifying *absolute necessity*' [emphasis in original].

A further challenge for Australia is the difficult process required to formally amend the Constitution under section 128 of the Constitution, which necessitates a referendum. Any powers that are constitutionally codified then become notoriously difficult to change. One of the key things about conventions is that they are designed to adapt and therefore are not readily amenable to solidification in an inflexible document. It was for this reason that Winterton's 'minimalist' model favoured giving the Commonwealth Parliament the power to regulate the exercise of the reserve powers (rather than constitutionalising these powers) with any such legislation requiring a two-thirds parliamentary majority for it to be amended (Murray 2010, p. 45).

What is evident is that the unpredictability of political turmoil and crises makes detailed constitutional prescription particularly problematic in the Australian constitutional context. What we see through the Australian experience is that constitutional conventions, like reserve powers, are vulnerable at times of constitutional change and that discordant views as to what norms must remain unchanged can obstruct the constitutional reform process. In the next section, the chapter unpacks the inter-relationship between constitutional conventions and constitutional identity, discussing how these are inevitably co-dependent in times of change.

Constitutional Identity and Republican Imaginings

Underlying the debate about the codification of the reserve powers is the question of whether it is possible to adopt a Republican model that keeps Australia within its constitutional comfort zone.[2]

This reality also intersects with the notion of national constitutional identity or identities. Constitutional identity is a complex thing wrapped in text, history, culture, political landscapes and national identity. Jacobsohn (2011, pp. 129–130, 139) describes how the creation of identity (or identities) is an ongoing process resulting from 'experience', 'aspiratio[n]' and 'disharmony' (see also Pitkin 1987, p. 167; Jacobsohn 2010, pp. 3–4; Tribe 1983, p. 440). Further, provisions that inhibit ready constitutional change (like section 128 in the *Commonwealth Constitution*) become barriers to too easy departures from this identity, even if not locking in a particular constitutional form (Jacobsohn 2011, p. 129). Jacobsohn (2011, p. 130) notes that constitutional identity or identities are far from constant and 'may manifest itself differently in different settings'. As the 1999 failed referendum showcased, it is often the case that constitutional identity becomes the most stark through moments of 'disharmony'. Similarly, 1975 played out different constitutional notions or understandings latent within Australian notions of responsible government.

2 Interestingly, the public's unwillingness to accept the politician's republican model in 1999 could be perceived as an inclination to depart from the well-known, in spite of expert reservations about this (Brett 1995, p. 6) – or was it perhaps merely a protest vote against the 'Politician's Republic'?

These differences persist, along with conflict with regard to whether the Governor-General did or did not 'do his duty'. For Jacobsohn (2010, p. 4) it is precisely historical moments such as these which allow us to witness 'continuities' within differing conceptions, ambiguities and disputations which draw on shared history and constitutional understandings.

As Winterton (2004, p. 5) expressed, '[r]espect for the Constitution and the governmental system are enhanced when constitutional arrangements are in harmony with national culture'. This arguably explains a lot of the difficulties that the republican question has presented. What emerges is the realisation that the problem is not simply about how to codify the reserve powers, or the method of appointing the President, or even the place of established constitutional conventions. Instead, it is about determining what Australia wants its constitutional identity to be. And while constitutionality identity is a complex mix of things, it feeds into debates over what the Republican model and its granular detail should be. As Jacobsohn (2011 p. 133) points out, '[a]s problematic as the idea of an immutable or static identity is, so too is the belief that the modifications of it are unconstrained by the traditions that carried it to its transformative moment'. These established traditions can be put under real 'stress' by processes of constitutional change or what Barry et al. (2019, p. 669) term 'constitutional softening'.

In embracing a direct election model, the public would be favouring a stronger say in who becomes the head of state and greater 'popular sovereignty' (Winterton 2001, p. 5), removing this decision from the control of parliamentarians. This could suggest a degree of popular frustration or a sense of feeling disempowered by the current governmental system (Winterton 2001, pp. 3–4). It also could suggest a wish for an Australian President to be more than just a figurehead. This says as much about Australian constitutional identity as the tensions which are suspended within it. If this is the case, it can also shape the powers the President is conferred with and the degree to which established constitutional conventions should continue once the monarchy is abandoned. But as Saunders (2010, pp. 54, 80) notes, we have to agree about 'the nature of the office that we want to create' and not, by default, fall back into making 'monarchical assumptions'.

The particular challenge presented by constitutional reform is understanding not only the current landscape of Australian constitutional identity or identities but what aspects the nation wants to hold onto. To what extent would losing the current flexibility associated with the reserve powers represent too much of a cleavage from our political identity and constitutional way of life? Harris (2019, p. 73), for instance, describes Australia's 'mystical attachment to the conventions'. Would losing these constitutional practices by codifying powers be a necessary and beneficial part of shifting to a republic? Or, can we understand conventions as ultimately safeguarding fundamental constitutional principles that can be ruptured without established conventions being in place? (Heard 2012, pp. 319, 330). Taking this 'principle-based approach' makes a lot of sense in understanding the importance of constitutional norms or practices and the instrumental role they play in 'protect[ing] and giv[ing] life to fundamental constitutional values' (Heard 2012, pp. 330, 338; Twomey 2018, p. 23).

If, like the Australian Choice Model, Australia decides to insert into the Commonwealth Constitution a provision that a sitting Prime Minister holding the confidence of the House of Representatives cannot be dismissed, Australia would be taking a position on the legality of Sir John Kerr's actions in 1975. Doing so is not just an exercise in forward state planning but becomes a reflection on our political history and the political tensions and morality wrapped within that (Barry & Miragliotta 2015, p. 204).

Similarly, the High Court has tended to avoid political controversies through the doctrine of non-justiciability and (if retaining this impartiality is seen as desirable) then particular attention must be paid to the design of constitutional reforms and whether a Constitutional Council would represent a good constitutional fit. Would providing for a Council to provide advice in a highly politicised crisis create an institutional power imbalance or accountability deficit? If concerted codification represents too much of a challenge, would it be possible to codify guiding principles or even some of the conventions governing the exercise of reserve powers? Or would that still leave too much unresolved? Australia needs to find reform solutions that recognise and attempt to respond to these uncertainties by actively designing a republican model with an appreciation of its significance for our identity as a nation.

In his writings prior to 1999, Winterton was keen to emphasise that Australia is not designing its Constitution anew and is 'not starting from scratch' (1993, p. 249). The core principles at the heart of the operation of the Australian state, and the conventions which exist within it, do not necessarily have to be abandoned. However, the constant question that has arisen since 1999 is the degree to which the Republic provides us with a chance to do just that – the chance to revise core elements of the constitutional framework. The Australian Republican Movement markets its 'Australian Choice Model' as a model that 'will not alter our fundamental constitutional order'. This makes a claim about Australia's constitutional identity and the Republic's relationship with it. It is precisely this claim which must be resolved as a pre-condition for reform. As Pitkin (1987, p. 167) makes clear, 'our constitution is less something we have than something we are'.

Conclusion

Reserve powers have been described as like 'fire extinguishers'; rarely used but 'there in an emergency' (Twomey 2018, p. 33, citing MacKinnon). In providing flexibility in times of crisis, the exercise of these powers, and the conventions guiding them, form a key part of Australia's constitutional identity, despite the fact these powers are rarely used. The Republican dilemma is ensuring that we are attuned to the need to embark on the consultation, drafting and education process with an awareness of what Australia is ready to abandon and what features, principles and practices need to be retained in the insertion of an Australian President. The question of whether and what to codify in an amended Commonwealth Constitution becomes tied up in how much discretion the Australian President is to have and how much tractability can be forgone in that process, while not rupturing existing conventions to too great a degree.

The Australian Republican imaginings, explored here, become a case study in how the impact of reform to established conventions, most specifically, the reserve powers, can pose a real threat to achieving constitutional change. As Brett (1995, p. 6) noted:

> The over-whelming popular demand for an elected head of state should be interpreted not as the result of ignorance about the balance of the Westminster system, but as an expression of the democratic desire of people to reconnect with national political life.

In claiming or re-creating a constitutional identity for Australia as a Republic, this process of reconnection can begin to come full circle. The predicament becomes how to allow the nation to move forward, if that is what it decides to do, without fundamentally rupturing all of its constitutional moorings and norms in that process.

References

Altman, Dennis. 2022. 'The Federal Government Has Appointed an Assistant Minister for a Republic', *ABC News*, 6 June, https://www.abc.net.au/news/2022-06-06/assistant-minister-for-republic-appointed-will-referendum-follow/101127738

Australian Republican Movement. 2022. 'The Australian Choice Model', https://static1.squarespace.com/static/5b531a35b98a78268300cad6/t/61fcc064b40c467706dcf334/1643954279725/The+Australian+Choice+Model+-+Detailed+Policy+2022.pdf

Barry, Nicholas, Narelle Miragliotta and Zim Nwokora. 2019 'The Dynamics of Constitutional Conventions in Westminster Democracies', 72 *Parliamentary Affairs* 664–683.

Barry, Nicolas and Narelle Miragliotta. 2015. 'Australia', in Brian Galligan and Scott Brenton (eds), *Constitutional Conventions in Westminster Systems: Controversies, Changes and Challenges* (CUP) 204.

Brennan, Gerard. 2004. 'Submission to Senate Legal and Constitutional References Committee', *Inquiry into an Australia Republic*, https://www.aph.gov.au/~/media/wopapub/senate/committee/legcon_ctte/completed_inquiries/2002_04/republic03/submissions/sub497_pdf.ashx

Brennan, Gerard. 2011. 'George Winterton Memorial Lecture', https://www.abc.net.au/radionational/programs/bigideas/2011-george-winterton-memorial-lecture-pathway-to/2993158

Brett, Judith. 1995. 'Political Cynicism and the Head of State', *Arena Magazine* 1–6, August–September.

Commonwealth of Australia. 1993. *An Australian Republic – the Options – Volume 2: The Appendices – the Report of the Republic Advisory Committee* (Commonwealth of Australia).

Donaghue, Stephen. 2022. 'In the Matter of the Validity of the Appointment of Mr. Morrison to Administer the Department of Industry, Science, Energy & Resources', SG No. 12 of 2022, 22 August, https://www.pmc.gov.au/sites/default/files/sg-no-12-of-2022.pdf

Fenna, Alan. 2010. 'The Incremental Republic', in Sarah Murray (ed), *Constitutional Perspectives on an Australian Republic: Essays in Honour of Professor George Winterton* (Federation Press) 126–143.

French, Robert. 2021. 'A True Australian Republic: True to Our History, Fit for Our Future', 2021 Toohey Oration, 19 August.

Harris, Bede. 2019. 'The Case for Codifying the Powers of the Office of the Governor-General', 16(1) *Canberra Law Review* 65.

Heard, Andrew. 2012. 'Constitutional Conventions: The Heart of the Living Constitution', 6 *Journal of Parliamentary and Political Law* 319–338.

Jacobsohn, Gary J. 2010. *Constitutional Identity* (Harvard University Press).

Jacobsohn, Gary J. 2011. 'The Formation of Constitutional Identities', in Tom Ginsburg and Rosalind Dixon (eds), *Comparative Constitutional Law* (Edward Elgar Publishing) 129–142.

Keating, Paul. 1995. *An Australian Republic – the Way Forward* (Australian Government Publishing Service), 7 June.

Morse, Dana. 2023. 'Constitutional Expert Believes Voice Vote Could Be the Last Referendum Held in Australia', *The Conversation*, 13 October, https://www.abc.net.au/news/2023-10-13/expert-believes-voice-could-be-last-referendum/102970978

Murray, Sarah. 2010. 'The Minimalist Winterton Model', in Sarah Murray (ed), *Constitutional Perspectives on an Australian Republic: Essays in Honour of Professor George Winterton* (Federation Press) 42–53.

Pitkin, Hanna Fenichel. 1987. 'The Idea of a Constitution', 37 *Journal of Legal Education* 167–169.

Real Republic Australia. 2022. 'Your Choice, the People's Choice', October, https://static1.squarespace.com/static/5a9e5ed4a9e028af26f1f247/t/634ff3347193ff44c2a1e9da/1666183994984/RRADiscPaperOct2022.pdf

Saunders, Cheryl. 2010. 'Beyond Minimalism', in Sarah Murray (ed), *Constitutional Perspectives on an Australian Republic: Essays in Honour of Professor George Winterton* (Federation Press) 54–80.

Tribe, Laurence H. 1983. 'A Constitution We Are Amending: In Defense of a Restrained Judicial Role', 97 *Harvard Law Review* 433.

Turnbull, Malcolm. 1993. *The Reluctant Republic* (William Heinemann Australia).

Twomey, Anne. 2018. *The Veiled Sceptre – Reserve Powers of Heads of State in Westminster Systems* (Cambridge University Press).

Ward, Alan, J. 1999. 'Australia and Parliamentary Orthodoxy: A Foreign Perspective on Australian Constitutional Reform', Senate Occasional Lecture Series, https://www.aph.gov.au/About_Parliament/Senate/Powers_practice_n_procedures/pops/pop35/c04

Williams, George and David Hume. 2010, *People Power: The History and Future of the Referendum in Australia* (UNSW Press).

Winterton, George. 1993. 'Reserve Powers in an Australian Republic', 12(2) *University of Tasmania Law Review* 249–262.

Winterton, George. 1994. 'A Republican Constitution', in George Winterton (ed), *We, the People: Australian Republican Government* (Allen & Unwin) 38–48.

Winterton, George. 2001. *The Resurrection of the Republic*, Law & Policy Paper No. 15 (Centre for International and Public Law, Australian National University).

Winterton, George. 2004. 'Submission to Senate Legal and Constitutional References Committee', *Inquiry into an Australia Republic*, https://www.aph.gov.au/~/media/wopapub/senate/committee/legcon_ctte/completed_inquiries/2002_04/republic03/submissions/sub319_pdf.ashx

Chapter 7

Populism and Constitutional Conventions

Nicholas Barry

In recent years, the resurgence of populism in many parts of the world has led to greater scholarly interest in the relationship between populism and constitutionalism (e.g., Muller 2016; Sadurski 2020; Krygier et al. 2022), and between populism and democracy (e.g., Mudde and Kaltwasser 2017: 79–96; Przeworski 2019; Urbinati 2019; Ostiguy and Moffitt 2020; Weyland 2020; Tushnet and Bugaric 2021). However, despite this, to date, there has been relatively little work examining the relationship between populism and constitutional conventions. This is surprising because these conventions are crucial components of the constitutional system in contemporary liberal democracies, so any assessment of the impact of populism on liberal democratic institutions needs to take constitutional conventions into account. This chapter aims to explore this gap in the literature, examining the extent to which populist government poses a threat to constitutional conventions in long-standing liberal democracies. In doing so, it aims to further our understanding of populism and its impact on liberal democracy, while also extending our understanding of conventions themselves by analysing the extent to which they shape the actions of political elites. In doing so, the chapter thereby aims to contribute to the recent "dynamic turn" in scholarship on conventions, which seeks to extend a new institutionalist lens to conventions, shifting focus onto the ways in which they shape, and are shaped by, law and politics (Barry, Miragliotta and Nwokora 2019; Chapter 1, this volume).

In order to address the central question motivating the chapter, a significant amount of theoretical background work is necessary because we need to be clear about the ways in which constitutional conventions work to constrain mainstream (i.e., non-populist) political elites in liberal democracies. This knowledge then enables us to assess – at the theoretical level – the extent to which these mechanisms are likely to hold when populist governments are elected. The final step is to empirically test this theory with detailed case study analysis. Although this kind of empirical testing is beyond the scope of this chapter, I do discuss some recent examples, drawing largely on the secondary literature, that seem to illustrate these dynamics in practice.

DOI: 10.4324/9781003506577-7

The structure of the chapter is as follows. In the first section, I explore some of the major mechanisms underpinning elite adherence to constitutional conventions under normal liberal democratic conditions. To do so, I draw on and further develop the two major perspectives in the literature: the strategic account, which explains elite adherence as the result of rational decision-making aimed at avoiding future reprisals from political opponents; and the moralistic account, which links adherence to an elite commitment to these conventions. I also identify a third, hybrid mechanism which views elite adherence to conventions as a rational strategy to avoid electoral punishment in circumstances when a large number of citizens have a commitment to the liberal democratic principles underpinning core conventions. The second section then outlines the three dominant accounts of populism in the existing scholarship – the ideational, the political–strategic, and the socio-cultural – before the third section applies these different accounts of populism to the mechanisms for adherence outlined in the first section. In this section, I argue that the strategic and moralistic mechanisms are likely to be ineffective when populist leaders/parties hold office. The hybrid (electoral) mechanism has some chance of success, but there are reasons for pessimism too given that the populist government has already attracted significant electoral support. In the fourth section of the chapter, I briefly discuss the relationship between populist governments and constitutional conventions in two recent cases – the Trump administration in the United States and the Johnson government in the UK – and I argue that both cases provide preliminary support for the theoretical argument developed in the chapter, while also pointing to some directions for future research.

Mechanisms of Constraint

This section aims to identify how constitutional conventions constrain political actors in long-standing liberal democracies. That is, it is concerned with explaining why political elites follow these features of a constitutional regime that are not set out in a codified constitution or (in normal circumstances) judicially enforced, particularly in cases where breaching these norms seems to be in their short-term interest. If we are interested in the impact of constitutional conventions on politics and law, this is one of the most important questions to address, but it has received much less attention in the literature than one would expect. The accounts that do exist can be divided using the distinction between strategic and moralistic accounts of conventions identified by Nwokora (Chapter 3, this volume). This section will further refine and develop this distinction, drawing particularly on recent accounts of norm adherence put forward by Elster (2014) and Postema (2022).

The strategic account explains the existence of constitutional conventions – and adherence to these conventions – with reference to the rational choices of political actors. As Elster explains in an illuminating analysis, strategic norms "are game-theoretic equilibria, in which each agent changes choses a certain behavior because it is the *best response* to the (anticipated) choices of others" (Elster 2014: 47). These conventions can be further divided into coordination equilibria and cooperation equilibria. As coordination equilibria, conventions are designed to coordinate the behaviour of political agents in a way that contributes to the smooth running of the political system. An example of this is the convention that emerged to determine who succeeds after the death of the reigning monarch (Elster 2014: 53–54, quotation at 53):

> The Salic convention is a convention in this sense. Abstractly speaking, there are several rules that might serve to decide what happens upon the death of a monarch. One might use the Salic rule, or allow for male succession through the female line, or allow for female succession. Each of these procedures serves the same coordinating function, just as driving on the left hand of the road serves the same purpose as driving on the right. What matters is that there is a consensus on one of them.

If support for the convention erodes and is not replaced by an alternative norm on which there is consensus, then this is likely to have a disruptive effect on the system, producing instability and conflict over the question of succession. In order to avoid this, it is rational for actors to uphold the existing convention that regulates this practice and to punish other actors who seek to defect from it.

Although coordination equilibria deal with important matters, many of the conventions that are of greatest relevance to political scientists and constitutional lawyers take the form of *cooperation* equilibria because these conventions "are often created by an expectation of alteration in power" (Elster 2014: 54). The idea is that conventions develop to regulate – and often constrain – the power of the government in ways that go beyond or even contradict, the formal provisions of a codified constitution. Conventions in this sense are linked to the broader liberal democratic idea of limited government. These conventions are respected by the government of the day because they know that they are likely to lose power at some point in the future, and they want to avoid a "tit-for-tat" response when their political opponents assume power. In this way, conventions as cooperative equilibria often have the form "of a repeated Prisoner's Dilemma" whereby the fear of future reprisals gives governments a rational reason not to defect from them, even when doing so has a short-term cost to them (by restraining their power). In this way, "[t]he shadow of the future . . . induces cooperative behavior" (Elster 2014: 55).[1]

1 Elster (2014: 55) also notes that "tit-for-tat arrangements may also arise for other reasons than alterations in power". The examples he give relate to conventions facilitating cooperation

However, this does not guarantee that politicians will always adhere to conventions as cooperative equilibria. Elster points out that "[c]ooperation is harder to achieve . . . than coordination" and "[i]t can break down if the temptation to defect is large, or if only the distant future casts a shadow over the present" (Elster 2014: 55). For example, if breaking a convention marks the difference between holding office or losing office, then the temptation to break it will be larger. Similarly, if a party becomes accustomed to holding government over a long period of time, then this is likely to reduce its fear of future reprisals – the threat will not seem credible if it thinks it is unlikely to become the opposition.

In addition to the factors identified by Elster, political parties also have an important role to play in understanding conventions as cooperative equilibria. In modern parliamentary democracies, governments are normally formed by a political party or coalition of parties, while in presidential systems, presidents generally also have a partisan affiliation. In both systems, most members of the legislature also tend to be aligned to a political party. This matters because political parties often constrain the actions of their elected politicians who represent them, and this may be an important factor underpinning convention adherence. For example, a powerful individual politician (e.g., a prime minister or president) might be confident that they can breach a convention without fear of future sanctions – if they lose office, there is a strong chance they will leave the political scene altogether and thereby avoid tit-for-tat reprisals when their political opponents assume office in the future. However, a political party is in a different position from an individual politician. As a collective organisation that is – or aspires to be – an enduring presence on the political scene, it cannot afford to ignore the risk of future reprisals. Politicians who plan to remain active political players in the future, along with the officials who head the party's administrative wing, have an incentive to think about the medium/long-term consequences for their party of engaging in actions that undermine long-standing conventions in the interests of the party's short-term advantage. This means they will tend to have a stronger reason to pressure the party leaders who threaten to defect from the conventions that restrain their power. Of course, whether they are able to do so in practice is also likely to depend on the power dynamics within the party, and there may be circumstances when a leader is so powerful the party is likely to be able to restrain them.

An example of the logic underpinning conventions as cooperative equilibria is the convention regulating the Senate's capacity to block supply in Australia. Governments in Australia usually command a majority in the lower

between different Cabinet ministries, and cooperation between senators from different states over federal appointments to state offices. In federal systems, we might add to Elster's list the possibility of cooperation between federal and state levels of government.

house of Parliament, but rarely have a majority in the upper house (the Senate). By Westminster convention, the Senate is not supposed to block supply (the money bills the government needs to fund its activities), although it constitutionally has the power to do so (see Barry and Miragliotta 2015). If this were to occur, the government would be forced to resign and/or would have to go to an election earlier than it otherwise would, so the opposition seems to have a strong incentive to break this convention, particularly if it is doing well in the polls. However, fear of future reprisals gives it a strong incentive to adhere to the convention rather than defecting. This is because when it finds itself in government in the future, it is unlikely to control the Senate, and would therefore be vulnerable to a tit-for-tat strategy from the opposition. Interestingly, in the Australian case, there has only been one occasion (the 1975 constitutional crisis) when the opposition has used its numbers in the Senate to block Supply, bringing down the government and forcing an election (see Winterton 2003). Since then, this situation has never come close to being repeated, and the major parties have maintained the convention against blocking supply (Barry and Miragliotta 2015: 213).

In contrast to the strategic account, the moralistic account holds that constitutional conventions are not simply "best-response behaviors" to the actions of others (Elster 2014: 56). Rather, conventions have a "non-instrumental" foundation – they are viewed as being the right standards for political elites to follow in a particular political community, rather than convenient rules that are followed to help maintain a smooth-running system, or practices that are upheld in order to avoid future reprisals. Conventions have a normative force, and political elites feel they should adhere to them because they have a duty to do so.

Although he uses different terminology, in a recent article, Postema (2022) has further developed the concept of a moralistic convention. He argues that political elites believe they have a moral obligation to uphold conventions because they are members of a political community in which these standards are dominant:

> Conventions are not merely rules typically followed by individuals; they are relatively stable nodes in a network of common norm-responsive activity. Moreover, members comply not for their own part only; rather, they see their conduct as something done in and by their community. It is "what we do," as they might say. Internalization of the norm is not a matter of an individual's private endorsement or acceptance; rather, it is a matter of willing participation in an activity characterized by a reciprocity of attitudes, judgments and actions.
>
> (Postema 2022: 107)

Being a member of the political community therefore means accepting these conventions as standards that should guide one's conduct, and recognising the need to hold others to account when they fail to follow them (Postema 2022: 107–109). On this account, constitutional conventions also have an "expressive" character in that they are publicly discussed and invoked in political debates, and they give the "values [of a political community] concrete, publicly visible reality" (Postema 2022: 108). They are also interconnected, existing "in a complex network of informal and formal norms, informal practices, and formal institutions".

It is also possible to identify a third approach which combines elements of the strategic and moralistic accounts. On this view, a large number of citizens are supportive of conventions (or the liberal democratic principles underpinning them), and this shapes the way they vote at elections. This gives elected politicians a strong instrumental reason to uphold key conventions because of the potential repercussions they will face from the wider public risk if they breach them (Elster 2014: 56–57, 59; see also Barry et al. 2025). In other words, on this account, it is citizens who have a commitment to the conventions, and this is what gives political elites a rational reason to adhere to them. Because this account rests on a combination of moral motivation from below and strategic motivation from above, I will refer to it as the "hybrid" mechanism for convention adherence.

These approaches provide different accounts of why political elites adhere to constitutional conventions. However, it is also important to note that they need not be mutually exclusive. Political elites might adhere to conventions because of strategic interest and because they have a commitment to them. For example, the decision not to block supply in Australia might reflect the desire to avoid future reprisals (as discussed previously), and a non-instrumental commitment to the idea that the party with a confidence of the lower house of Parliament is entitled to remain in office. Having outlined the mechanisms that underpin adherence to conventions, the next section turns outlines the three leading accounts of populism, before turning to the question of convention adherence in the third section.

The Nature of Populism: Three Accounts

There has been a "huge proliferation" of studies of populism in recent years that has refined scholarly accounts of the concept (Kaltwasser et al. 2017: 10). Nonetheless, significant disagreements remain about how it should be understood. There are three main approaches that have been identified in the literature – the ideational, the political–strategic, and the socio-cultural (Kaltwasser et al. 2017). These accounts lead, at times, to different conclusions about precisely which types of governments and political parties should be classified as populist, what the motivations of populists are, and how they function when they obtain office.

The ideational account of populism is probably "the most broadly used in the field today" (Mudde 2017: 28). It identifies populism with reference to a core set of political ideas. Some within the ideational camp would regard populism as akin to an ideology, although there is disagreement on this point (Mudde 2017 and cf. Freeden 2017). Nonetheless, at its core, the ideational account holds that populism is

> an ideology that considers society to be ultimately separated into two homogenous and antagonistic groups, "the pure people" versus "the corrupt elite", and which argues that politics should be an expression of the volunte generale (general will) of the people.
>
> (Mudde 2017: 29)

Central to this understanding of populism is the idea that the division between the elite and the people is ultimately a moral definition. As Mudde (2017: 32) puts it, although "the people" as a term

> is certainly very flexible, it is not completely empty: first of all, as populism is essentially based on a *moral* divide, the people are "pure"; and while purity is a fairly vague term, and the specific understanding is undoubtedly culturally determined, it does provide some context to the signifier.

What this means in a given country or community is shaped by the cultural context and other ideological influences on the populist movement. The cultural context matters because "if populists want to become politically relevant, they will have to define the people in terms of some of the key features of the self-identification of the targeted community" (Mudde 2017: 32). Other ideological influences matter because populism is generally combined with a "host" ideology, which adds another dimension to the way in which "the people" is defined. For example, right-wing forms of populism are likely to define populism in terms of race or nation, while left-wing forms are more likely to define it in terms of class (Mudde 2017: 32).

On the ideational account, the aim of populist leaders and parties is to win office and introduce the policies that achieve "the singular common good, that the people discern" (Muller 2016). They are not opposed to democratic institutions or liberal democratic constraints, unless these institutions block them from achieving their goals. As Muller puts it, "[p]opulists are fine with representation as long as the right representatives represent the right people to make the right judgment and consequently do the right thing" (Muller 2016: 25). However, if representatives or institutions frustrate them from achieving their goals, then populists will challenge the legitimacy of these institutions and, potentially, attempt to dismantle or weaken them (Muller 2016). One of the key means of doing this in office is to "colonize or occupy the state" by appointing supporters to key posts in the judiciary or bureaucracy (Muller 2016: 44–46). They also tend to engage in other practices that run counter to core liberal democratic values, including mass clientelism, the systematic repression of civil society by harassing or silencing non-governmental organisations (NGOs) that are critical of the government, and by engaging in "discriminatory legalism" that uses the law to target their political opponents (Muller 2016: 46–49).

The major alternative to the ideational account of populism is the "political–strategic" account. Rather than associating populism with a loose set of ideas or language, this account focuses on the actions of populist leaders, arguing that populism is best understood as "a political strategy through which a personalistic leader seeks to exercise government power based on direct, unmediated, unconstitutionalized support from large numbers of mostly unorganized followers" (Weyland 2017: 49). This shifts the focus away from the rhetoric populists use, and onto "what they actually do, especially how they pursue and sustain political power" (Weyland 2017: 49). On this account, the key political agent is an individual politician rather than a populist political party or a wider political movement (Weyland 2017: 56). This individual might initially come to prominence (or win power) as the leader of a political party, but they "can achieve populist leadership if . . . [they establish] personal preeminence and independence" (Weyland 2017: 56).

The other central element of the populist political strategy is its principal power capability. Whereas other strategies of rule rely on giving special weight to the preferences of business or the military to retain power, populism's principal power capability is mobilising large numbers of people through mass rallies, opinion polls, and ultimately, plebiscites and elections:

> To prove and boost their distance from "the establishment", populist politicians keep mobilizing their mass support, their main base of sustenance. For this purpose, they hold frequent elections and plebiscites, constantly advertise their popularity ratings, and rally their backers for street demonstrations, especially when they confront a political challenge.
>
> (Weyland 2017: 56–58, quotation at 57–58)

In order to gain the support of large numbers of citizens, populist leaders try to develop an "unmediated, quasi-direct appeals" to the mass public, presenting themselves "as the embodiment of 'the people'" through the mass media, particularly television, and, more recently, social media (Weyland 2017: 57). This in turn can give citizens the sense that they have a personal bond with the leader that in some cases ends up becoming "quasi-religious" (Weyland 2017: 58; Hoschild 2016).

Populist leaders also attempt to mobilise the people by warning of the dangers that external enemies (such as foreign leaders) pose to their interests. Although this has parallels to the ideational account, proponents of the political–strategic account of populism emphasise that "Manichean rhetoric does not form of populism as a potentially bottom-up movement, but serves as a top-down instrument for personalistic leaders" (Weyland 2017: 58). On the strategic account, populist leaders are opportunistic rather than ideological – they announce policies based on what they think will best mobilise voters rather than because of a deep commitment to them, which also explains why they often fail to properly implement major policies they announce or adopt major shifts in approach to key policy issues (e.g., economic management) (Weyland 2017: 62–63).

A third account of populism is the socio-cultural approach, which understands populism to be "the 'flaunting of the low'" (Ostiguy 2017: 73) It views populism as being relational in character, and concerned with political style and the performance of an identity, rather than ideology (Moffitt 2016; Ostiguy and Moffitt 2020). Although this can take different forms depending on the context, populist politicians and parties present themselves as outsiders to the political status quo; representatives of "the Other":

> This project's so-called "Other" can be recognized as such if it provokes shame or embarrassment for "decent," "politically correct," "proper," or "well-educated" people. The political entrepreneurs *flaunting this other*, in turn, claim to be speaking in the name of a "repressed truth" (especially in Europe) or (more often in Latin America) of "previously excluded social sectors" or (in the US) the "silent majority."
>
> (Ostiguy 2017: 76)

Although this has similarities to the ideological and political–strategic views, its proponents emphasise that it is performative, with populist politicians deliberately engaging in actions and speech that "is almost always transgressive: of the 'proper' way of doing politics, of proper public behavior, or of what can or should be publicly said" (Ostiguy 2017: 76).

Key to this account of populism is the distinction between "the high and the low in politics", which is a means of categorising "ways of *being* and *acting* in politics" that become markers of political identity (Ostiguy 2017: 77, emphasis in original). Populist politicians use discourse and behaviour associated with the "low," which means engaging in transgressive forms of discourse and behaviour that communicates their identity as a member of "the other" – those who see themselves as marginalised by dominant social groups. The use of "low" forms of language and behaviour become a way for populist leaders to mobilise these voters and challenge the power of dominant groups.

Do Populists Adhere to Constitutional Conventions?

The three dominant accounts of populism outlined in this chapter disagree about some key issues – particularly with regard to the ultimate motivation of populist leaders – but they share a common belief that populism is about (claiming to represent) the interests of the people against the elite by challenging aspects of the status quo, whether this is for ideological, strategic, or performative reasons. From the outset, this notion of opposition to the status quo seems to conflict with the liberal democratic idea that there should be institutional checks on the power of the government of the day, which seems to suggest that populist politicians are likely to violate constitutional conventions. However, the situation is more complex than it first seems. For a start, although populist politicians often use inflammatory rhetoric, whether this results in actual attempts to weaken or dismantle institutional checks is another question. After all, one of the motivations for having these institutions is to restrain overbearing leaders who threaten to misuse their power, so the mere fact that such an illiberal politician has been elected does not automatically result in the institutions being dismantled, particularly in long-standing liberal democracies with robust institutions (note Weyland 2020). Linked to this, although constitutional conventions are (usually) non-justiciable, they have also proven to be highly resilient. Most politicians and political parties, not just populists, will be able to achieve short-term gains by violating conventions, and yet, major instances of outright convention abrogation in long-standing liberal democracies are relatively rare. Lastly, although populist politicians generally adopt an oppositional stance towards the existing system, they also have a complicated relationship with legal and political institutions. As Krygier (2022: 4) notes, "most of the contemporary range of populist regimes have created distinctive, complex, and often paradoxical relationships with pivotal elements of democracy and of law." One of the key elements of this has been a kind of "autocratic legalism" where populist governments act lawfully and constitutionally but change the law and constitution in illiberal ways that weaken institutional checks on their power (Scheppele 2018). Examining whether populist governments are likely to adhere to constitutional conventions is therefore an important task that helps shed light on the dynamics of conventions and helps clarify the extent to which populism poses a threat to liberal democracy. The remainder of this section investigates this question at the theoretical level by examining whether the mechanisms underlying convention adherence, outlined in the first section of this chapter, are likely to be effective against populist leaders, using the three different theoretical accounts of populism outlined in the second section.

On the ideational view, populism is a matter of ideological commitment rather than a political strategy. If this is correct, then the normal mechanisms that drive elite adherence to constitutional conventions are unlikely to hold. This is most obvious with regard to the moralistic account of convention adherence, which holds that elites adhere to conventions because of a commitment to them. On the ideational account, populist politicians sit outside the norm community, and for this reason, they are unlikely to be restrained from violating conventions by a strong internal commitment to them. Instead, they view themselves as the embodiment of the people's will, so they have an ideological opposition to institutional constraints that limit their power and stop them from being able to implement their agenda (Muller 2016). For these reasons, they are unlikely to adhere to constitutional conventions that restrain their power or hold them accountable for their conduct and their policies.

The strategic mechanism may initially seem a more effective restraint on populists in office. That is, the desire to avoid future reprisals by political opponents might seem to be an effective way of restraining a populist leader from violating constitutional conventions. However, whether this is the case is likely to depend on the extent to which the leader prioritises short-term advantage (electorally and in advancing their agenda) over the long-term interest of their party, and on the extent to which they are able to dominate their party. On the first criterion, the Manichean view of politics associated with the ideational view of populism means that they are likely to place high value on avoiding a short-term loss to political opponents whom they view as enemies of the people. This tends to militate against a risk-averse strategy that is focused on the longer-term implications for their party. Moreover, as previously noted, on the ideational account, populist leaders usually tend to dominate their party, so it is unlikely that the party will be much of a restraint on them. A more likely eventuality – at least in a parliamentary system – is that the populist leader will be replaced altogether. However, unless and until it gets to this point, the strategic reasons for convention adherence are unlikely to be effective against populist leaders, at least on the ideational account of populism.

The third possibility is the hybrid mechanism – the idea that political elites will adhere to conventions because they fear electoral repercussions from voters motivated by a commitment to liberal democratic values. In general, this is also likely to be ineffective – if a leader's commitment to populism is primarily ideological and this has resulted in electoral victory in the recent past, then they are likely to be reluctant to compromise in the interests of electoral pragmatism. They believe in the program they are pursuing; they are ideologically hostile to liberal checks, and they have recently enjoyed electoral success running with a populist message, so they are likely to be reluctant to abandon this approach because of short-term political difficulties. There may nonetheless be exceptions to this in cases of strong public opposition over a long period of time, which might drive a shift towards convention adherence in the interests of electoral pragmatism. In a parliamentary system, this may even result in a populist, convention-violating leader being replaced because they are viewed as an electoral liability or, in a presidential system, the impeachment of the president.

Turning to the political–strategic account of populism, we can once again see why a populist leader is unlikely to be constrained by the usual mechanisms that underpin elite adherence to constitutional conventions. For reasons of electoral pragmatism, they use a strategy that emphasises their own pre-eminence as a leader and engage in mass mobilisation by challenging the status quo and creating a sense of imminent threat and elite conspiracy. A commitment to this electoral strategy is unlikely to sit alongside a strong ideological commitment to upholding liberal democratic values and respecting institutional restraints. In fact, as Weyland (2020: 391) puts it, "[t]o maintain and boost their leadership, they [populist leaders] constantly need to prove and enhance their own preeminence. Because institutions hem in their wilfulness, they disrespect or try to dismantle checks and balances."

Nonetheless, even if a populist leader, on the political-strategic account, lacks an ideological commitment to upholding constitutional conventions, perhaps their political party will be able to pressure them to abide by conventions in order to avoid tit-for-tat reprisals from their political rivals? However, this is also unlikely. On the strategic–political account of populism, the leader tends to build direct connections with voters rather than developing strong organisations, such as parties that create mediated linkages. If they take over an existing party or build a new one, they are likely to view it merely as an instrument for realising their own leadership ambitions (Weyland 2017: 56), resulting in weak party structures that are unable to restrain an electorally successful leader. Finally, given that the populist leader's electoral strategy is based on challenging existing norms, and that this has been successful at a recent election, it seems unlikely that they are going to be concerned about losing votes because they violate constitutional conventions. This means that the hybrid mechanism underpinning convention adherence is also likely to be ineffective.

We reach similar conclusions if we are viewing populism through a socio-cultural framework. This account of populism is centred around the idea that populist politics is transgressive, associated with the performance of "low politics." This has important implications for political decision-making and leadership, with an emphasis on "very personalistic, strong (often male) leadership" (Ostiguy 2017: 81). The discourse associated with the populist low tends to valorise "decisive action" rather than the restraints imposed by the rule of law and to emphasise the need for a close relationship – "a 'fusion' between the leader and the masses" (Ostiguy 2017: 82). Once again, there is clear tension here between populism and liberal democracy, with populists viewing "classic institutional limitations . . . as undesirably limiting popular sovereignty and the people's will" (Ostiguy 2017: 82). For this reason, populist leaders, on the socio-cultural account, are unlikely to have a moral commitment to upholding constitutional conventions. Respect for liberal democratic restraints is the kind of status quo behaviour that is associated with "high politics."

Given the emphasis on personalistic connections with voters and the need for decisive action, the socio-cultural account also means that populist leaders are likely to dominate over their party. This means it is unlikely that the party is going to be able to restrain the leader from violating conventions, to prevent tit-for-tat retaliation from a rival party when they lose power in the future. If the socio-cultural account is correct, then the hybrid mechanism is also likely to be ineffective. It focuses on the ability of populist leaders to build their identity around a transgressive political identity – violating the norms of "high politics" is part of their electoral appeal, so their support base is unlikely to be motivated to shift their vote because of the violation of constitutional conventions. Even were this to occur, it is going to be difficult for a populist political leader to plausibly flip their identity to one associated with support for liberal democratic restraints and long-standing conventions.

Thus, whether the ideational, political–strategic or socio-cultural account of populism is correct, the normal mechanisms underpinning elite adherence to constitutional conventions are unlikely to be effective in the case of populist leaders. Part of the problem is that populist leaders on all three accounts (Table 7.1) are likely to reject the ideological commitment to the kinds of liberal democratic standards that constitutional conventions embody, rendering the moralistic mechanism ineffective, while they are also likely to dominate over their party, reducing the likelihood that it will be able to restrain the leader in the interests of avoiding future retaliation. The mechanism that has the greatest chance of success is the (hybrid) electoral mechanism, but even here, the odds that it will restrain a populist leader are low – it depends in large part on voters who are committed enough to liberal democratic principles to vote a populist leader out of office, and this is risky in a political context that has recently seen populist leaders elected. In addition, if populism is fundamentally about an anti-establishment electoral strategy, as the rational-strategic account suggests, or about the performance of a transgressive political identity, as the socio-cultural approach claims, then it is going to be difficult for a populist leader to alter their approach to win over voters alienated by their rejection of liberal democratic values. If this is correct, then it suggests that removal from office at an election or by their party, is likely to be the only secure way of protecting constitutional conventions from being violated by populist leaders. As long as populist leaders remain in power, conventions will be highly vulnerable. Given that all liberal democratic systems depend on unwritten conventions, not just codified constitutional law, to regulate the system and constrain the power of governments, this highlights another major way in which populism poses a threat to liberal democracy.

Constitutional Conventions in an Era of Resurgent Populism

Having outlined a theoretical account of the relationship between populism and constitutional conventions, the next step is to test this account empirically by applying it to detailed case studies of populist governments. There

Table 7.1 Variants of Populism and Mechanisms of Elite Convention Adherence

	Moralistic: Internalised Standard Among Elites	*Strategic–Cooperative Equilibrium (Tit-for-Tat)*	*Hybrid (Citizens' Commitment to Conventions Gives Elites an Electoral Incentive to Adhere)*
Ideational	Ineffective: lack of principled commitment to constitutional conventions (populists sit outside the norm community).	Ineffective: (1) Manichean view of politics results in greater emphasis on short-term political advantage; and (2) leader dominance over the party weakens its capacity to restrain the leader to avoid medium-/long-term retaliation.	In general, ineffective because of recent electoral success, but possible exception in cases of very strong and sustained public opposition.
Political–Strategic	Ineffective: populist politicians are motivated by electoral pragmatism and a strategy focused on mass mobilisation and leader pre-eminence, rather than a strong commitment to liberal democratic norms.	Ineffective: (1) leader is likely to have a focus on their own short-term electoral success, not the long-term interests of the party; and (2) leader dominance over the party means it is unlikely to be a restraint.	Ineffective: an electoral strategy based on mass mobilisation by challenging existing norms, means that it is unlikely that the populist support base is going to be motivated to shift their vote because of the violation of constitutional conventions.
Socio-Cultural	Ineffective: the political identity of populist politicians is built around norm transgression – populists sit outside the norm community.	Ineffective: emphasis on personalistic leadership and unmediated (or weakly mediated) links to the mass public suggests a short-term focus, with parties unlikely to be a restraint.	Ineffective: leader's identity is built on transgression, which means it would 1) be difficult to shift away from this identity; and 2) doing so would be likely to alienate large sections of the populist support base.

is not space here to engage in the kind of systematic empirical analysis that is required; however, in the final substantive section of the chapter, I want to begin the process by providing a brief sketch of some recent cases of populist government in long-standing liberal democracies where constitutional conventions might be thought to be more robust, and use this to illustrate some of the theoretical claims outlined above. This does not offer a systematic test of the theoretical account developed in this chapter, but it does provide some preliminary evidence in support of its main claims, as well as identifying some areas where further theoretical development is needed.

The first case of populist government is the Donald Trump administration in the United States (2017–2021). The Trump administration engaged in a variety of actions that violated constitutional norms in the United States (for a more detailed account, see Pfiffner, Chapter 8 in this volume). Two of the most high-profile examples were violating the convention against presidential interference in Department of Justice investigations and violating a number of conventions relating to the appointment of Supreme Court nominees (Levitsky and Ziblatt 2018; Postema 2022). Trump's willingness to violate these conventions – along with many others – showed that the mechanisms underpinning convention adherence were ineffective. He clearly lacked a commitment to liberal democratic constitutionalism, and did not feel any need to follow constitutional conventions that constrained his power. It is also notable that the threat of electoral defeat was also insufficient to deter him from violating conventions, even after the Republican Party's poor showing at the 2018 mid-term Congressional elections, so the hybrid mechanism was also ineffective.

Although there were some dissenting voices within his own party, they were ultimately unable to prevent numerous violations of constitutional conventions. In part, this is a reflection of the authority Trump came to wield over the party, but it is also a result of a longer-term trend in the U.S., pre-dating Trump's presidency, which has seen the two major political parties, particularly the Republican Party, increasingly willing to violate long-standing conventions (Livitsky and Ziblatt 2018). There is also evidence that some members of the Trump Administration tried to restrain his actions (Woodward 2018), while in the civil service, there were also attempts to at least speak up against what was occurring (Kucinskas and Zylan 2023). However, for the most part, over the longer term, these efforts seemed to prove ineffective in preventing the violation of key constitutional conventions, and many of the key members of his Administration who sought to restrain him either resigned or were dismissed. Some of the civil servants who sought to push back (within the boundaries of civil service norms) also found it more difficult to do so the longer his presidency progressed, and some ultimately transferred to less controversial government departments or agencies (Kucinskas and Zylan 2023).

Ultimately, the biggest check on the Trump administration came from electoral defeat at the 2020 presidential election. There are a variety of reasons for this, but survey results suggest that attitudes toward Trump were a key factor shaping voter behaviour. In fact, Jacobson (2021a: 492) goes so far as to say that national election results have "[n]ever before . . . been shaped so comprehensively by a single political figure." Despite ultimately losing the election, and the stream of damaging revelations about Trump that emerged during his presidency, it is important to note that "more than 74 million Americans, 46.9 percent of the electorate, voted to give him another four years in the White House," while his approval rating among Republicans in October 2020 was 94 percent (Jacobson 2021b: 13, 15). This highlights the vulnerability of constitutional conventions if electoral mechanisms are the main mechanism relied upon to restrain leaders.

The second illustrative case of populism in a long-standing liberal democracy is the Johnson government in the UK. In office, Johnson engaged in actions that violated a variety of constitutional conventions (Sanders 2023). The most high-profile example of this was Johnson's attempt to prorogue the Parliament in order to avoid Parliament preventing him from signing a no-deal Brexit (the UK's exit from the European Union). He also refused to resign when he had clearly lied to Parliament and when it was revealed that he had broken the law by attending a party at 10 Downing Street during the COVID-19 lockdown, when gatherings such as this were banned. He also broke conventions relating to appointments to the House of Lords, appointing Conservative Party donors as well as his own brother.

This illustrates that the normal mechanisms underpinning convention adherence were ineffective. Clearly, Johnson had no ideological commitment to these conventions, while the threat of electoral sanction also appeared insufficient to restrain him, perhaps reflected in his comment, following a by-election defeat for his government, that he would "not undergo a 'psychological transformation'" (cited in Amos 2022). Alongside the fact that challenging norms was long part of Johnson's public appeal, part of the reason he may not have taken the electoral threat seriously is the fact he was re-elected with a large majority in 2019 (Ford et al. 2021). However, Johnson ultimately did face major restraints and/or sanctions. In particular, although conventions are usually non-justiciable, the British Supreme Court ruled that Johnson's attempt to prorogue the Parliament was illegal (Russell and James 2023). Most importantly, Johnson was ultimately pressured to resign after losing the support of his own party (Amos 2022). This is partly a reflection of the fact that Britain is a parliamentary system, so prime ministers can be removed mid-term if they have lost the confidence of their party or the parliament. In the month before announcing his resignation, Johnson faced criticism from a backbench MP for a lack of "integrity, competence, and vision" (Hunt, cited in Amos 2022), while two of the senior ministers who initially resigned from his cabinet (in a tactic aimed to pressure Johnson himself to resign) also criticised the Prime Minister for lacking integrity (Quinn 2022). Although it is possible to view this as a principled stance from members of the Conservative party room, it is important to note that Johnson had engaged in many breaches of convention before he was actually pressured to resign and that this occurred after a series of by-election defeats and bad polling that indicated that his government was likely to lose the next general election. This suggests that in all probability, it was a concern about electoral defeat that ultimately motivated Conservative MPs to remove him.

Although further investigation is necessary, I would tentatively suggest that the case of the Johnson government points in a similar direction to that of Trump and supports the theoretical analysis in the third section – members of the political elite (especially the leader's own party) are the best hope for restraining or sanctioning the violation of constitutional conventions, but these restraints are likely to be weak when dealing with a populist leader who has recently enjoyed electoral success. In the end, it is electoral defeat – or the risk of electoral defeat – that seems to be the most powerful safeguard against populist leaders. However, this is not because they exercise self-restraint in the face of potential electoral defeat; rather, it comes from their removal from office, either by the electorate at large (in the case of Trump) or their party, in the face of potential electoral defeat (as in the case of Johnson).

In light of this, there is a variety of possible conclusions one could reach. It might be argued that populists who violate conventions pose no long-term threat to long-standing liberal democracies because they are likely to be checked by electoral defeat or removal by their party. However, this conclusion is too hasty. The problem is that there is no guarantee that populist leaders will necessarily lose office, even if they routinely violate constitutional conventions. Both Trump and Johnson were elected and, in Johnson's case, re-elected, and in both cases, their populist message was key to their image and appeal. In addition, a major part of the problem with the violation of constitutional conventions is that this becomes a means of undermining other liberal safeguards that are inscribed in statute law or the written constitution. A clear example of this is the way Trump's violation of conventions relating to judicial appointments allowed him to alter the composition of the Supreme Court in a way that is proving highly consequential for public policy and the likelihood that the Court will rein in a future populist president.

An alternative conclusion is that constitutional conventions are too flimsy a device to restrain populist leaders, and that we should turn to the hard provisions of a higher law constitution instead. However, this response is also open to a number of objections. For a start, constitutional conventions are virtually unavoidable – every constitutional system relies on widely agreed-upon norms to shape how the written text of the constitution operates in practice, so it will be impossible to completely do away with them. In addition, the effectiveness of "hard" legal and constitutional restraints on governments is also highly dependent on having a judiciary that is prepared to act independently of – and, where appropriate, critically towards – the government. The problem is that extended periods of populist rule tend to result in judicial appointments that undermine this independence (see, for example, Sanchez-Urribarri 2022 on the Venezuelan case and Bodnar 2022 on Hungary).

A further problem is that if a constitution is too easy to change, then although this makes it easier for conventions to be codified, it also makes it easier for populist governments to introduce their own constitutional changes – or even a new constitution altogether – to weaken constraints on their power and enhance their capacity to further their policy agenda. This is a more difficult proposition in an established liberal democracy where constitutions have often been in place for long periods of time and there tends to be a high level of public resistance to constitutional change, but it has proven to be a major issue in new democracies that have experienced populist rule in recent times, such as Poland and Hungary (see Sadurski 2020; Weyland 2020). Were established liberal democracies, including the US and UK, to experience sustained periods of populist rule, then there seems a high chance that they would go down a similar path. In this way there is a paradox in the idea of convention codification – the harder it is to amend the constitution, the harder it is to codify conventions; while conversely, the easier it is to codify conventions, the easier it is for populists to alter the constitution.

What this points to is the important role played by political parties and the values and attitudes of citizens (see also Bugaric 2019). Once a system gets to the point that a democratically elected government is routinely flouting conventions and being re-elected despite this conduct, then the explicit restraints associated with legal statutes, a codified constitution and the courts are also likely to be highly vulnerable. The widespread violation of constitutional conventions may not be a sign of faulty institutional design that could be repaired by the hard codification of conventions; rather, it may be a sign that political elites – and perhaps a significant proportion of the electorate – no longer support fundamental liberal democratic values. In this context, it is likely that formal institutions – including courts and higher law constitutions – will also come under serious strain. In other words, the sustained and widespread violation of long-standing constitutional conventions by political elites might be one of the best indicators of a liberal democratic system that is on the precipice of disaster.

Conclusion

This chapter has examined the extent to which populist government poses a threat to constitutional conventions. In doing so, it has also developed an account of the three major mechanisms underpinning elite adherence to constitutional conventions, building on the moralistic and strategic approaches in the sparse existing literature on this topic. It outlined the three dominant ways of understanding populism in the literature and examined their implications for convention adherence by populist leaders. It found that the three major mechanisms underlying elite convention adherence are likely to break down, whichever account of populism one adopts. The moralistic mechanism fails because populism is based on a rejection of liberal democratic norms. The strategic mechanisms that would otherwise restrain them are also likely to be ineffective, given the populist tendency to view political opponents as enemies of the people, resulting in a high priority on short-term electoral considerations, while the dominance of the leader weakens the capacity of political parties to act as a restraining influence. The hybrid mechanism has more chance of restraining a populist leader – but even here, the chances of this are low given the success the populist leader has had with a political campaign built on challenging the status quo. Although further empirical investigation is needed to test these theoretical claims, I argued that the recent experience of the Trump presidency and the Johnson government in two long-standing democracies offers preliminary support for these claims. In both cases, it was ultimately removal from office that reset the system with leaders who largely adhered to constitutional conventions. Although it would be easy to conclude from this that conventions are flimsy devices that should be replaced by hard law, I sounded a note of caution suggesting that although written constitutional checks might be more effective than conventions in restraining leaders in the short term, ultimately, they are also vulnerable to populist government. In this way, the systematic violation of constitutional conventions may indicate less that conventions are weak institutional constraints, and more that the liberal democratic system is in crisis.

References

Amos, O. 2022. Boris Johnson Resigns: Five Things That Led to the PM's Downfall. *BBC News*, 7 July. https://www.bbc.com/news/uk-politics-62070422.

Barry, N., Miragliotta, N., Murray, S. and Nwokoro, Z. 2025. Care-Taking of Conventions in Australia: A Role for Citizens and Media. In Civic Engagement in Australian Democracy, ed. Sarah Murray and Lachlan Umbers. London and New York: Anthem Press.

Boznar, E. 2022. Disarming the Guardians – The Transformation of the Hungarian Constitutional Court After 2010. In *Anti-Constitutional Populism*, ed. Martin Krygier, Adam Czarnota and Wojciech Sadurski. Cambridge: Cambridge University Press, pp. 254–293.

Bugaric, B. 2019. Central Europe's Descent into Autocracy: A Constitutional Analysis of Authoritarian Populism. *International Journal of Constitutional Law* 17(2): 597–616.

Elster, J. 2014. Political Norms. *Iyyun: The Jerusalem Philosophical Quarterly* 63: 47–59.

Ford, R., Bale, T., Jennings, W. and Surridge, P. 2021. The Red Wall Falls. In *The British General Election of 2019*. Cham: Palgrave Macmillan.

Freeden, M. 2017. After the Brexit Referendum: Revisiting Populism as an Ideology. Journal of Political Ideologies 22(1): 1–11.

Hoschild, A. 2016. The Ecstatic Edge of Politics: Sociology and Donald Trump. Contemporary Sociology 45(6): 683–689.

Jacobson, G.C. 2021a. Driven to Extremes: Donald Trump'sExtraordinary Impact on the 2020 Elections. Presidential Studies Quarterly 51(3): 459–521.

Jacobson, G.C. 2021b. The Presidential and Congressional Elections of 2020: A National Referendum on the Trump Presidency. Political Science Quarterly 136(1): 11–45.

Kaltwasser, C.R., Taggart, P., Espejo, P.O. and Ostiguy, P. 2017. Populism: An Overview of the Concept and the State of the Art. In *The Oxford Handbook of Populism*, ed. Cristobal Rovira Kaltwasser et al. Oxford: Oxford University Press, pp. 1–24.

Krygier, M. 2022. Introduction: Anti-Constitutional Populism. In *Anti-Constitutional Populism*, ed. Martin Krygier, Adam Czarnota and Wojciech Sadurski. Cambridge: Cambridge University Press, pp. 1–24.

Krygier, M., Czarnota, A. and Sadurski, W (eds.). 2022. *Anti-Constitutional Populism*. Cambridge: Cambridge University Press.

Kucinskas, J. and Zylan, Y. 2023. Walking the Moral Tightrope: Federal Civil Servants' Loyalty, Caution, and Resistance Under the Trump Administration. *American Journal of Sociology* 128(6).

Levitsky, S. and Ziblatt, D. 2018. *How Democracies Die: What History Reveals About Our Future*. London: Penguin Books.

Moffitt, B. 2016. *The Global Rise of Populism: Performance, Political Style and Representation*. Stanford: Stanford University Press.

Mudde, C. 2017. Populism: An Ideational Approach. In *The Oxford Handbook of Populism*, ed. Cristobal Rovira Kaltwasser et al. Oxford: Oxford University Press, pp. 27–47.

Mudde, C. and Rovira Kaltwasser, C. 2017. Populism: A Very Short Introduction. New York: Oxford University Press.

Muller, J.W. 2016. *What Is Populism?* University of Pennsylvania Press.

Nwokora, Z. This volume. *Morality Versus Strategy: Constitutional Conventions Through the Lens of Political Motivation*.

Ostiguy, P. 2017. Populism: A Socio-Cultural Approach. In *The Oxford Handbook of Populism*, ed. Cristobal Rovira Kaltwasser et al. Oxford: Oxford University Press, pp. 73–96.

Ostiguy, P. and Moffitt, B. 2020. Who Would Identify with an 'Empty Signifier? The Relational, Performative Approach to Populism. In *Populism in Global Perspective: A Performative and Discursive Approach*, ed. P. Ostiguy, F. Panizza and B. Moffitt. Oxford: Taylor and Francis Group, pp. 47–72.

Pfiffner, J.P. This volume. *The Breakdown of Constitutional Norms in the United States*.

Postema, G.J. 2022. Constitutional Norms – Erosion, Sabotage, and Response. *Ratio Juris* 35(2): 99–122.

Przeworski, A. 2019. *Crises of Democracy*. New York: Cambridge University Press.

Quinn, T. 2022. Boris Johnson Didn't Want to Quit. So How Did They Get Rid of Him? The Washington Post, 8 July.

Russell, M. and James, L. 2023. *The Parliamentary Battle Over Brexit*. Oxford: Oxford University Press.

Sadurski, W. 2020. Constitutional Design: Lessons form Poland's Democratic Backsliding. *Constitutional Studies* 6: 59–79.

Sanchez-Urribarri, R. Populism, Constitutional Democracy, and High Courts – Lessons from the Venezuelan Case. In *The Oxford Handbook of Populism*, ed. Cristobal Rovira Kaltwasser et al. Oxford: Oxford University Press, pp. 185–219.

Sanders, D. 2023. One Man's Damage: The Consequences of Boris Johnson's Assault on the British Political System. *The Political Quarterly* 94(2): 166–174.
Scheppele, K.L. 2018. Autocratic Legalism. *The University of Chicago Law Review* 85(2): 545–84.
Tushnet, M. and Bugaric, B. 2021. *Power to the People: Constitutionalism in the Age of Populism*. New York: Oxford University Press.
Urbinati, N. 2019. *Me the People: How Populism Transforms Democracy*. Cambridge, MA: Harvard University Press.
Weyland, K. 2017. Populism: A Political-Strategic Area. In *The Oxford Handbook of Populism*, ed. Cristobal Rovira Kaltwasser et al. Oxford: Oxford University Press, pp. 48–72.
Weyland, K. 2020. Populism's Threat to Democracy: Comparative Lessons for the United States. *Perspectives on Politics* 18(2): 389–406.
Winterton, G. 2003. 1975: The Dismissal of the Whitlam Government. In *Australia's Constitutional Landmarks*, ed. Hoong Phun Lee and George Winterton. Melbourne: Cambridge University Press.
Woodward, B. 2018. *Fear: Trump in the White House*. New York: Simon and Schuster.

Chapter 8

The Breakdown of Constitutional Norms in the United States

James P. Pfiffner

The Framers of the Constitution were aware of the propensity of men to aggrandize their own power, and they sought to mitigate this human tendency by arranging a constitutional structure in which "ambition must be made to counteract ambition." They did this by creating three branches of government – legislative, executive, and judicial – whose members would protect their own prerogatives and thus prevent the other branches from becoming too powerful. At the same time, they understood that formal structures of government were only "parchment barriers" to overweening ambition. Thus fundamentally, the preservation of the polity would depend on "republican virtue" in the character of government officials and the wisdom of citizens in electing persons of virtue. That is, republican norms – as well as the formal provisions of the Constitution – were essential to the preservation of the republic.

Despite the written Constitution, the actual conduct of politics requires the observance of informal norms of behavior (i.e., conventions), rather than using the letter of the law, to gain partisan advantage. Much of the stability of the U.S. political system has been based on such expectations, practices that are not specified by law and cannot be litigated but which restrain political behavior in ways that allow the system to settle disagreements peacefully.

The survival of the Union and the Constitution was challenged by the Civil War of the 1860s, fought over the issue of slavery. But in the 21st century, the survival of the republic and rule of law were again challenged by increasing strains on the system, particularly the presidency of Donald Trump.

Donald Trump ignored many of the constitutional norms to which previous presidents of both parties had adhered, both during and after his term as president (Pfiffner 2021). Although Trump violated many norms of presidential behavior in his four-year term, this chapter will focus on his greatest threat to democracy: his refusal to accept his electoral defeat and his attempt to overturn the 2020 election.

This chapter (based on Pfiffner 2022) will examine Trump's most egregious norm breaking, his refusal to accept the clear outcome of the 2020 election, in which he was defeated by Joe Biden. After he left the presidency

DOI: 10.4324/9781003506577-8

his continued assertions that he actually won the 2020 election, the "Big Lie," created the most serious threat to the United States as a constitutional republic since the Civil War. The actions of Donald Trump after the 2020 election illustrate how fragile are the Constitution and rule of law in the United States. Were it not for the brave actions of many Republican officials after the 2020 election, Trump might have been able to stay in control of the government, even though he had lost the election.

Trump's Attempts to Overturn the 2020 Election

The peaceful transition of power is the *sine qua non* of democracy. For more than two centuries (with the exception of during the Civil War, from 1861–1865), the United States has enjoyed the consensus that elections are the means to change the leadership of the country. The 2020–2021 transition of the presidency marks an exception to that consensus. President Trump, elected with a minority of votes in 2016, refused to accept the reality of his 2020 defeat at the polls, despite the fact that Joseph Biden won more than 7 million more votes than Trump and won the Electoral College by a vote of 306–232.

Traditionally in the modern presidency, the loser conforms to the norm of accepting the outcome of the election; the loser graciously concedes defeat, congratulates the winner of the election, and affirms the results of the democratic process. Never in U.S. history has a president who lost the election attempted to stay in office by undermining the electoral process after the election has taken place – yet President Trump took a number of actions that he hoped would keep him in power, despite his having lost the 2020 election. The following subsections specify the ways in which Trump violated the norm of accepting the outcome of presidential elections as he tried to undermine and overturn the presidential election of 2020.

Trump Undermined U.S. Norms of Confidence in the Electoral Process in the Summer of 2020

No other president has violated the norm of maintaining confidence in the integrity of the U.S. electoral process, Trump violated this norm even before the election, which he lost. In the summer of 2020, President Trump began to lay the groundwork for rejecting the outcome of the forthcoming November election if he did not win. When asked if he would accept the outcome of the election if he lost, he said "I will look at it at the time" (Healy and Martin 2016). Trump expected that he might lose and began to undermine the legitimacy of mail-in ballots. He asserted that mail-in ballots would favor Democrats and would be corrupt, saying things such as that the 2020 election "will be, in my opinion, the most corrupt election in the history of our country" (Haberman et al. 2020) and "The only way they can take this election away from us is if this is a rigged election" (Crowley 2020). It was unprecedented for a president to violate the norm of agreeing to accept election results and equivocate about whether he would accept the election outcome and a peaceful transfer of power if he lost.

Rather Than Adhering to the Norm of Losers Accepting the Outcome of Elections, Trump Falsely Claimed That He Won the Election

On the day of the election, it appeared that Biden had won sufficient states to win the Electoral College, but final counts were delayed as states tabulated all of the mail-in and absentee ballots. Trump, however, preemptively and falsely claimed victory. At 12:49 a.m. Eastern time on November 4 (in the early hours of the morning immediately following election day). Trump tweeted, "We are up BIG, but they are trying to STEAL the Election" (Kessler 2020). Despite Trump's unwillingness to publicly admit defeat, internally reality was beginning to sink in. Trump asked his aides, "How did we lose to Joe Biden? What happened? What went wrong" Can we still win?" (Woodward and Costa 2021, p. 133). His aides, Hope Hicks and Kellyanne Conway, and his political allies, Senator Phil Graham and Chris Christie, tried to get Trump to accept that he had lost (Woodward and Costa 2021, p. 143). But unlike other modern presidential candidates who conceded to their opponents after very close elections, as did Richard Nixon in 1960, Al Gore in 2000, and Hillary Clinton in 2016, Trump declared, "this election is far from over" (Chiacu 2020).

On November 4, Christopher Krebs, the Trump-appointed director of the Department of Homeland Security (DHS) Cybersecurity and Infrastructure Security Agency (CISA), which is in charge of coordinating with state and local governments for election security, released a statement about the 2020 national elections. Noting that all of the states with close election results had paper records of each vote, the statement said, "The November 3rd election was the most secure in American history . . . . There is no evidence that any voting system deleted or lost votes, changed votes, or was in any way compromised" (Krebs 2020).

Ironically, the election was not relatively close. Three presidential elections since 1960 have been won by a smaller Electoral College vote margin than the Biden margin of victory, and five candidates have won with fewer electoral votes than Biden won (Brinkley et al. 2021). Even Trump's own appointed attorney general, William Barr, said On November 16, after briefings by election experts from the FBI and DHS, concluded that tampering with election outcomes was virtually impossible. "It's all bullshit," Barr declared (Woodward and Costa 2021).

In 2000, immediately after the Supreme Court stopped the recount of votes in Florida, Al Gore, despite winning 500,000 more popular votes, congratulated George W. Bush. In his public remarks he said, "Just moments ago I spoke with George W. Bush and congratulated him on becoming the 43rd president of the United States . . . . This is America and we put country before party. We will stand together behind our new president" (*New York Times* 2000).

Similarly, in 2016, Hillary Clinton won 2.9 million more popular votes than Trump, though she losing the electoral vote. At 2:35 a.m. following election night, she called Trump to concede the election. In her concession speech, she said, "I congratulated Donald Trump and offered to work with him on behalf of our country. I hope that he will be a successful president for all Americans" (CNN 2016).

Even Richard Nixon, despite a very close election in which he could have challenged John F. Kennedy's margins in Illinois and Texas, refused to do so. When he, as Vice President, presided over the electoral vote count in Congress, he remarked,

> I do not think we could have a more striking and eloquent example of the stability of our Constitutional system and of the proud tradition of the American people of developing, respecting and honoring institutions of self-government . . . . In our campaigns, no matter how hard-fought they may be, no matter how close the election may turn out to be, those who lose accept the verdict, and support those who win.
>
> (Brockell 2021)

The U.S. presidential norm of the losing candidate conceding graciously after losing very close elections was broken by Donald Trump in the 2020 election.

Trump Filed Meritless Lawsuits Without Evidence

Previous losing presidential candidates seldom – if ever – violated the norm of accepting the outcome of elections. In an election involving more than 160 million voters and more than 230,000 polling places in the United States (National Conference of State Legislatures 2020), it is probable that there would be some irregularities, some miscounting, or other problems. Nevertheless, Trump's lawyers were not able to document any problems significant enough to question the outcome of the election results in any state. There were scattered instances of individuals trying to cast more than one ballot, including three Republican voters in Pennsylvania. But many searches in response to President Trump's allegations of widespread fraud were unable to uncover any significant fraud (Helderman, Swaine, and Lee 2020). In losing more than 60 lawsuits challenging votes in the election, Trump's lawyers could not convince any court (of judges appointed by Trump, as well as by other presidents) that illegal votes were cast for Biden or that election counting procedures shifted the election away from Trump. Thus, Trump violated the norm of not pursuing meritless legal challenges to an election.

Trump Personally Pressured State and Local Officials to Not Certify Election Outcomes

No other president has attempted to exert pressure on local election officials to reverse their decisions about an election outcome. This strong norm was violated in 2020 by President Trump, who inserted himself in the usually *pro forma* procedures for counting votes in presidential elections. After votes are cast in each polling station in presidential election years, the results are tabulated and certified by local officials, then forwarded to the state capital, where governors must certify the outcome of the election. State laws specify the procedures by which votes are counted, and these actions are most often routine and accompanied by little partisan interference. But in 2020, President Trump broke all precedents by trying to intervene at local levels in battleground states to try to stop vote counts from being certified.

After Trump lost Michigan by more than 150,000 votes, he personally called a Republican member of Wayne County's Board of Canvassers to convince her not to cast her vote to certify the election, though he was unsuccessful. Inspired by Trump's claims of fraud, armed protestors threatened state officials, Democrat and Republican, in Michigan, Georgia, Vermont, and Pennsylvania (Armus 2020).

In the close race in Georgia, which Biden won by only about 12,000 votes, Georgia voting administrator Gabriel Sterling, a Republican who voted for Trump, specifically refuted allegations of voting improprieties in the Georgia election (Astor 2021). Georgia Secretary of State Brad Raffensperger announced on December 7: "We have now counted legally cast ballots three times, and the results remain unchanged" (Fausset and Corasaniti 2020).

Three days before Congress was to meet to count electoral votes, Trump personally called Raffensperger and pressured him to "find" enough votes to change the election outcome in Georgia. Trump said, "there's nothing wrong with saying that, you know, um, that you've recalculated . . . . So look. All I want to do is this. I just want to find 11,780 votes, which is one more than we have because we won the state" (Fausset and Corasaniti 2020).

Trump Pressured Governors and State Legislatures to Nullify State Elections

Article II of the Constitution provides that, "Each State shall appoint, in such Manner as the Legislature thereof may direct" the electors who will cast electoral ballots for president. All states have laws providing that voters in the states determine the slates of electors who cast ballots for president. No president had ever put pressure on governors or state legislatures to violate state laws and ignore the states' voters and declare the loser to have won the state's electoral votes. Trump thus violated the norm of allowing individual states to decide their own election outcomes.

In his efforts, Trump brought the leaders of the Michigan legislature to the White House to try to convince them to have the Michigan legislature throw out the popular vote and appoint their own slate of electors to cast their ballots for Trump. Despite losing Pennsylvania by more than 80,000 votes, Trump personally addressed by phone a meeting of State Senate Republicans to try to convince them to ignore the popular vote and award Pennsylvania's electoral votes to him (Gardner 2020). Although two recounts confirmed the initial count of votes, Trump called Republican Georgia Gov. Brian Kemp and urged him to have the legislature ignore the popular vote in the state and appoint its own set of electors to cast their ballots for Trump (Gardner 2020).

Part of Trump's plan to overturn the 2020 election was a scheme to have Republicans in the seven closely contested "battleground" states that he lost to Biden submit false slates of electors who were purported to represent votes for Trump. The plan involved Trump campaign representatives who tried to convince Republican electors who had been pledged to vote for Trump, but who did not win the votes in their states, to meet illegally and submit their votes to the Senate to be counted for Trump instead of Biden. The problem was that the voters in those seven states had chosen the Biden electors, and their selection was certified by the governors of those states. So the Trump "electors" had no legal standing to cast any presidential electoral ballots. In effect, these were attempts to defraud the United States and alter the election. Nevertheless, the attempt by Trump to gin up fake electoral votes continued through January 6, when the official ballots were to be counted in the joint session of Congress. Trump continued to put pressure on Mike Pence, who as vice president also served as president of the Senate, to recognize the fake ballots and not count the legitimate Biden ballots.

As one Trump lawyer explained in an email: "We would just be sending in 'fake' electoral votes to Pence to count the pro-Trump slates, reject those saying Mr. Biden had won and thus unilaterally keep the former president in Office" (Feuer and Benner 2022). Trump thus broke the strong norm of losing presidential candidates of adhering to the law.

Trump Broke a Strong Norm Against Using the Military to Interfere in Elections

In late December, Trump continued his efforts to overturn the election. In a six-hour meeting late on December 18, Sidney Powell, Michael Flynn, and Patrick Byrne argued (completely without basis) that voting machines had been programmed to change votes from Trump to Biden at the direction of President Hugo Chavez of Venezuela. They urged Trump to order the military to seize voting machines in the states in order to change the election outcomes (Haberman and Kanno-Youngs 2020).

Flynn had publicly suggested that Trump could impose martial law in the swing states and that "he could take military capabilities, and he could place those in states and basically rerun an election in each of those states" (Sonmez et al. 2020). Flynn and Powell drafted an executive order for Trump that would authorize military authorities to seize voting machines. White House counsel Pat Cipollone, his deputy Eric Herschmann, and Staff Secretary Derek Lyons joined the meeting (Haberman 2022). When Cipollone asked for evidence of fraud and there was none, he said, "at some point, you have to put up or shut up" (Feuer et al. 2022) Attorney General Barr had said that he saw "no basis now for seizing machines by the federal government" (Olorunnipa and Wootson 2020).

There is a strong military norm that U.S. military forces should not be used within the United States except in exceptional circumstances. Trump's consideration of using military force was so alarming that all ten of the living former Secretaries of Defense wrote a public letter stating that, "any efforts to involve the U.S. armed forces in resolving election disputes" would be dangerous and potentially criminal (Former Secretaries of Defense 2021).

After vociferous arguments at the meeting on December, the "team normal" White House staffers were able to dissuade Trump from seizing voting machines. But the meeting that night was a turning point for Trump, and he began to make plans to summon his supporters to Washington, D.C. to pressure Congress to overturn the election.

Breaking a Long-Standing Norm, Trump Pressured the Justice Department to Overturn the Election

The U.S. Department of Justice (DOJ) had a long-standing practice (norm) not to investigate allegations of election irregularities until after votes were certified so as not to insert itself into the politics of campaigns. This norm was followed by the DOJ in 2020. After the post-election investigations, Attorney General Barr told Trump on December 1 that Justice Department had "not seen fraud on a scale that could have effected a different outcome in the election" (Benner and Schmidt 2020).

Nevertheless, in his pressure campaign to overturn the election, Trump "directly and repeatedly asked DOJ's acting leadership to initiate investigations, file lawsuits on his behalf, and publicly declare the 2020 election corrupt" (Majority Staff Report 2021). After the election, the president began talking with Jeffrey Clark, Assistant Attorney General for the Civil Division of the DOJ, who agreed with Trump that the election had been marred by fraud.

On December 28, after talking with Trump, Clark emailed Acting Attorney General Jeffrey Rosen and Principal Associate Attorney General Richard

Donoghue, attaching a draft letter ("Georgia Proof of Concept") saying that the DOJ had taken notice of irregularities in the 2020 election and that the state should call a special session of the state legislature to "consider appointing a new slate of Electors." He further suggested that similar letters be sent to "each relevant state" (Majority Staff Report 2021). Rosen and Donoghue rejected Clark's proposal, after which Clark disclosed that Trump had offered to fire Rosen and replace him with Clark. The implied threat was that if Rosen did not send the letter, Trump would fire Rosen and replace him with Clark.

Donoghue told Trump that he and seven DOJ assistant attorneys general (all Trump appointees) would resign if Clark were appointed to replace Rosen. Cipollone, called Clark's proposal a "murder-suicide pact," and said that he and his deputy would also resign if Trump carried out his plan to replace Rosen with Clark (Majority Staff Report 2021). At the end of the meeting, Trump decided not to replace Rosen with Clark. In this case, DOJ appointees enforced the norm of not interfering with an election against Trump's threats.

Trump Summoned a Mob to Pressure Congress to Change the Vote Outcome, Violating the Norm of the Peaceful Transfer of Power After an Election

In the United States, there is a norm not to use violence to affect the outcome of an election.

The law governing the counting of electoral ballots on January 6, the Electoral Count Act (3 USC 15) and the Constitution make it clear that the role of the Vice President is merely to count the electoral votes submitted by the states, not make judgments about which votes to count. Nevertheless, Trump incorrectly asserted that "The Vice President has the power to reject fraudulently chosen electors" (Haberman and Karni 2021). But Pence refused to agree to change the electoral votes when they were to be counted on January 6.

Desperate to stay in power, Trump urged his followers to come to Washington to put pressure on Congress as they formally counted electoral votes on January 6. In a series of tweets, Trump planned for the insurrection. On December 19 he wrote: "Big protest in D.C. on January 6th. Be there, will be wild" (Barry and Frenkel 2021). On January 1, 2021, he wrote: "The BIG Protest Rally in Washington, D.C. will take place at 11:00A.M. on January 6th. Location details to follow. StopTheSteal!" (Barry and Frenkel 2021).

On January 5, Trump ally and former White House official Steve Bannon predicted "all hell is going to break loose tomorrow" (Broadwater 2021). n a podcast, Bannon called his followers to action, saying, "We are going into uncharted waters. We're going into something that's never happened before in American history. Tomorrow it's going – we're pulling the trigger" and "It's all converging, and now we're on the point of attack tomorrow" in order to "kill the Biden presidency in the crib." (Bump 2021). In a coordinated effort, right-wing militias traveled to Washington, many with weapons, to keep Congress from counting the electoral votes. They were encouraged by Republican members of Congress. On January 2, more than 100 Republican representatives and 12 senators promised to object to the vote count in Congress, misleading Trump supporters into believing that Vice President Pence and Congress could somehow overturn the election (Woodward and Costa 2021).

In a call to Pence on January 6, Trump said, "You can either go down in history as a patriot, or you can go down in history as a pussy" (Baker, Haberman, and Karni 2021). Trump was putting great pressure on Pence, but on January 6, Pence released a letter explaining why he would not do Trump's bidding: "no Vice President in American history has ever asserted" authority to ignore or throw out slates of electoral votes (Woodward and Costa 2021, p. 240).

As the crowd assembled on the morning of January 6, Trump addressed them in the Ellipse south of the White House. In his remarks, Trump said, "all of us here today do not want to see our election victory stolen by bold and radical left Democrats which is what they are doing. We will never concede. It doesn't happen. You don't concede when there's theft involved." The crowd chanted, "Fight for Trump! Fight for Trump!" (ABC News 2021).

In his speech to the mob, Trump lashed out at the Vice President, saying that Pence did not have "the courage to do what should have been done to protect our country and our Constitution" (Hsu, Weiner, and Marimow 2021). Although Trump was told by the Secret Service that many in the mob had weapons, Trump insisted that they be allowed onto the grounds where he was speaking, saying: "I don't fucking care that they have weapons. They're not here to hurt me" (NPR 2022). After his speech riling up the mob, Trump told them that he would go with them to the Capitol, but his Secret Service detail refused to take him because of the security threat. Trump returned to the White House and spent most of the next several hours (187 minutes) in a dining room close to the Oval Office watching Fox News on television.

As he watched the mob at the Capitol chant "hang Mike Pence!" it was clear that Pence's life was in danger, and he was removed to a secure location by his Secret Service detail (some Secret Service agents made farewell calls to their loved ones). But instead of acting to protect his Vice President, Trump egged the mob on by tweeting, "Mike Pence didn't have the courage to do what should have been done to protect our Country and our Constitution" (Bump 2022). When Mark Meadows, Trump's chief of staff, was told about the mob's chant, "hang Mike Pence!" he did not contact the president, but said he "think[s] Mike deserves it. He doesn't think they're doing anything wrong" (Brockell 2022).

As the mob attacked the Capitol, Trump's White House aides, family members, members of Congress, and outside advisors pleaded with him to call off the mob, but he refused. He did not contact the Pentagon, Homeland Security, or any other government official in order to protect the Capitol. Rather he called several Senators to encourage them to obstruct the counting of electoral ballots. According to a White House lawyer, "the president didn't want anything done" to stop the mob (Broadwater and Haberman 2022).

It was only after it was clear that the Capitol Police and National Guard troops were dispersing the mob, and Trump's plans to prevent Congress from counting the electoral ballots had failed, that Trump was finally convinced to make a public statement to the mob. Trump refused to present a scripted statement, which included stating that the election was over and encourage the mob to leave peacefully. In his statement, Trump deviated from the script to justify the violence. "These are the things and events that happen when a sacred landslide election victory is so unceremoniously and viciously stripped away from great patriots who have been badly and unfairly treated for so long," He finished with, "Go home with love and in peace. Remember this day forever!" (Haberman 2021). In his recorded video, he said: "I know you're hurt . . . . We had an election that was stolen from us. It was a landslide election and everyone knows it, especially the other side. But you have to go home now. We love you. You're very special" (Haberman 2021).

After the violent mob had been cleared from the Capitol, the counting of electoral votes continued at 8 p.m. Despite the violent attack, 139 House Republicans and eight senators voted to challenge several slates of electors that had been certified by the states (Armus 2021). After the challenges failed, Joe Biden's status as president-elect was confirmed by Congress; the session adjourned at 3:45 a.m., January 7, 15 hours after it convened (Helderman, Swaine, and Lee 2020). One hundred fifty Capitol Police officers were injured, and five officers died as a result of the attack.

After 2020, Trump Continued the "Big Lie" That He Had Won the Election

There is a norm in the United States that losing presidential candidates do not claim that that they have actually won the election. The 2020 presidential election was one of the most carefully watched elections in U.S. history, and Trump supporters were not able to produce sufficient evidence to convince any court of law that fraud had been committed. Nevertheless, Trump continued his campaign to overturn the 2020 election and to promote the "Big Lie" that President Biden was not legitimately the president. Despite the lack of evidence of fraud, sizable majorities of Republicans believed Trump and his congressional supporters that the election had been stolen (Monmouth University Poll 2021), and that the rioters were led by anti-Trump activists and members of Antifa (Lange 2022). After the violent attack on the Capitol, Georgia Republican, Representative Andrew Clyde, characterized the mayhem as "a normal tourist visit" (Shammas 2021).

Based on the myth of the stolen election, Republican state legislators proposed more than 250 laws in 43 states intended to limit voting, such as restricting absentee voting, limiting hours of polling places, and requiring stricter identification for voting (Gardner et al. 2021). As of September 2021, 33 of those proposals in 19 states were enacted into law (Brennan Center for Justice 2021). Referring to Democratic proposals to make absentee voting easier during the pandemic, Trump said: "They had things – levels of voting that, if you ever agreed to it, you'd never have a Republican elected in this country again" (Blake 2020).

Perhaps more importantly, Republican legislatures in many states proposed and enacted new laws and procedures to take more direct control of the administration of elections. They changed election and appointment procedures for positions such as secretaries of state and local election officials, as well as giving state legislatures more discretion to affect the outcome of elections (Corasaniti and Epstein 2021). Some of these changes in state laws may have laid the groundwork for legislatures to appoint alternative slates of presidential electors to send to Congress in states in which the popular vote might go against the Republican presidential candidate in the future (Levitt 2021).

Trump's lies were so effective that many of his followers were willing to threaten violence. Hundreds of election administrators in 17 states were threatened with death and other violence, and had to be given special protection (Brennan Center for Justice 2021). Reuters documented more than 800 threats of bodily harm or death to election officials and school board members. The FBI even opened up a "threat tag" to track threats of violence against school officials (So and Szep 2021). Arizona Republican, Representative Paul Gosar was censured by the Democratic majority in the House for posting an animated video of himself slashing the neck of New York Democrat, Representative Alexandria Ocasio-Cortez with a sword, and attacking President Biden (Edmondson 2021).

As of November 2021, a major poll (N = 2508) found that 31% of Americans and two-thirds of Republicans believed that Trump won the 2020 election, while 30% of Republicans (and 18% of Americans) believed that "true American patriots may have to resort to violence in order to save our country" (PRRI 2021). According to data gathered by the Center for Strategic and International Studies, between 2015 and 2021, right-wing violence has caused 91 deaths and 267 plots, whereas far-left plots and violence have led to 19 deaths and 66 plots (O'Harrow, Tran, and Hawkins 2021). Neither former President Trump nor his supporters among members of Congress were willing to denounce the threats of violence.

Trump Broke the Norm That Candidates for the Presidency Accept the Rule of Law

There is a norm in American politics that presidential campaigns focus on doing positive things for the nation if elected – but a major theme in Trump's 2024 campaign was to take revenge on his enemies if elected. In appealing to his base, Trump declared, "I am your warrior, I am your justice. And for those who have been wronged and betrayed, I am your retribution" (Samuels 2023). In exacting his retribution, Trump declared that he would not let the law or traditional norms stop him.

From the beginning of the republic, U.S. politicians have adhered to the norm that the United States is governed under the rule of law. Donald Trump often explicitly violated that norm in his rhetoric and as he ran for election in 2024. In complaining about the supposed fraud in the 2020 election, Trump posted on Truth Social, "A Massive Fraud of this type [his loss of the 2020 election] and magnitude allows for the termination of all rules, regulations, and articles, even those found in the Constitution" (Holmes 2022). Trump continued to violate the norm of respect for freedom of the press by denouncing what he called the "fake news media" as "the enemy of the people," and vowing to exact revenge on them if he became president again.

There is a norm in the United States not to call for the death of people of whom the president disapproves. Yet Trump implied that Mark Milley, the Military Chairman of the Joint Chiefs of Staff, was guilty of treason because Milley called his Chinese counterpart to assure him that the United States was not contemplating an attack on China. "Mark Milley . . . turned out to be a Woke train wreck . . . in times gone by, the punishment would have been DEATH!" (Cooper 2023). In March 2024, he predicted, "Now, if I don't get elected, it's going to be a bloodbath for the whole – that's going to be the least of it. It's going to be a bloodbath for the country" (Astor 2024).

In the wake of the assault on the Capitol on January 6, 2021, hundreds of people were convicted of breaking the law and were imprisoned. Trump called those who had been convicted of crimes "political prisoners" and promised to pardon them if he won the 2024 election. "I will look very, very favorably about full pardons . . . And I mean full pardons with an apology to many" (Grayer and LeBlanc 2022).

In campaigning for a second term, Trump promised to politicize the DOJ more effectively than in his first term and use it against his political enemies. "If I win and somebody wants to run against me, I call my attorney general. I say, listen, indict them. 'Well, he hasn't done anything wrong that we know of' – I don't know, indict him on income tax evasion, you'll figure it out" (C-SPAN 2023). Using the DOJ to punish political enemies breaks an important norm in the United States that justice should be impartial.

No other president has claimed to have absolute immunity from accountability for crimes that a president might commit while in office. Yet Trump violated that norm in his claim that he was not liable for actions he took while president. "A PRESIDENT OF THE UNITED STATES MUST HAVE FULL IMMUNITY . . . . EVEN EVENTS THAT 'CROSS THE LINE' MUST FALL UNDER TOTAL IMMUNITY" (Trump, cited in Wolf 2024).

Conclusion

The Framers of the Constitution were well aware of the threat that a demagogue might become president and violate the letter as well as the norms of the Constitution. At the first level, they thought that Congress would defend its own prerogatives and rein in an overreaching executive.

James Madison argued that "some provision be made for defending the Community agst [i.e., against] the incapacity, negligence or perfidy of the chief Magistrate" (Farrand 1966, p. 65). And if a president abused his power egregiously, the Constitution provided a final backstop by giving the House of Representatives the power to impeach and the Senate the authority to remove the president from office. Impeachment is a political charge ("high crimes and misdemeanors"), rather than a criminal charge of breaking the law, though it might include breaking the law (Hamilton 1992, Federalist 65). Thus, the Framers of the Constitution intended impeachment and removal to include the egregious violation of norms.

What the Framers did not foresee was the development of political parties and the polarization of Congress in the late 20th and early 21st centuries. Partisan polarization allowed Trump to be acquitted in his second impeachment (as he had been in his first), despite majorities in both Houses of Congress voting to remove him from office. The Senate vote was 57–43 against Trump, ten votes short of the two-thirds majority needed to convict. Thus, if one chamber of Congress is held by the president's party, and the Trump precedent holds, it is unlikely that any future president could be impeached and removed from office.

President Trump found flaws in the system that allowed him to refuse to admit his electoral defeat. He rejected the customary civility of defeated candidates in dealing with his successor. Most importantly, a large majority of the members of his party in Congress went along with Trump and refused to recognize the outcome of the election by supporting his specious claims that the election was stolen. Consequently, the broad base of the Republican Party believed their leaders and denied the legitimacy of the election. These fervent beliefs, along with Trump' incitement, led to the violent occupation of the Capitol by the mob and continued threats of violence.

If one of the major parties in a two-party constitutional republic refuses to accept the clear-cut outcome of an election and is willing to encourage or condone violence to keep or attain power, that democratic system is in trouble.

References

ABC News, 2021, "President Trump Speaks at Save American Rally in Washington," *ABC News*, 7 January.

Armus, Teo, 2020, "Michigan Closes Legislative Buildings Due to 'Credible Threats of Violence' Ahead of Electoral College Vote," *Washington Post*, 14 December.

Armus, Teo, 2021, "House Rejects Challenge to Biden's Win in Pennsylvania," *Washington Post*, 7 January.

Astor, Maggie, 2021, "Georgia Election Official Debunked Trump's Claims of Vote Fraud, Point by Point," *New York Times*, 4 January.

Astor, Maggie, 2024, "Trump Defends 'Blood Bath' in Speech," *New York Times*, 19 March.

Baker, Peter, Maggie Haberman, and Annie Karni, 2021, "Pence Reached His Limit with Trump: It Wasn't Pretty," *New York Times*, 12 January.

Barry, Dan, and Sheera Frenkel, 2021, "'Be There. Will Be Wild!': Trump All but Circled the Date," *New York Times*, 6 January.

Benner, Katie, and Michael Schmidt. 2020. "Barr Acknowledges Justice Dept. Has Found No Widespread Voter Fraud," *New York Times*, 1 December.

Blake, Aaron, 2020, "Trump Just Comes Out and Says It: The GOP Is Hurt When It's Easier to Vote," *Washington Post*, 30 March.

Brennan Center for Justice, 2021, "Voting Laws Roundup: October 2021," 4 October, https://www.brennancenter.org/our-work/research-reports/voting-laws-roundup-october-2021.

Brinkley, Doug, et al. 2021, "Historians' Statement on Congressional Certification of the 2020 Presidential Election", 4 January, https://www.politico.com/f/?id=00000176-d218-d162-a7ff-f31c5b8c0000.

Broadwater, Luke, 2021, "Bannon Found in Contempt of Congress," *New York Times*, 22 October.

Broadwater, Luke, and Maggie Haberman, 2022, "Jan. 6 Panel Presents Evidence of Trump's Refusal to Stop the Riot," *New York Times*, 22 July.

Brockell, Gillian, 2021, "'Grace and Humor': The Vice Presidents Who Certified Their Own Election Losses," *Washington Post*, 2 January.

Brockell, Gillian, 2022, "Trump Wasn't the First to Decry His Vice President," *Washington Post*, 21 July.

Bump, Philip, 2021, "Bannon's Jan. 6 Role Walks the Thin Line Between Revolutionary Rhetoric and Revolution," *Washington Post*, 20 October.

Bump, Philip, 2022, "Trump Put Pence in More Danger Than We Knew," *Washington Post*, 16 June.

Chiacu, Doina, 2020, "Trump says 'This Election Is Far From Over'," *Reuters*, 7 November.

CNN, 2016, "Hillary Clintons Concession Speech," *CNN Politics*, 9 November.

Cooper, Helene, 2023, "Wars, Pandemic, Insurrection, U.F.O.s: Gen. Mark Milley's Term Had It All," *New York Times*, 27 September.

Corasaniti, Mick, and Reid Epstein, 2021, "How Republican States Are Expanding Their Power Over Elections," *New York Times*, 19 June.

Crowley, Michael, 2020, "Trump Won't Commit to 'Peaceful' Post-Election Transfer of Power," *New York Times*, 23 September.

C-SPAN, 2023, "Former President Trump Speaks at South Dakota Monumental Leaders Rally," *C-SPAN*, 8 September.

Edmondson, Carl, 2021, "House Democrats Press for Censure of Republican Over a Video," *New York Times*, 17 November.

Farrand, Max, 1966, *The Records of the Federal Convention of 1787*, vol. II, Yale University Press, New Haven, CT, p. 65.

Fausset, Richard, and Nick Corasaniti, 2020, "After Three Counts, Georgia Recertifies Biden's Win," *New York Times*, 8 December.

Feuer, Alan, and Katie Benner, 2022, "The Fake Electors Scheme, Explained," *New York Times*, 27 July.

Feuer, Alan, Maggie Haberman, Michael S. Schmidt, and Luke Broadwater, 2022, "Trump Had Role in Weighing Proposals to Seize Voting Machines," *New York Times*, 31 January.

Former Secretaries of Defense: Ashton Carter, Dick Cheney, William Cohen, Mark Esper, Robert Gates, Chuck Hagel, James Mattis, Leon Panetta, William Perry, and Donald Rumsfeld, 2021, "The Time for Questioning the Elections Results Has Passed," *Washington Post*, 4 January.

Gardner, Amy, 2020, "How Trump Drove the Lie That the Election Was Stolen, Undermining Voter Trust in the Outcome," *Washington Post*, 20 December.

Gardner, Amy, Rabinowitz, Kate and Stevens, Harry, 2021, "How GOP-Backed Voting Measures Could Create Hurdles for Tens of Millions of Voters," *The Washington Post*, 11 March.

Grayer, Annie, and Paul LeBlanc, 2022, "Trump Says He Will 'Very, Very Seriously' Consider January 6 Pardons if He Runs and Wins in 2024," *CNN*, 2 September. Haberman, Maggie, 2021, "Trump Told Crowd 'You Will Never Take Back Our Country with Weakness'," *New York Times*, 6 January.

Haberman, Maggie, 2022, "Tears, Screaming and Insults," *New York Times*, 12 July.

Haberman, Maggie, and Annie Karni, 2021. "Pence Said to Tell Trump That Votes Can't Be Blocked," *New York Times*, 6 January.

Haberman, Maggie, and Zolan Kanno-Youngs, 2020, "Trump Discussed Making Conspiracist Special Counsel," *New York Times*, 20 December.

Haberman, Maggie et al., 2020, "Trump's False Attacks on Voting by Mail Stir Broad Concern," *New York Times*, 24 June.Hamilton, Alexander, 1992, "Federalist 65," *The Federalist*, Every Man's Library, Rutland, VT, pp. 355–359.

Healy, Patrick, and Jonathan Martin, 2016, "Donald Trump Won't Say if He'll Accept Result of Election," *New York Times*, 19 October.

Helderman, Rosalind, Jon Swaine, and Michelle Ye Hee Lee, 2020, "Despite Trump's Intensive Hunt for Voter Fraud, Officials in Key States Have so Far Identified Just a Small Number of Possible Cases," *Washington Post*, 23 December.

Holmes, Kristen, 2022, "Trump Calls for the Termination of the Constitution in Truth Social Post," *CNN*, 4 December.

Hsu, Spencer, Rhel Weiner, and Anne Marimow, 2021, "Retired Firefighter Accused of Attacking Police, Man Carrying Confederate Flag Charged in Capitol Riots," *Washington Post*, 14 January.

Kessler, Glen, 2020, "Trump's White House Statement: Falsehood upon Falsehood," *Washington Post*, 5 November.

Krebs Christopher, 2020, "Trump Fired Me for Saying This, but I'll Say It Again: The Election Wasn't Rigged," *Washington Post*, 1 December.

Lange, Jason., 2022, "Half of U.S. Republicans Believe the Left Led Jan. 6 Violence: Reuters/Ipsos Poll," 10 June, https://www.reuters.com/world/us/half-us-republicans-believe-left-led-jan-6-violence-reutersipsos-2022-06-09/.

Levitt, Justin, 2021, "Failed Elections and the Legislative Selection of Presidential Electors," *New York University Law Review*, vol. 96, no. 30.

Majority Staff Report, 2021, "Subverting Justice: How the Former President and His Allies Pressured DOJ to Overturn the 2020 Election, Senate Committee on the Judiciary 2021," October, https://www.judiciary.senate.gov/imo/media/doc/Interim%20Staff%20Report%20FINAL.pdf.

Monmouth University Poll, 2021, "National: Majority Back Capitol Riot Commission," 17 March, monmouth.edu/polling-institute/documents/monmouthpoll_us_031721.pdf/.

National Conference of State Legislatures, 2020, "Polling Places," https://www.ncsl.org/research/elections-and-campaigns/polling-places.aspx.

New York Times, 2000, "Text of Gore's Concession Speech," *New York Times*, 13 December.

NPR, National Public Radio, 2022, "Here's Every Word from the Jan. 6 Committee on It Investigation," *NRP*, 22 July.

O'Harrow, Robert, Andrew Tran, and Derek Hawkins, 2021, "Data Shows a Surge in Homegrown Incidents Not Seen in a Quarter-Century," *Washington Post*, 12 April.

Olorunnipa, Touluse, and Cleve Wootson, 2020, "In Challenging Election Defeat, Trump Cements His Control Over the Republican Party," *Washington Post*, 12 December.

Pfiffner, James P., 2021, "Donald Trump and the Norms of the Presidency," *Presidential Studies Quarterly*, March, pp. 96–124.

Pfiffner, James P., 2022, "How Donald Trump Tried to Overturn the 2020 Election," *Rivals for Power*, James Thurber (ed.), 7th edition, Rowman and Littlefield, Lanham, MD, pp. 53–82.

PRRI, Public Religion Research Institute, 2021, "Cultural Change and Anxiety in America," *PRRI Research*, 1 November, https://www.prri.org/research/competing-visions-of-america-an-evolving-identity-or-a-culture-under-attack/.

Samuels, Brett, 2023, "Trump Signals He's Out for Revenge in a Second Term," *The Hill*, 16 November.

Shammas, Brittany, 2021, "Congressman Compared Capitol Rioters to Tourists," *Washington Post*, 18 May.

So, Linda, and Jason Szep, 2021, "Reuters Unmasks Trump Supporters Who Terrified U.S. Election Workers," *Reuters*, 9 November.

Sonmez, Felica, Josh Dawsey, Dan Lamothe, and Matt Zapotosky, 2020, "A Frustrated Trump Redoubles Efforts to Overturn Election Result," *Washington Post*, 20 December.

Trump, Donald, 2024, "Truth Social," quoted in Susan B. Glasser, "Trump isn't Even Hiding His Plans to Go 'ROGUE'," *New Yorker*, 18 January.

Wolf, Zachary B., 2024, "Trump's Absurd 'Total Immunity' Argument for Law-Breaking Presidents, Deconstructed," *CNN*, 18 January, https://edition.cnn.com/2024/01/18/politics/immunity-court-trump-what-matters/index.html.

Woodward, Bob, and Robert Costa, 2021, *Peril*, Simon and Schuster, New York.

Chapter 9

Strategic Development of Constitutional Conventions on Succession Under Authoritarian States

The Case of China

Baogang He

Introduction

One could easily form the impression that constitutional conventions do not matter or do not really exist in China's authoritarian system; one could even make a claim that the only norm in an authoritarian system is the violation or manipulation of conventions and norms by autocratic leaders, or abandonment of them altogether. Authoritarianism is – by its nature – a system in which the top authority has exclusive powers to make exceptions to the rules and create their own rules.

I challenge this conventional view by developing a nuanced understanding of the strategic development and operation of constitutional conventions on succession in China. My aim is to deepen our understanding of how authoritarian constitutionalism operates through the case study of Chinese authoritarian conventions.

In a comparative study of succession politics, Frantz and Stein (2017: 935–936) found that the development of leadership succession rules was a constant under authoritarian systems, such that Party or state constitutions incorporate institutionalised mechanisms of succession. Such rules are designed to ease the unsettling process of appointing successors, lessen infighting, and "convey political legitimacy and offer guidelines for how politics should progress". Graeme Gill (2021) also demonstrated that a series of rules are well-developed and operated under ten authoritarian regimes. In the early 2000s, other studies on succession politics had examined whether China had begun developing constitutional conventions on succession. Shambaugh (2001) and Nathan (2003), for instance, noted how the process of succession in the wake of the Deng Xiaoping era came to be regulated through the institutionalisation of succession politics (Zeng 2014). Fewsmith (2003, 2021), however, did not believe this to be the case. He was of the view that the Chinese authoritarian system faced enormous obstacles in establishing a legitimate institutionalisation of succession politics because individual leaders and factions were still beholden to a secretive and manipulative Marxist–Leninist system, as was evident in the ongoing tensions between different factions.

DOI: 10.4324/9781003506577-9

This chapter aims to advance the previous studies by developing a nuanced understanding of the operation of constitutional conventions in authoritarian states. Rather than seeing the authoritarian state as either a facilitator of succession conventions or a hindrance to them, my argument is that authoritarian states have strategically selected and developed constitutional conventions on succession. Taking the case study of China, I examine a variety of formal constitutional or informal succession conventions and categorise them into three groups. The first group concerns the qualifications and ideological positions of successors, their work experience, and the age-limit rule. The second group covers the methods of election and selection of successors, and the third group concerns operational conventions such as the distribution of powers, majority rule, and civilian control over the army. Through an empirical study, I examine and explain why and how rules such as those concerning democratic selection and the two-term rule have failed to develop into constitutional or operational conventions, while other rules like those concerning the ideological orientation of the successor, power distribution, Party–military relations, and the age limit for successors have become operational conventions. Through the case study of Chinese authoritarian conventions, the chapter demonstrates that the operations of succession conventions are deeply rooted in the Chinese authoritarian system.

The chapter also aims to advance our understanding of authoritarian constitutionalism by identifying the pattern of the strategic selection and development of specific succession rules. Mark Tushnet's (2015) theory of authoritarian constitutionalism illustrates how authoritarianism has developed and maintained its constitutionalism, an intermediate normative model between liberal constitutionalism and authoritarianism. More recently, scholars were invited in Helena Alviar García and Günter Frankenberg's *Authoritarian Constitutionalism: Comparative Analysis and Critique* (2019) to examine how authoritarian power is constituted, exercised, and transferred in different countries, including Hungary, apartheid South Africa, China, Venezuela, Syria, and Argentina. This chapter focuses on just one variant of party–state constitutionalism and its rule on succession. Like Vietnam, North Korea, Laos, Cuba, and many other socialist countries, China has developed party–state constitutional conventions on succession.

This chapter therefore adopts an historical method using the case study of China. This historical angle will help us to identify long-established patterns of party–state behaviour concerning succession through the confirmation or disconfirmation of certain conventions or rules. For this purpose, I have used a practical testing method using the regular Party Congresses every five years (total of four Party Congresses from 2002–2022) to observe how often specific rules have been followed or violated (see Table 9.1). Here I deploy a quantitative approach to the formation of the norm. Rules written in a constitution but never practised do not qualify as a norm. Convention refers to customised practices with a stabilised pattern. While some succession rules are constitutionally and legally defined, others are informal and non–legally binding practices. They can constrain power holders and regulate political behaviour even if they are informal or non–legally binding. To study these customised practices, a quantitative method is necessary for the simple reason that if a rule is practised once, it is far from being a norm. It is proposed that what qualifies as a "norm" must be practised at least three times. In connection with the Party Congresses to be examined subsequently, the term "three times" spans more than a decade and encompasses two leadership periods, allowing us to assess whether the incoming leader will adhere to the precedents set by their predecessor. "Three times" also shows a relatively stabilised pattern, increasing the probability of the norm being followed. Yet, the possibility of abandoning an existing rule remains even if it has been practised three times or more. It is also acknowledged that while some succession rules have been written in the State Constitution or the Party Constitution, not all are institutionalised and/or legalised. The age-limit rule in China, for instance, is informal and deliberately non–legally binding, leaving it open to being downplayed, but it nevertheless continues to play an important role in succession politics.

The chapter consists of three sections. The first following section offers a historical overview of succession politics from Mao to Xi. It focuses on the institutionalisation of succession and describes the basic features of China's constitutional provisions on succession. The next section tests the efficacy of certain succession conventions through demonstration of at least three practices of it, as mentioned previously. It examines how and why the Chinese Communist Party (CCP) has developed certain succession conventions but has failed to develop succession conventions that are more critical. In the concluding section, I summarise the key features of authoritarian succession conventions and address whether these rules can regulate – and even tame – the power of the CCP.

Politics of Succession Plans From Mao to Xi

In the commentary on institutionalisation of succession politics, Mao's effort to institutionalise succession has often been overlooked. Perhaps this is because it was a significant failure. Mao's chosen candidates were originally Liu Shaoqi and Lin Biao. He later turned against them at a tremendous social cost. It is worth revisiting these times with a short overview of history, drawing key lessons from the particulars of succession politics in Mao's era. This will help us understand the dynamics of succession that are in play today.

Mao first attempted to institutionalise succession rules in 1956. The plan was to appoint four co-serving vice-chairmen to the Party. Having previously held a number of highly ranked positions in the Party, Liu Shaoqi was long considered the next in line to succeed Mao and was appointed to the position of the First Vice-Chairman of the Party (Deputy Chairman). The institutional arrangement was such that Liu Shaoqi was twice elected as the State President, first in 1959, when Mao ceded state responsibilities, and then in 1965 (Dittmer, 2015). After Mao decided to abandon his post as President in 1959, a position he held since it was established in the 1954 constitution, he was concerned he had created two power centres: one was around Party organisation under Mao, and the other was around state institution under Liu. It was a situation with which Mao became increasingly uncomfortable. This led to a growing mistrust of Liu, who was censured and then placed under house arrest, later dying in 1969.

Liu was replaced by Lin Biao in 1966. He was the new designated successor to Mao. It was not until the 9th Party Congress in 1969 that the status of Lin Biao as a successor was written into the Party Constitution. Lin's official appointment nonetheless seemed to fuel paranoia in Mao that Lin could through his military positions and supporters take power from him any time, so that by 1970, Mao proposed abolishing the post of President of the State. While many leaders had opposed this, especially Lin Biao, Mao went ahead with his plan. On 17 January 1975, at the first session of the Fourth National People's Congress (NPC), the posts of President and Vice-President of the State were officially abolished in the constitution. In the end, Lin Biao died mysteriously in an airplane crash in 1971. Hua Guofeng, Mao's last preferred successor, took office in 1976 on Mao's death.

In sum, Mao's institutionalisation of succession had set the tone for succession politics in China. Two key conclusions can be drawn from it: (1) the possibility of a rival power centre makes leaders reluctant to designate successors or to provide a time frame for succession while in power; and (2) succession rules formally written into the constitution typically carry no weight because leaders can weaken or overturn the rules.

Deng Xiaoping had sought to overcome the problems associated with Mao's succession plans. On 18 August 1980, Deng gave a seminal speech on the "Reform of the Party and State Leadership System" in which he argued that bureaucracy, the excessive concentration of power, the patriarchal system, and the tenure of cadre leadership must be reformed. At the Twelfth Party Congress in September 1982, the posts Chairman and Vice-Chairman of the Party were abolished at least in terms of their first and second rankings with the leading official figure in the Party now called the General-Secretary, thus leaving no indicator as to who would be next in line to the General-Secretary. The Twelfth National Congress also approved the establishment of the Central Advisory Committee of the Communist Party of China as a transitional institution for the abolition of the tenure system of leading cadres. In December, the Fifth Session of the Fifth NPC passed the 1982 Constitution; one article stipulates that "the term of office shall not exceed two consecutive terms" for the President, Vice-President, Premier of the State Council, Vice-Premier, and the Chairman of the Standing Committee of the NPC. The 2006 General Office of the Central Committee of the CCP issued the "Interim Provisions on the Term of Office of Leading Party and Government Cadres" qualified the rule regarding the length of the terms. Article 3 stipulates that "each term of party and government leadership positions is five years". Article 6 further stipulates that "Party and government leading cadres serve two consecutive terms in the same position, and will no longer be recommended or nominated, or appointed to the same position" (the General Office of the Central Committee of the CCP, 2006). However, the Party Constitution does not have such a provision for the Party General-Secretary.

Deng Xiaoping's succession politics was characterised by regular promotion through establishing limits of two terms in office, a retirement age, a rotation of roles, and the selection of young leaders as successors (Harding, 1987). Both Jiang Zeming and Hu Jintao put these succession rules into practice and improved some of them. China had witnessed a peaceful transition of political power from Jiang Zeming to Hu Jintao in 2002 and then from Hu Jintao to Xi Jinping in 2012. This is a direct reflection of the normalisation of many of the succession rules initiated by Deng Xiaping. Jiang Zeming, for example, had transferred the posts and the heads of the Party and State to Hu Jintao in 2002 but kept the post of the Chairman of the Central Military Commission until 2004; Hu Jintao and Wen Jiabao were the first leaders to take office through constitutional processes – and the first to assume positions of national responsibility. This garnered much praise from Kissinger (2011: chap. 18). Hu Jintao's efforts could be seen as setting the example for a peaceful transition of power within the two-term limit by ultimately transferring all posts and powers to Xi Jinping in 2012. In a comparative context, the six instances of succession under the Soviet Union – Lenin/Stalin, Stalin/Khrushchev, Khrushchev/Brezhnev, Brezhnev/Andropov, Andropov/Chernenko, and Chernenko/Gorbachev, only came about because the first five were precipitated by the death of the leader, and the sixth was overthrown as leader (Gill, 2018).

The two-term rule has only been observed once under Hu Jintao (2002–2012), based on my suggestion that a rule that has not been practised more than three times is not a convention, even if it was written in the constitution. The two-term rule was not even followed entirely by Jiang Zeming. Jiang held power for 13 years from 1989–2002, or 15 years from 1989–2004 if we count his final retirement from the post of Chairperson of the Central Military Commission of the CCP.

Hu was a weak political leader, however. He only gave up all his powers in the transition because Jiang Zeming had forced his hand. Tellingly, Hu had installed his loyal supporters (like Li Keqiang and Wang Yang) in top positions before transferring posts. Jiang's influence had extended well into the current leadership. Xi Jinping had been lucky in setting out to consolidate his power as Jaing's influence had begun to wane with his ageing. On taking office, Xi's main tactic to silence the opposition and unify the Party following the 18th Party Congress was to deploy anti-corruption measures which targeted his political opponents. While Xi sought to reduce Jiang's influence further at the 19th Party Congress by negotiating and compromising with the Youth League faction, he put a complete end to the faction at the 20th Party Congress, which was symbolised by escorting former Party Secretary Hu Jintao out of the closing ceremony of the meeting on 22 October. Clearly, then, the ascendency of Xi Jinping reveals severe problems with Deng's institutionalisation of succession.

On designating Hu Jintao as Jiang's successor in 1992, Deng had introduced a practice of "successors in training". Both Hu and Xi waited ten years in all before becoming national leader, both had to be "trained". Training practice, as such, was very paternalistic in that it was generational – the leader was considered an elder to the young leader in the making. Deng's "successor in training" plan was one that violated the principle of power operation. The training process quickly became an instrument of intense interference, e.g., Jiang Zhemin's meddling during the Hu Jintao era (Cheek et al., 2021: 193–212).

Besides the training, the more egregious error on Deng's part in institutionalising succession was failing to enshrine the two-term rule in the Party Constitution. This allowed Xi to exploit this loophole. Deng's paternalistic model of succession remained a severe problem for Xi. Prior to being designated successor, Xi had already gone through a lengthy process climbing the Party ranks; it followed that his political manoeuvrings were very cautious and conservative before taking power. So, when he became the General Party Secretary, he spent at least 2–3 years in the first term consolidating his power. While Deng's succession method was designed to open the way for a harmonious power transition, it had severely constrained Xi's ambitious plans. If Xi Jinping had followed the two-term rule, he would have had to pass some of his powers on to the next leader in his second term. Not being able to realise his plans provides a justification for Xi to break the two-term rule.

To reiterate the quantitative measure mentioned earlier, a rule that has not been practised more than three times is not a norm, even though it is included in the constitution. This is the case with the two-term rule, which has only been observed once – and that was under Hu Jintao (2002–2012). The rule was clearly broken by Xi Jinping, but it was also broken by Jiang Zeming. Jiang held power for roughly three terms. However, a modification of the rule of the two terms might be deemed acceptable in Jiang's case: first, he took the Party Secretary position in 1989, which was regarded as an exceptional circumstance, and second, noticeable was the slow decline of Jiang's power from 2002–2004, during which he could not officially attend Politburo meetings, nor did he control economic affairs in this period. He only controlled military organisations and affairs. One might suspect that he would have used the Taiwan issue to provide an excuse to consolidate his military power, but it did not happen.

Nevertheless, unlike Jiang, Xi Jinping had strategically sought to end the two-term rule in 2018 (much like Leonid Brezhnev did to Nikita Khrushchev's three-term limit) by exploiting the weakness of the existing institutional rule. The Constitution of the Communist Party of China did not impose a term limit on the positions of General-Secretary of the Central Committee of the Chinese Communist Party (CPC) and Chairman of the Central Military Commission. Xi's abolishment of the term limit simply confirms that no sacred rule exists under the authoritarian system. He is now serving his third term, confirmed at the 20th Party Congress in 2022.

In both the 19th and 20th Party Congresses, no successor was nominated by Xi. It is likely that he will continue for at least another five or even ten years, as there does not appear to be any succession plan on the horizon. If Xi chooses to be a life-Party Secretary, only the loyalists will be offered key positions to maintain the autocrat's rule. Thus, the age-limit rule is likely to be further eroded. As discussed later, the broken two-term rule is consistent with further autocrat developments to weaken and abandon the age-limit rule.

One might offer a comparative justification for Xi's behaviour. In the United States, the two-term limit had been informal for a long time until 1951, when it was formalised in the 22nd Amendment. Both presidents Ronald Reagan and Donald Trump attempted to repeal it. The Westminster system by comparison did not introduce a two-term limit at all. For example, both John Howard (1996–2007) and Lee Hsien Loong (2004–2024) took more than the two terms. Using any of these examples as a justification for Xi, however, would be superficial and misleading. In the case that prime ministers have more than two terms, the tremendous difference is procedural justice – it is legitimately done through the election process.

Xi, by contrast, had abolished the two-term rule through a forced process without elite and public deliberation on the matter. Against the power transition model established under Hu Jintao, Xi's departure has been constantly questioned and lacks legitimation and justification. Moreover, Xi's abandonment of the two-term rule continues to be the source of intra-Party friction. *People's Daily* published an article on 1 March 2018, saying that the revision of the presidency regulations is aimed at improving the leadership system of the Party and the state; it "does not mean changing the retirement system for the leading cadres of the party and the state. It also does not mean the life tenure of leading cadres".

Subsequently, Xi deployed Party disciplinary mechanisms and anti-corruption measures to force elites to abolish the two-term rule, weakening collective leadership practice and undermining frank remonstration practice. Also, through societal suppression and public propaganda, he shut down avenues for citizens to challenge the amending of the two-term rule. In modern society, the lives of Chinese citizens are affected by this kind of succession politics but lack any opportunity to express their voice. Xi, in the absence of elite and societal legitimacy, develops and sustains Hobbes' politics of coercion.

While Xi has not designated his successor, several potential successors are among the Politburo Standing Committee (PSC) members. They include Li Qiang, Cai Qi, Ding Xuexiang, and Li Xi. Li Qing became Premier in March 2023, but undertaking the premiership does not guarantee being a successor. Although Hua Guofeng and Zhao Zhiyang gained the top Party position from the Premier posting, former Premiers like Zhou Enlai, Zhu Rongji, Li Peng, and Wen Jiabao did not.

Moreover, a designated successor is not always the one who is best qualified. Mao chose Wang Hongwen and Hua Guofeng because they were loyalists and lacked a power basis; they did not constitute a serious challenger. Xi appears to be following a similar pattern of putting political loyalty first and meritocracy second.

Xi is increasingly seen as a new dictator or autocrat. Susan Shirk (2022), for example, said, "Mr. Xi fell into the same trap that has ensnared dictators throughout history". However, despite Xi's successful consolidation of his power in 2022, senior and retired leaders have successfully defended Article 6 of the Party Constitution that banned "any form of personality cult". Xi had failed to insert the words "*Renmin lingxiu*" ("people's leader") into the amended Party Constitution in 2022 (Nakazawa, 2022). This means that he cannot simply develop a new pattern of autocracy at whim. When he decides who the successor is, which he inevitably will, he faces the same sort of problem as Mao and Deng. So as not to risk concentrating power in a factional or individual competitor, thus avoiding the early taking of power from the others, Xi is unlikely to designate successor earlier. At the same time, he must work with the existing institutions and conventions. It remains uncertain whether Xi's ending of the two-terms rule has instigated a slow erosion of all the existing constitutional conventions on succession or whether Xi will strategically select and maintain the existing constitutional conventions, or even improve them, and, if so, how could do this. This will be complicated. The task would be a complex, unpredictable journey for Xi.

The Succession Conventions

I will now assess why some rules have become the conventions and others have failed to do so – and how likely they are to play a particular role in the politics of succession under Xi.

Qualification Norm I: Ideology

Confucian ethics has been a guiding principle in selecting successors in the dynasties of China. In the Qing dynasty, the Daoguang Emperor chose

Xianfeng over his younger brother, Yiteng, as a successor because he was much more benevolent. Today, the ideology of socialism is the lifeblood of party–state constitutionalism. While Beijing may not have a developed normative theory of succession, it has a distinctively normative force in the politics of succession in that the selection of top leaders is guided by its socialist ideology and the candidates in turn must demonstrate their commitment to socialism.[1] In the Deng era, in the face of the collapse of the Soviet Union, the renowned senior leader, Chen Yun, vigorously developed the new rule that only the children of the veteran cadres be selected as successors to ensure that the "red" (socialist) country is passed on from one generation to the next. Former Prime Minister Li Peng also insisted on this rule to prevent a Chinese "Gorbachev" from occurring. These days, Xi Jinping promotes a neo-socialism with Chinese characteristics to usher in and buttress a new age of socialist culture, thus preventing pro-West officials from being successors.

The Party Constitution developed the "ideology rule" that all successors must be committed to socialism. The rule is ostensibly a departure from the hereditary rule tradition in China under which the succession of imperial power in dynasties was carried out. Although the People's Republic of China (PRC) had abolished the hereditary rule, Chen Yun's rule is really nothing more than a refined hereditary rule in disguise. Given that Xi Jinping is the son of a famous Long Marcher and Vice-Premier, Xi Zhongxun, one may attribute his rise to power to covert hereditary rules rather than meritocracy. Xi has also urged people to inherit the "red gene".

Nevertheless, a special normative force has shaped the succession conventions beyond the wish of individual leaders. The core idea of Chinese socialism rejects the very notion of one family's inheritance and monopoly of power. Xi cannot put his daughter forward to the Party as his successor. It is hard to imagine powerful political families ruling China for three or four generations, like those in Japan, India, and the Philippines. The Cultural Revolution has destroyed the cultural foundation of this kind of family politics, although its revised versions are likely to take place.

In contrast, North Korea leaders still inherit political power: one that has passed from Kim Il-sung (1966–1994) to Kim Jong-il (1994–2011) and then to Kim Jong-un (2011–present). In the communist world, North Korea is the anomaly. The Soviet Union, China, Vietnam, Cuba (from Fidel Castro to Raúl Castro in 2006, then to Miguel Díaz-Canel in 2018) and many others have abandoned hereditary succession.

In imperial Chinese history, it was customary to honour emperors by designating a unique name or term to summarise their life in the ancestor temple. A similar custom takes place in the contemporary world, whereby

1 In some liberal countries, by comparison, there is an informal requirement of the candidates to show allegiance to the nation's main religion.

each Party Secretary is honoured for their ideological work. Mao Zedong Thought (Mao Zedong Thought was removed in the 1956 Eighth Party Congress), Deng Xiaoping Theory, the theory of three representatives by Jiang Zemin, and the theory of scientific development by Hu Jingtao are acknowledged in the Preamble of the Party Constitution. There is an implicit norm that all ideological work belongs to the top leader. Bo Xilai had violated this norm however during his ruling in Chongqing by gathering several prominent scholars to promote a specific "red" ideology.

The acknowledgement of the ideological contribution by Jiang and Hu was in their final terms or after retirement. In the 19th Party Congress, Xi Jinping Thought was written into the Party Constitution in his second term with the words of "Xi Jinping Thought on Socialism with Chinese Characteristics for a New Era". This may appear to indicate Xi's status as the core of the leadership, as it did with Mao Zedong Thought; however, the following qualifications deserve special attention. First, the Preamble of the Party Constitution stresses that the Party develops Xi's thought as a guideline. Second, Xi's thought is not a timeless doctrine, it is merely for "the new age". Third, his thought is about new socialism with Chinese characteristics, as compared with Mao Zedong Thought, which has no qualifying words in the preamble. Interestingly, the amended 2022 Party Constitution did not shorten "Xi Jinping Thought on Socialism with Chinese Characteristics for a New Era" (16-character ideology) into "Xi Jinping Thought", which would have put it on par with "Mao Zedong Thought" and above "Deng Xiaoping Theory" (Nakazawa, 2022). This is more evidence for the resistance to Xi's personality cult within the Party.

Qualification Norm II: Political Experience

Apart from the described ideology rules or conventions, there is another implicit informal rule: to be a successor, one must have had experience as the Party Secretary at the provincial level or in a municipality directly under the central government and/or have had experience working in critical national organisations. This norm has its origins in early meritocratic China, which required its rulers to be capable and practical. Central to governance in modern times, this rule is a functional necessity of managing a big state. In this respect, the accumulation of political experience in big provinces and critical departments of the Zhongnanhai is essential for mastering the ability to coordinate different organisations and manage power relations required by the operation of the party–state machine.

Although only informally practised, the political experience qualification rule has been applied at least four times between the 17th and 20th Party Congresses, thus meeting our quantitative criteria constituting a norm. In terms of selecting national leaders, the rule enables a big pool of potential successors to be narrowed down to a more manageable list of candidates. The position for the next Premier at the 2022 Party Congress, for example, came down to the experience of the last two candidates remaining. Based on merit, it appears that Li Qiang was chosen over Ding Xuexiang because of his provincial work experience in Zhejiang and Shanghai. This was key but not necessarily the decisive factor in the final decision, however. While Ding had lacked provincial work experience, he had worked in critical national organisations. Of these two long-time loyalists, Li was successful in the end primarily because of the subjective preference of Xi Jinping at this point in time. The rule had been slightly altered to match Xi's choice because Li Qiang had not yet worked in a national government capacity.

Qualification Norm III: Age-Limit Norm

The long-standing age-limit rule for a PSC member is that those aged 67 or younger at the time of the Party Congress can stay on this role, whereas anyone aged 68 or older must go. This age limit, though, is not the compulsory retirement age for members. It is the age limit for the last round of the five-year term at the point of being appointed to the committee. According to the rule, for example, Hu Jintao, who was 65 years of age during the 17th Party Congress in 2007, had to retire from the Politburo at age 70 at the 18th Party Congress in 2012. This rule has since been practised more than four times, accounting for all standing members of the Politburo except Jiang Zemin, who was 71 years old in 1997, when the 15th Party Congress was held. Since the retirement of Hu from the Politburo in 2012, and others before him, the rule was confirmed again with the retirement of Wang Qishan, 69 years old, at the 19th Party Congress, and Li Zhanshu (72 years old) and Han Zheng (68 years old) at the 20th Party Congress. In sum, the norm for members of the Politburo aged 68 and older at the entry point to a five-year term is to retire. The rule has been consistently sustained since 2002 (Miller, 2013, 2018). The reasoning behind it was to prevent a Brezhnev-type ageing problem from occurring in Beijing.

Despite the consolidation of the age-limit norm in all the circumstances mentioned previously, there were incidents at the 2022 Party Congress in which this norm had been twisted. Li Keqing and Wang Yang, both younger than 68 years of age, lost their PSC positions. More bizarrely, Wang Yi, 69 years old, was promoted to the Politburo member in charge of international affairs, while Zhang Youxia, 72 years old, kept his position as the vice-president of the Central Military Commission. On top of this, the age-limit rule for provincial leaders had also been violated. The retiring age for provincial leaders is 65 years older at the start of a five-year term, but around ten leaders born in the early 1950s had been reinstated. It is expected that more exceptions will be made to the age-limit rule to meet Xi's personal preferences and needs in the 21st Party Congress.

Method Norm I: Electoral Procedure for Succession

The CCP has used several methods in the past to select or elect successors. Decisions have been made by individual leaders alone, or by a small elite group within the Party, or by the vote of the Central Committee members. The dominant and influential method has been the decision or preference of the individual leader, as evidenced by Mao and Deng exercising their powers in selecting successors. Often a small group of senior ranking officials in the Party has also been consulted to support the leader's decision. In 1987, the 13th Party Congress introduced the element of a semi-competitive election process for the Central Committee members to decide on succession. Under Hu Jintao's reign, the CCP elite drew up a list of nominations for potential successors. In all these circumstances, the glaring absence is the citizens' perspective. There is no mechanism for ordinary citizens to express their opinion or cast a vote on succession. This is an abysmal record, especially in the 21st century. It is quite extraordinary that in the long history of Chinese dynasties to today, succession ultimately still comes down to the preferences of individual leaders. China is to yet design and develop a modern, fair, and workable system of succession. Beijing's current methods are completely outdated for the ordinary Chinese citizens.

Under the guise of democracy, Mao seeded a popular norm that the will of a leader is a constitutional right and that because a leader naturally knows the interests of people, the leader can decide what they need. This has nothing to do with democratic succession; it is a blatant misuse of democratic principles and sentiments. Xi seems to be following this Maoist practice by reproducing such popular conventions with a nationalist ethos.

From Mao to Deng, paramount leaders, usually with the support of a small elite, have dominated the succession process by personally designating who should succeed them. The norm is that the decision made by paramount leaders provides a source of legitimation (this differs from the Western election-based legitimacy). As I have noted, Mao designated four people: Liu Shaoqi, Lin Biao, Wang Hongwen, and Hua Guofeng. Deng Xiaoping did the same thing: Hu Yaobang, Zhao Ziyang, Jiang Zemin, and Hu Jintao. Xi, on the other hand, has yet to designate successors, concentrating instead on consolidating his power by promoting loyalists to the top decision-making body, the PSC. It is a tragedy that that after two decades of institutional building, Xi has reverted to the individualistic and personalised succession politics of old – it seems now that any small movement at the Party level in the direction of democratic election conventions have been further eroded under Xi. It remains to be seen when Xi will designate successors and just how many he will designate.

Although Xi Jinping's power may seem deep and far-reaching, Xi will need to create a new balance of factions to prevent one faction or one individual leader from dominating others. Here, a critical new condition is already afoot with the formation of new factions under Xi. A rivalry may take place between a provincial faction and a new military industry faction called the "aerospace clique". Seventeen local officials from Zhejiang Province have now been made members of the Central Party Committee. Xi has also placed more than ten former officials from state-owned companies with ties to the defence sector in the critical Party and state positions. Members of this "aerospace clique" include Jin Zhuanglong, the Minister of the Ministry of Industry and Information Technology; Huai Jinpeng, the education minister; and Ma Xingrui, the Party Secretary of the Xinjiang Uyghur autonomous region (Tabeta, 2022).

It is well known that democracy provides a set of succession rules, it regulates the transfer of political power through elections, and it settles any succession disputes through a constitutional court. In contrast, Chinese laws and higher courts have no part in settling any succession dispute. Party–state constitutionalism is a system in which the CCP dominates, and elections play a minor and symbolic role. The state leaders are elected and approved by the NPC, but such elections are indirect, non-competitive, and controlled. The Party's Organization Department nominates candidates and controls the process. The CCP sets up its apparatus within the NPC and uses the Party's discipline to direct its members to elect and approve Organization Department–designated candidates. This manipulative electoral system is a prerequisite for the operation of the party–state system.

Such elections are only valuable as a means of eliminating an unwelcome incumbent leader. Take, for example, the procedural rule that an individual's standing as a member of the pool of potential national leaders should be confirmed by the election to the Party's Central Committee. This rule implies that any promising successor must win internal elections within the Party. Deng Liqun, dubbed the Party's "underground General-Secretary", lost all hope of being a successor when he was not elected as a member of the Central Committee in 1987 and 1992. This is not a hard and fast rule, however; it can be amended any time.

Moreover, the gap between elected members and the listed names is tiny: it was 8.3% for the 17th Party Congress, 9.3% for the 18th Party Congress, 8.8% for the 19th Party Congress, and 8.3% for the 20th Party Congress. Furthermore, while this semi-competitive election for the Central Committee has been practised more than four times as a norm, the election method itself can be easily changed. In the 20th Party Congress, the constitutional amendment vote was by a show of hands.

The Method of Selection Through an Elite Opinion Questionnaire

In the 17th and 18th Party Congresses, about 300 leaders gathered in the Central Party School to complete a questionnaire and rank potential candidates for standing Politburo members. The process was called a "democratic recommendation system" but Alice Miller (2018: 9) said it was merely "a straw poll". Even though the so-called "democratic recommendation" gave elite individuals outside the oligarchy more opportunity to weigh in on potential leaders, they were still voting from a list that the oligarchs had provided.

The "Democratic recommendation system" was abandoned in the 19th and 20th Party Congresses. During the 19th Party Congress, Xi Jinping adopted a face-to-face consultation ("*miantai*") method instead. It is reported that Xi consulted vital top leaders, past and present, more than 57 times between April and June 2017 and that his team had organised 258 consultation sessions with senior national, military, and provincial leaders. For the 20th Party Congress, Xi held merely 30 "*miantai*" consultations; this time, he did not consult retired senior leaders. Observers see face-to-face consultation as a retreat from the previous "democratic recommendation system" (Xinhua News, 2022).

Reportedly, it has been proposed that a "Three-Three-System" plan be piloted. The core idea is that in deciding on the next generation of leaders, the current General Secretary has one-third of the decision-making power, and the other two-thirds of decision-making power is split among a group comprising of current and retired Politburo members and a group comprised of members of the Central Committee, the Standing Committee of the NPC, and the Standing Committee of the Chinese People's Political Consultative Conference. Considering the way Xi exercised his power in the 20th Party Congress, it seems highly unlikely that he would accept such an arrangement. Doubtless, his choice will have the most significant weight in deciding his next successor.

However, it is not as if the subject of democracy is never raised in the top echelons of the Chinese government. Back in 2014, Xi himself had promoted the view that whether national institutions are democratic entirely depends on whether the national leadership undergoes an orderly change in power according to law. In 2019, after the two-term provision was abolished, an article published by the Party's theoretical journal *Qiushi* had strategically emphasised the same idea. In a short article in the *People's Daily* on 4 December 2021, Chen Xi, the director of the Central Party Organisation of the CCP, again raised the seemingly "urgent issue" of succession. It is not entirely clear why the Party machinery is raising the issue of democratic institutions or mechanism, but one suspects it is a means to ameliorate negative perceptions of Xi's rule as a dictatorship or as a result of internal Party fighting. Despite calls for these kinds of proposals for instituting a democratic model of succession, democratic mechanisms have never been properly tested to settle succession issues. This is mainly due to the nature of party–state constitutionalism. Succession politics in China is mostly the "muddled thought" of a small selectorate behind closed doors. Chinese succession is often managed as a means of control over large numbers of competitors seeking top leader positions. The national leader is not going to be open to democratic political competition.

Distributive Convention

The two power centres based around Mao and Liu during Mao's period as discussed earlier were not unique. Even under Deng and Jiang, there was a short time of two power centres again. For example, in the early period of Hu's reign as the General-Secretary, Jiang was the Chairman of the Central Military Committee (2002–2004). Unlike Mao, who had relinquished his head of state post to Liu, thus creating another power centre, the emergence of two power centres under Hu was the direct result of Jiang retaining his long-held post as Chairman of the Central Military Committee in the transfer of power. While Jiang had relinquished the President of the State post, along with General-Secretary, he continued to hold the chairman position from 2002–2004 before relinquishing it to Hu. Since 2004, the PRC had put a stop to this issue from occurring again by establishing the three-in-one leadership system: the General Party Secretary, the President of the State, and the Head of the Military Commission all now combined as the sole roles and responsibilities of a leader.

As power holders below the national leader, it is worthwhile to detail the historical makeup of PSC members to illuminate the workings of distributive power in the CCP. The number of standing members typically varies from 5–9 or even more. It is an odd number in most cases, although it has had an even number of six on five occasions. The practice of the odd number is related to a majority rule. A majority vote is a basic rule for the standing members of Politburo meetings. Thus, the "Gang of Four" can be explained as four-fifths of the simple majority that Mao Zedong needed to override the other four members of the Standing Committee during the Cultural Revolution.

Since 2012, the number of standing members of the Politburo has stabilised at seven despite reportedly reducing standing Politburo members from seven to five in 2017. In contrast, the number of standing members of the Politburo under the Soviet Union system (over a similar historic timeline to the CCP up to its 1991 collapse) had varied greatly. It had 18 Politburo members at the 21st Party Congress in 1959, 15 at the 22nd Party Congress in 1961, 11 at the 23rd Party Congress in 1966, 18 at the 24th Party Congress in 1971, 21 at the 26th in 1981, and 19 at the 27th in 1986.

The distributive norm in China is all about allocating vital political positions to the standing members of the Politburo. After the 14th Party Congress in 1992, four of the standing members of the Politburo held the four most critical positions as the President of the PRC and Chair of the Central Military Commission, the Premier of the State Council, the Chairperson of NPC, and the Chairperson of CPPCC (Chinese People's Political Consultative Conference). This pattern symbolises the strength of party–state constitutionalism; these four influential organisations have a close working relationship under the leadership of the CCP. Similarly, in Vietnam, the four most senior members of the Politburo hold the four top party–state leadership posts as the Secretary-General of the Party, the State President, the Prime Minister, and the Chair of the National Assembly.

While the 19th Party Congress had confirmed the distributive norm for those key posts previously mentioned, it had introduced a new practice which was naming a member of the PSC the Chairman of the Central Commission for Discipline Inspection. It was the first time a standing member was appointed to this position. This arrangement reflects the feature of party–state constitutionalism – a reliance on the internal Party discipline for political control. This practice was confirmed again in the 20th Party Congress with the promotion of another Politburo member to this post.

The Minister of Foreign Affairs is not typically a standing Politburo member. Historically, Zhou Enlai was the only exception. Under the Soviet Union, by contrast, the Minister of Foreign Affairs was often a Politburo member. Moreover, despite Mao's famous saying that "women hold up half the sky", women are seldom elected as standing Politburo members. The CCP remains a patriarchy. In its 100-year history, it has yet to appoint a woman to its core decision-making body, the PSC (even Jiang Qin, the wife of Mao Zedong, merely became a member of the Politburo). The percentage of women in the Central Committee has also decreased from 7.9% in the 19th Party Congress to 5% in the 20th Party Congress.

Civilian Control Convention

Civilian control over the People's Liberation Army has been in place for more than 75 years. The controlling agent was the head of the state in the 1954 Constitution, then the Central Committee of the CCP in the 1975 and 1978 Constitutions, and finally, the Chairman of the National Military Commission. While civilian control over the army is the norm, a prudential rule has been to get and maintain support of the People's Liberation Army (PLA) in succession politics (Teiwes, 1984: 96). There is an implicit rule that no military leader can be a successor through coups. Military coups or military governments are illegitimate and unacceptable. To exclude military coups from succession politics, Chinese leaders have enforced the rule that successors cannot be military officers. The Party Constitution specifies that the chairperson of the Central Military Commission must not have any military title, which implies that civilians should be leaders of the military. The 19th and 20th Party Congresses reconfirmed the chairman control system: the "CCP upholds absolute control of the PLA and other people's forces". There have been more subtle attempts to reduce the influence of military power in succession politics, like cutting down the number of military leaders in the Politburo and introducing more civilian control over the army. No military leader has been a standing Politburo member since the 15th Party Congress.

Table 9.1 summarises and charts the frequency of the different succession conventions. It identifies the formal constitutional provisions and informal practices, recaps the significance and impact of succession politics, and offers comparative perspectives to give some insight into China's succession conventions.

Concluding Discussion

Table 9.1 highlights the patterns of authoritarian succession politics. Now let me sum up the distinguishing features of constitutional conventions in authoritarian constitutionalism.

First, the widespread view that succession conventions do not exist in China is a mistake. The view that authoritarian leaders disregard norms is a simplistic viewpoint. Authoritarianism needs conventions, and Xi Jinping needs constitutional conventions to rule. Although the succession conventions in China are weak, flexible, and under-institutionalised, they have constraining functions. Chinese succession rules played essential roles under both the Jiang and Hu governments. The latter was the first successful story of transferring power peacefully and completely. The existing succession conventions regulate and affect the behaviour of individual leaders and political institutions. Potential leaders like Deng Liqun are ruled out through the electoral rule, and others are ousted through lack of work experience qualifications or because of their age. The ideology norm for any successor is rooted in party–state constitutionalism, and this has become a standard practice in China's political system. The distributive norm decides who is most likely of the key leaders to hold critical official posts. These succession conventions are operative and workable and help strengthen party–state constitutionalism. Understanding this fundamental difference can help us problematise the assumption that China will follow the collapse of the Soviet Union – that the CCP will soon end its domination. The CCP has outperformed the former Communist Party of the Soviet Union in both its regulation of conventions and norm development. It circulates generational leadership, established an ideological norm that has replaced the traditional hereditary rule, and has maintained power distribution and Party–military conventions. As Frantz and Stein (2017: 940) find, "authoritarian regimes with succession rules last twice as long, on average, compared with those without them". However, with Xi's breach of specific rules, the risk for the Party is apparent. The weaker the succession conventions, the shorter the likely lifespan of such an authoritarian system.

Second, leaders in authoritarian regimes always have the discretionary power to make exceptions to rules and are quick to dismiss or abolish rules that constrain their power; hence, they show little interest in establishing a

Table 9.1 Succession Rule or Conventions and Frequency

Rules and Functions	*Constitutional Provisions*	*17th Party Congress (2007)*	*18th Party Congress (2012)*	*19th Party Congress (2017)*	*20th Party Congress (2022)*
Qualification Norm I: ideology norm (any successor is required to be committed to socialism)	All State and Party constitutions confirm socialism, Marxism-Leninism and Mao Zedong Thought, and the ruling class proletarian	√	√	√	√
Qualification Norm II: experience norm (the successor must work as the Party Secretary at the provincial level or a municipality and in critical national organisations)	Informal	√	√	√	√
Qualification Norm III: agelimit norm	Written into the Party document	√	√	√	√ (some modification)
Method Norm I, the election method: an election is indirect and limited, but an election can rule out unpopular leaders	Constitutionally, the NPC elects the President of the PRC, but it is only a semi-competitive election for the Central Committee	√	√	√	√
Method Norm II, the selection method: an elite opinion questionnaire introduced under Hu but abandoned under Xi	Informal practice	√	√	X	X
Operation Norm: distribution of the key organisations, forming a party–state system, and perfecting the model of the Soviet system	The 1982 Constitution confirmed President as the head of the state. The three-in-one leadership system has been established since 2004	√	√	√	√
Operation Norm, civilian control rule: prevents the formation of military regime	All the state and Party Constitutions confirm the civilian control rule	√	√	√	√
Operation Norm, two-term limit: the regularised peaceful transfer of political power	It was first introduced in the 1982 Constitution but was abolished in 2018		Hu-Xi	Xi ended the rule.	

set of clearly defined rules on succession matters. The main priority of leaders has instead been to maintain power, and even extend their power if possible. While there was a peaceful and orderly power transition from Jiang Zeming to Hu Jintao, this was essentially because Deng had pre-selected Hu as a successor to Jiang. Jiang faced resistance from within the Party if at any point he overturned Deng's decision. Hu's transition of power to Xi was an exceptional case primarily due to his weaker power status, the intervention of Jiang, and his personal characteristics without an ambitious desire.

Moreover, top leaders are at liberty to ignore the age-limit conventions. Deng had imposed the age-limit rule at a time it was an exception that he himself stay in power. The great irony was that to introduce and enforce the age-limit rule, Deng must maintain his power and stay longer. Jiang Zemin, too, had made himself an exception in 1997. The implicit rule is that all Politburo members except the Party Secretary should not seek another term at the age of 68. The examples of Deng and Jiang left the door open for Xi to make himself an exception. If he had followed the two-term limit rule, he would have retired at the 20th Party Congress in 2022 at the age of 69. Now that he has extended his tenure to another term, questions will persist as to whether he retires in 2027 at the 21st Party Congress at the age of 74 or at the 22nd Party Congress in 2032 at the age 79. The contemporary Chinese practice is of leaders thinking of themselves as exceptions to the age-limit rule. Such a practice of making an exception has historical roots in Chinese dynasties. The power and authority of emperors was so exceptional that no rules or laws could touch them.

Third, succession conventions are authoritarian and are often strategically selected and maintained to serve the purpose of the authoritarian system and its leaders. There are operative conventions such as the credential-based "work experience" norm which reflects the strength of a potential successor's ability to control the sizeable party–state machine. Similarly, the age-limit rule has been generally followed by almost all senior leaders except one top leader, as noted previously, because there is a large pool of potential leaders; the reproduction of young generation leaders helps to maintain the system. The distribution norm is also followed. A well-designed power arrangement is a good public image for the CCP, even though top leaders can still exercise their powers such as setting up small leadership teams to further concentrate power. The new conventions, like constitutional provisions for successors or the conventions concerning the democratic election of successors, are far from established. Written constitutional conventions do not matter to CPP. It has repeatedly demonstrated this. Lin Biao's status as a successor to Mao was written into the Party Constitution. The two-term rule which had long been written into the state constitution was finally abolished by Xi in 2018. Authoritarian leaders often violate the core norms that constrain their power but enforce other norms that can bolster the authoritarian system. The CCP has not produced democratic norms in succession politics.

References

Cheek, Timothy, Klaus Mühlhahn and Hans van de Ven. 2021. *The Chinese Communist Party: A Century in Ten Lives*, Cambridge University Press, Cambridge.

Dittmer, Lowell. 2015. *Liu Shaoqi and the Chinese Cultural Revolution*, Routledge, London.

Fewsmith, Joseph. 2003. "The Sixteen National Party Congress: The Succession That Did Not Happen", *The China Quarterly*, 173: 1–16.

Fewsmith, Joseph. 2021. *Rethinking Chinese Politics*, Cambridge University Press, Cambridge.

Frantz, Erica and Elizabeth A. Stein. 2017. "Countering Coups: Leadership Succession Rules in Dictatorships", *Comparative Political Studies*, 50(7): 935–962.

García, Helena Alviar and Günter Frankenberg, eds. 2019. *Authoritarian Constitutionalism: Comparative Analysis and Critique*, Elgar Publishers.

General Office of the Central Committee of the CCP. 2006. "*dǎng zhèng lǐngdǎo gànbù zhíwù rènqí zhàn háng guīdìng*" (*Interim Provisions on the Term of Office of Leading Party and Government Cadres*), https://news.12371.cn/2015/03/12/ARTI1426126246992108.shtml, accessed on 7 November 2022.

Gill, G. 2018. *Collective Leadership in Soviet Politics*, Palgrave Macmillan, Cham.

Gill, G. 2021. *Bridling Dictators: Eules and Authoritarian Politics*, Oxford University Press, Oxford.

Harding, H. 1987. *China's Second Revolution: Reform After Mao*, Allen & Unwin, Sydney.

Kissinger, Henry. 2011. *On China*, Penguin Press.

Miller, Alice. 2013. "The Work System of the Xi Jinping Leadership", *China Leadership Monitor*, 41, Spring.

Miller, Alice. 2018. "The 19th Central Committee Politburo", *China Leadership Monitor*, 55, Winter.

Nakazawa, K. 2022. "China's Elders Defend Party Charter from Xi Onslaught", *Nikkei Asia*, 3 November.

Nathan, Andrew. 2003. "China's Changing of the Guard: Authoritarian Resilience", *Journal of Democracy*, 14(1): 6–17.

Shambaugh, David. 2001. "The Dynamics of Elite Politics During the Jiang Era", *The China Journal*, 45: 101–111.

Shirk, Susan. 2022. "Xi Jinping Has Fallen into the Dictator Trap", *New York Times*, 14 October.

Tabeta, S. 2022. "Xi Promotes 'Aerospace Clique' to Counter U.S. as a Defense Power", *Nikkei Asia*, 22 October.

Teiwes, Frederick C. 1984. *Leadership, Legitimacy, and Conflict in China: From a Charismatic Mao to the Politics of Succession*, M.E. Sharpe, New York.

Tushnet, Mark. 2015. "Authoritarian Constitutionalism", *Cornell Law Review*, 100(2): 391–461.

Xinhua News. 2022. http://austoday.com.au/thread-610748-1-1.html, accessed on 7 November 2022.

Zeng, Jinghan. 2014. "Institutionalization and the Authoritarian Leadership in China: A Power Succession System with Chinese Characteristics", *Contemporary Politics*, 20(3).

Chapter 10

Constitutional Conventions in Czechia and Hungary

When Two Are Doing the Same, It Is Not Always the Same

David Kosař and Attila Vincze

In 2013, the then-Czech President Miloš Zeman claimed that "the concept of constitutional convention is completely idiotic". He added that "if they were really, constitutional conventions, they would somehow be enshrined in the constitution" – but because they are not, he is not bound by them and "has the sacred right to change conventions that are not enshrined in the constitution" (Werner & Wirnitzer, 2013). He was immediately rebuffed by politicians. For instance, Petr Pithart, a former Chairman of the Senate (upper chamber of the Czech Parliament), opposed that "paradoxically, what is not written in the constitution actually holds it together" (Pithart, 2013, 16). Scholars entered the debate soon after (Brunclík, 2021; Brunclík et al., 2023; Hájek, 2023).

The very fact that the president of the country publicly discusses constitutional conventions, albeit in a very specific manner, suggests that this concept has found some traction in Central Europe. However, it does not tell us much about how constitutional conventions are conceptualized in civil law countries. We examine two jurisdictions in Central Europe, Czechia and Hungary, to explore this question. We chose these two countries on the basis that they were the most similar cases (Hirschl, 2005). They share their communist and Austro-Hungarian legacies and both entered the European Union in the same year (2004), but their political development has varied significantly since 2010. While Hungary has witnessed the most severe de-democratization in the CEE (Halmai, 2012; Uitz, 2015; Scheppele, 2018), Czechia is still "careening"[1] rather than backsliding.[2]

The aim of this chapter is thus to explore whether there are any differences between the individual Czechia and Hungary cases concerning constitutional conventions, and if so, what explains these differences and what repercussions these differences have for the legal and political life of these countries. It

1 On the concept of democratic careening in general, see Slater (2013).

2 See Cianetti and Hanley (2021). Of course, there are considerable differences between Czechia and Slovakia (see Kosař & Vyhnánek, 2021).

DOI: 10.4324/9781003506577-10

shows that there are actually significant differences between these two countries. Czechia has embraced constitutional conventions – albeit in relatively few areas – and the Constitutional Court, as well as the Supreme Administrative Court, found some of them justiciable and even decisive for the outcome of some cases. In contrast, Hungary has so far resisted justiciability, as well as a thorough discussion of constitutional conventions.

We tentatively argue that this divergence between these two countries can be explained by the different levels of majoritarianism, the degree of stability of the political landscape and constitutional text, and the existence of an explicit rule of recognition in the constitution (that limits the sources of law to written law). In other words, a lower level of majoritarianism that requires greater cooperation between different constitutional actors, a stable political landscape and constitutional text, and the non-existence of an explicit rule of recognition in the constitution prioritizing codified law contribute to the emergence and embeddedness of constitutional conventions.

This chapter proceeds as follows. The first section briefly explains how Austrian and German legal thinking, which heavily influenced how Central European lawyers think about the law, treats constitutional conventions. The second section analyzes the conceptualization and use of constitutional conventions in Czechia. The third section explains the life of constitutional conventions in a hostile political context in Hungary. The fourth section provides preliminary explanations for why the transplantation of the concept of constitutional conventions yielded such different results in Central Europe. The fifth section concludes.

German and Austrian Legal Thinking Casts a Long Shadow on CEE Countries

Central European countries, the main focus of this study, were part of the Austro-Hungarian dual monarchy up until the end of the First World War. Due to this close historical, political, and cultural proximity, the constitutional traditions of Austria and Germany influenced the evolution of constitutional thinking in Central Europe to a great extent (Balthasar & Vincze, 2021).

Hence, to understand the role of constitutional conventions in Central Europe, it is necessary to briefly address how Austrian and German legal traditions treat them. For the purpose of this chapter, it suffices to say that Austrian and German legal thinking – as part of the civil law tradition (Merryman & Pérez-Perdomo, 2007) – prioritizes legal formalism, codification of law, a closed and clear system of the sources of law, and legal certainty.[3] This

3 Conventions or customs might be referred to if the codified law allows that, see e.g., § 10 Austrian Civil Code or § 346 German Code of Commerce (see Hufeld, 2014).

in turn framed how Central European lawyers think about sources of law, the relationship between law and the state, the division between law and politics, and the role of constitutional courts. All of these elements have repercussions on the conceptualization and the role of constitutional conventions.

In general, constitutional conventions in German-speaking countries are much less robust than those of the common law world. The main reason lies in the essentially codified nature of the law in those countries with an aspiration to achieve an all-encompassing written constitution, which is therefore rather hostile towards conventions, customs, and customary law (Kischel, 2015, 389-477). This is in stark contrast to most common law systems.

The traditional German and Austrian constitutional theory presupposes that a constitutional order was established to control, constrain, and organize the state and its organs, which were set up and constituted by the constitutions, meaning that they exist because the constitution says so. In doing so, they execute the powers conferred to them by the constitution. Hence, it would be a theoretical contradiction if constitutional bodies were allowed and empowered to set the rules they are obliged to follow (the classical opposition of *pouvoir constituant* and *pouvoir constitué*). These rather detailed rules have to explain how the constitutional bodies *should* work – regardless of how they actually work – because mere factuality or normality should not constitute any normativity.[4] Moreover, the continental constitutions are not only written but are rather detailed, leaving no need or little room for a constitutional convention to be established,[5] even if the length and the degree of definitiveness of the constitution in civil law countries varies.

Importantly, European civil law constitutional courts are also keener on adjudicating in politically sensitive conflicts of constitutional bodies, and the political question doctrine has not found much traction here.[6] This in turn further reduces the room for constitutional conventions and the need to foster them.[7] Finally, the German and Austrian constitutions are (relatively) easy to amend, especially in comparison with the U.S. Constitution. Precisely because the formal amendment of the legal framework is a more available

4 Hans Kelsen's pure theory of law is the most rigid one in this sense. German constitutional thinking, or at least a considerable fraction of it, is more sensible to factuality, e.g., Jellinek (1906, 1914).

5 E.g., the role and involvement of parliament in the conclusion of international treaties is governed by written rules, and therefore there is no need for a convention like the former so-called Ponsonby convention in the UK. The same applies to parliamentary approval to employ the armed forces, which is also governed by written provisions, in contrast to the war power in the UK (see McCormack, 2019).

6 The political question doctrine deems certain matters to be inappropriate for judicial review because discretionary power over them should be left to the politically accountable branches of the government (see Lechner & Zuck, 2011, 44–45).

7 Explain the establishment of conventions regarding the presidential powers in the USA by the limited availability of judicial review (see Bradley & Morrison, 2013).

tool, there is no such need for constitutional conventions to do the hard work and keep the constitution working (Masing, 2005).

In sum, Austrian and German constitutional thinking is rather hostile towards the concept of constitutional conventions, because constitutional conventions are perceived as political rather than legal phenomena. Therefore, they are theoretically also less relevant among legal scholars and judges. Nonetheless, contrary to theoretical opposition, a good many unwritten rules can be found in both constitutional systems, though they are less recognized by constitutional legal scholarship. Consequently, a practice that falls within the ambit of constitutional conventions in common law countries is not conceptualized that way in Germany and Austria. Constitutional conventions are undertheorized, their defining features – as well as their intellectual underpinnings – are rather blurry, and the distinctions among usages, constitutional conventions, customs, and customary law is rather fuzzy, which their rather marginal legal significance tries to explain (Morlok, 2002).

This analysis of how Austrian and German legal thinking approach constitutional conventions is crucial for understanding the divergent paths of constitutional conventions in Czechia and Hungary, including those discussed in what follows. However, despite geographical and cultural proximity, each country has had a slightly different historical trajectory. We explore these different paths in the following section.

Czechia: The Embracing of Constitutional Conventions by Courts, Downplayed by Other Actors

Czechia became an independent state only in 1993 after the division of Czechoslovakia. Although Czechoslovakia introduced many features of socialist law during the communist era,[8] Czechia historically belongs to the civil law tradition and, more specifically, to its Austrian subfamily.[9] Thus, the Czech legal culture has traditionally been reluctant to accept unwritten sources of law.

Despite this fact, constitutional conventions are crucial, especially in the framework-of-government part of modern Czech constitutionalism, as they provide the necessary glue for the smooth functioning of inter-branch and intra-branch relationships. Some of those conventions have even been found justiciable by Czech courts. At the same time, it is fair to say that constitutional conventions are the most contested source of Czech constitutional law,

8 We leave aside here whether socialist law is a separate family of law, distinct from the civil law family, or merely a subfamily of the civil law tradition. For a concise summary of these debates, see J. Quigley (1989).

9 Note that Czech lands were part of the Austrian Empire from the end of the Thirty Years' War in 1648 until 1918.

and that their normative implications in interpreting constitutional norms have been disputed.

On the one hand, the Czech Constitutional Court and apex ordinary courts have on several occasions confirmed the binding nature of constitutional conventions and sometimes even engaged in nuanced debates about the extent to which constitutional conventions may change the meaning of written constitutional norms.[10] As early as in 1997, the Constitutional Court held that constitutional conventions are sources of Czech law, albeit without further elaboration.[11] The first big case in which constitutional conventions played a key role concerned the President's power to appoint a Governor of the Czech National Bank. When President Václav Havel intended to appoint a new Governor in 2000, the then-Prime Minister (PM) Miloš Zeman challenged this act before the Constitutional Court. Zeman argued that the President could not appoint alone but had to seek countersignature from the PM. The majority of the Constitutional Court eventually sided with Havel, arguing that the newly established constitutional convention altered the meaning of the Constitution.[12] The minority disagreed because this rule had not been observed for long enough by several presidents and there were even some examples of the opposite practice. According to them, the *usus longaevus* requirement of the constitutional convention thus had not been met. Paradoxically, Zeman himself benefited from this ruling a decade later, when he became President, as he could choose the Governor he wanted without consulting the PM.

A perhaps even more consequential dispute concerned the appointment of judges. In 2005, President Václav Klaus refused to appoint 34 judges nominated by the government, allegedly because they were too young. Most of the rejected judicial nominees sued the President in administrative courts, but only Mr. Langer pursued this dispute until the end. Here it suffices to say that, according to the Supreme Administrative Court, a constitutional convention had evolved that the President, when faced with a governmental recommendation of a certain candidate to be appointed as a judge, had either to appoint him or her as a judge or issue a reasoned individual decision justifying his refusal on statutory grounds.[13] This constitutional convention thus limited the President's unfettered discretion.

10 For example, in Judgment of the Constitutional Court of 20 June 2001, Pl. ÚS 14/01, *Appointment of the Governor of the Czech National Bank*; and Judgment of the Supreme Administrative Court of 21 May 2008, 4 Ans 9/2007, *Langer.*

11 Judgment of the Constitutional Court of 17 December 1997, Pl. ÚS 33/97, *Lapse of Time.*

12 See Judgment of the Constitutional Court of 20 June 2001, Pl. ÚS 14/01, *Appointment of the Governor of the Czech National Bank.* Note that there is a lively debate to what extent constitutional conventions were decisive for the outcome of this judgment (see Kysela, 2008; Kindlová, 2008).

13 See Judgment of the Supreme Administrative Court of 21 May 2008, 4 Ans 9/2007, *Langer.*

On the other hand, some key constitutional actors have not accepted this position and reject constitutional conventions. For instance, Václav Klaus did not respect the *Langer* judgment. He never appointed Mr. Langer to judicial office and he never issued a reasoned decision justifying his position. Mr. Langer received some compensation and the *Langer* judgment has not been implemented. A subsequent Czech President, Miloš Zeman, went even further. He labeled the concept of constitutional convention "idiotic" and made it clear that he would not let himself be bound by unwritten rules (Werner & Wirnitzer, 2013).

Czech scholars initially lagged behind the apex courts in addressing constitutional conventions. Most traditional scholars trained in the communist era dismissed unwritten sources of law such as customs and conventions, or spent only few lines on them.[14] The case law of the Constitutional Court and the Supreme Administrative Court spurred a lively debate among younger legal scholars, however, more recently joined by political scientists. What complicates the debate, however, is unclear conceptualization. While scholars agree that constitutional conventions are relevant to the Czech constitutional system, the terminology and elements – as well as repercussions of conventions – are blurred. The majority of scholars use the term "constitutional conventions" (*ústavní zvyklosti*) (Kindlová, 2008; Klíma, 2016; Gerloch, 2021; Brunclík & Kubát, 2021; Brunclík, 2021; Hájek, 2023), but others also refer to "legal customs" (*právní obyčej*) (Kysela, 2008, 2014; Píša, 2014; Škop et al., 2019; Gerloch, 2021), "observations" (*observance*) (Filip, 2003), "political conventions" (*politické zvyklosti*) (Klíma et al., 2005), "parliamentary conventions" (*parlamentní zvyklosti*) (Wintr, 2010, 2022; Škop 2018; Škop et al., 2019), or "ceremonial conventions" (*ceremoniální zvyklosti*) (Pavlíček, 2015). Unfortunately, some authors distinguish between these concepts, whereas others use them synonymously. To make things even more challenging, the English term "convention" can be translated into Czech in two different ways (*zvyklost* and *konvence*), which is particularly tricky as some authors give each of these two words a different substantive meaning (Kysela, 2008, 2014; Píša, 2014).

As to the elements of constitutional conventions, only political scientists have been clear and transparent in their conceptualization and operationalization of constitutional conventions. Their starting point is the three-prong Jennings test, but they tend to prioritize the number of precedents as a determinative element of the existence of constitutional conventions (Brunclík & Kubát, 2021; Brunclík, 2021; Hájek, 2023). In contrast, legal scholars either (often implicitly) pay more attention to the reason behind the convention

14 E.g., see Knapp (1995), Boguszak (2004) and Gerloch (2021) For an exception to this rule among senior scholars, see Filip (2003). For a more generous role of unwritten law advocated by younger legal theorists, see Sobek (2008).

and the acceptance of the rule by the relevant actors (Kindlová, 2008; Wintr, Antoš & Kysela, 2016; Píša, 2014; Kysela, 2008, 2014), or specify two defining features of conventions based on customary international law[15] – *usus longeus* and *opinio juris* (Gerloch, 2021) – but they tend to prioritize the number of precedents as a determinative element of the existence of constitutional conventions (Brunclík & Kubát, 2021; Brunclík, 2021; Hájek, 2023). Interestingly, unwritten law has also attracted renewed attention from civil law scholars as the new Civil Code, adopted in 2012, embraces conventions and customs both in civil and commercial law (Melzer, 2011; Tichý, 2014; Melzer & Tégl, 2013; Lavický, 2014; Horák, 2022). This might have a spill-over effect on the debate on constitutional conventions in the near future.

The status of constitutional conventions in Czech constitutionalism is thus not settled. The precise requirements for practice to become a constitutional convention with normative consequences are also unclear. Some justices of the Constitutional Court tried to transplant the criteria for customary international law, namely *usus longeus* and *opinion iuris*, into Czech constitutionalism.[16] However, the majority of the Constitutional Court has employed much looser criteria in its case law.[17] The same applies to the Supreme Administrative Court.[18]

We must add one more caveat here. We may distinguish between two types of constitutional conventions in the Czech Republic. The first type concerns the development of constitutional conventions in areas that typically end up before the Constitutional Court, such as the appointment of judges or key members of "the fourth branch"[19] constitutional bodies such as the Governor of the Czech National Bank or the president of the Supreme Audit Office. In these separation of powers issues, the Constitutional Court has a major say and may contribute to the formation of constitutional conventions. The only constitutional organ against which it is sometimes difficult to

15 This test was introduced to the Czech legal scholarship by Miloslava Kindlová, who was trained in Oxford (see Kindlová, 2008).

16 Dissenting Opinion of Jiří Malenovský in Judgment of the Constitutional Court of 20 June 2001, Pl. ÚS 14/01, *Appointment of the Governor of the Czech National Bank*.

17 Apart from the judgments Pl. ÚS 33/97 *Lapse of Time* and Pl. ÚS 14/01 *Appointment of the Governor of the Czech National Bank* discussed previously; see also Pl. ÚS 6/07; Pl. ÚS 24/07; Pl. ÚS 13/05 zákon o střetu zájmů; disent EW k Pl. ÚS 87/06 Brožová v. Klaus IV; disent JMus&PR k Pl. ÚS 24/07, § 12; Pl. ÚS 87/06 Brožová v. Klaus IV; Pl. ÚS 36/17 Návrh na zrušení amnestie 2013, § 34 a 36; a Pl. ÚS 6/21 Veto, § 59.

18 See Judgment of the Supreme Administrative Court of 21 May 2008, 4 Ans 9/2007, *Langer*; Decision of the Supreme Administrative Court of 13 December 2017, Vol 84/2017–175, § 94; and Joint Dissenting Opinion of Judges Zdeněk Kühn, Radan Malík and Miloslav Výborný in Decision of the Supreme Administrative Court of 24 June 2014, Vol 16/2014–78, § 18.

19 On fourth branch institutions, see (Tushnet, 2021; Khaitan, 2021).

enforce the Court's ruling is the President, but even he is under pressure from other politicians and public opinion.

The second type of constitutional convention arises in situations that are typically outside the reach of the Constitutional Court, because the relevant constitutional actors do not want to involve the Court and prefer to sort out their conflicts politically. These situations include in particular the relationship between the other two branches, namely between the President and the Parliament and between the President and the government. In this area, three strong personalities – Václav Havel, Václav Klaus, and Miloš Zeman – in the office of the President, each having a different vision, have led to a divergent practice that has problematized the establishment of stable constitutional conventions. For instance, President Miloš Zeman, in an unprecedented way, intervened in the composition of Bohuslav Sobotka's government (2014–2017) by de facto vetting several ministers on political grounds, despite the broad consensus that the President cannot arbitrarily decide to reject a candidate who has been proposed by the PM. The fact that it took Zeman 83 days to swear in Sobotka's government broke the emerging convention that the President must act without undue delay. To mention another example, on two occasions Zeman allowed the government appointed by him to run the country without passing a vote of confidence for several months, and the Chamber of Deputies could not force the appointed by not approved government to face a vote of no confidence. This practice encroached upon the powers of the Chamber of Deputies, to which the government is supposed to be responsible (Kosař & Vyhnánek, 2021).

In other cases, also outside the ambit of judicial review, Czech presidents, by refusing to follow the Constitution, have forced other actors to create a convention in return. For instance, under the Constitution, the President must either sign a bill or return it to the Parliament for reconsideration. This is a standard suspensive veto. However, President Klaus and President Zeman, when they disagreed with the law, sometimes neither signed nor vetoed a bill. Sometimes they behaved in this way because they knew that their veto would be overruled. In other cases, they appealed to the Czech electorate and used this move as a political gesture to attract the attention of their voters. These acts of defiance led to a new convention that assumes that when the President neither signs nor vetoes a bill within 15 days this "non-signature" does not affect the validity of the statute which enters into force even without the President's signature. This was actually the only possible solution, as otherwise the President, by doing nothing, would have an absolute veto.

Hungary: The Uneasy Life of Constitutional Conventions in a Hostile Political Context

The Hungarian constitutional development has been quite bumpy during the last century, a fact that has worked against establishing long-lasting conventional or customary rules. Up until the end of the Second World War, Hungary, as a monarchy, had an uncodified historical constitution full of doctrines and conventions similar to the British constitution. This old-fashioned constitutionalism was replaced by a codified one conceived under the communist party dictatorship that perceived law as an instrument for exercising political power rather than constraining it. Therefore, the black letter law, as an emanation of the will of the party, was to be obeyed. This was an extremely formalistic attitude casting a long shadow on legal thinking in Hungary. Law is still perceived as a normative text, which needs to be interpreted, but in doing so actual practice or institutional design is taken less into account.

Nonetheless, the hastily drafted Constitution of 1989 left many lacunae which were to be clarified. Therefore, the question also arose as to whether customs, conventions, or memoranda of understanding could play any role in constitutional interpretation as a bridge between the text and the practice. This question was decided very early on in 1991, as the ambit of the powers of the President as the commander-in-chief was questioned. The President understood this position as a power to command the armed forces – contrary to the view of the government, which perceived the President as a mere ceremonial figurehead without any actual influence on the armed forces. The President put forward the idea that this question should be decided as a memorandum of understanding between him and the PM. The Constitutional Court made very clear that no conventions, usages, or memoranda could govern politics, because that would contradict the very sense of a constitution which has to be followed and not constructed by the politicians.[20] The constitution was – quite naïvely – understood as a closed and single system of rules, which was to be interpreted solely by the Constitutional Court and not by other actors.

This had several consequences. First, it officially rooted out any customary or conventional rules from constitutional scholarship, and they are not referred to among the sources of law at all (Jakab, 2020, 913–915; Petrétei, 2013, 161–162). Second, it also led to a modus operandi in which the Constitutional Court was supposed to resolve every political conflict employing an abstract interpretation of the constitution. Kim Lane Scheppele famously referred to this regime as "courtocracy" (Scheppele, 2007, 2005), highlighting that the interpretative decisions of the Constitutional Court went as far as to produce informal constitutional changes (Drinóczi, 2020).

Although the Constitutional Court claimed that practices, usages, and routine mechanisms are not part of the constitutional system, it could not get rid of them completely. The most vivid example was the so-called theory of living law, which equated the content of legal rules with their actual

20 Decision of the Constitutional Court of Hungary 48/1991 (IX. 26.) AB.

application (Sólyom, 2001, 296–299). By applying this theory, the Constitutional Court – probably unwillingly – also acknowledged customary law[21] and even the concept of *desuetude*.[22] Although this decision made a big splash, the Constitutional Court did not develop any doctrinal underpinning for that theory and applied it only once.

Despite the theoretical opposition, some constitutional conventions have been established, mainly under the radar of the Constitutional Court and the scholarship. The exercise of the powers of the President or parliamentary affairs became subject to habits and usages which later hardened into convention even if nobody called them that: the appointment of the PM (Horváth, 2014), the nomination of candidates for key constitutional posts (chief justice, ombudsman), and ministerial as well as cabinet responsibility were especially governed by unwritten rules (Vincze, 2021a). These were partially created or specified the ambit of power (*consuetude*), like nominating the leader of the strongest parliamentary coalition for the position of the PM, or derogated from existing powers (*desuetude*) and constrained the exercise of powers existing on paper, like the power of the President to initiate a referendum, which has never been exercised since 1989, and is not expected to be exercised in the future.

The significance of conventional rules became particularly apparent if there was no historical precedent to follow like in 2004, when the PM stepped down (Vincze, 2021a, 2021b), and all actors were insecure how to proceed. The same nervousness prevailed between 2005 and 2010 as the then-President, László Sólyom, decided not to follow the earlier established practice of consulting the parliamentary parties before nominating key constitutional functionaries. The parties retaliated to this disregard of convention by not voting for them, regardless of their skills, competences, and merits. The conventions remained, however, few in number and undertheorized.

Since the landslide victory of the right-wing coalition of the Hungarian Civic Alliance (Fidesz) in 2010, the whole constitutional system has been redesigned. Although the newly enacted 2011 Hungarian Basic Law contains many elements of the 1989 Constitution and has implemented a huge chunk of the case law of the Constitutional Court (formalizing the former informal constitutional changes) (Vincze, 2012; Jakab & Sonnevend, 2013), the 2011 Basic Law was a fresh start in several respects: the ruling coalition commanded a two-thirds majority in Parliament, which allowed it to tailor-make

21 Decision of the Constitutional Court of Hungary 57/1991 (XI. 8.) AB. Interestingly, the Constitutional Court had not had a properly enacted order of procedures for more than two decades, and it was substituted for by customary law.

22 For this concept, see Richard Albert (2014). A rare example of *desuetude* was the duty of the PM to report on European Council meetings, which had never been observed and was later also formally repealed. The power to decide on conflict of powers of constitutional bodies has only been law in the books and never been applied (see Vincze, 2009).

any laws (including the Basic Law), as well as to appoint whomever to whatever position according to current needs and priorities without the minority's consent. This of course reduced the need to seek compromises or to observe conventions and usages, culminating in an instrumental approach to the law as a tool for achieving political goals. This understanding is embedded in a formalistic legal culture explicitly enumerating the sources of law, and denying the legal quality of other sources like conventions.[23]

The election of the President of the Supreme Court demonstrates this very vividly. Although it has not been an explicit requirement, the Chief Justice has, since the end of the Second World War, always been elected from among the judges of the general courts. This practice turned into a convention. This was also the ground – or at least the smokescreen – for not appointing Mr. András Baka, a former judge of the European Court of Human Rights (ECtHR), as the Chief Justice of the Hungarian Supreme Court in 2008, because he had no previous experience within the Hungarian judiciary. Baka was appointed eventually in 2009, but he was elected only under the pretext that he had in the meantime gathered the necessary experiences on the national bench. The Act on the Judiciary in 2011 made this requirement more explicit, stipulating that a candidate had to have five years' experience as a judge in Hungary to be eligible to become Chief Justice of the new Supreme Court, called Kúria.

Nonetheless, this was again amended in 2019 to make way for Mr. Varga, who is a professor of law and has worked as a deputy general prosecutor and a constitutional justice, but never as a sitting judge (Kazai & Kovács, 2020). The Hungarian Judicial Council, a consultative body of judges, pointed out that he lacked experience in the general judiciary, which is by convention a prerequisite for becoming Chief Justice.[24] The rule has not only been observed for several decades but also has a rationale: a successful career within the general judiciary is the key for augmenting reputation and respect which are necessary conditions for effective leadership of the general judiciary. Orbán's government brushed aside this argument, arguing that the black letter law did not require any such work experience.[25] Nevertheless, this formalist response did not end the conflict. The ongoing conflicts between the Chief Justice and the Hungarian Judicial Council – e.g., regarding judicial ethics, judicial appointments, and the promotion of his wife – show that Mr. Varga, as well as Orbán's government, have paid the price for disobeying the conventional rule.

23 Article T of the 2011 Basic Law.

24 The Hungarian National Judicial Council (*Országos Bírói Tanács*) should not be conflated with the National Judicial Office (*Országos Bírósági Hivatal*) established by Viktor Orbán in 2012 and packed with his protégés.

25 This was criticized "as an attempt to submit the judiciary to the will of the legislative branch, in violation of the principle of separation of powers" Rule of law Report, Hungary 2021 (see Kazai & Kovács, 2020).

Interestingly, even though the new 2011 Basic Law expressly refers to historical traditions and requires the Basic Law to be interpreted in accordance with them, this was not taken as an inspiration for acknowledging the existence of constitutional conventions (Vincze, 2020). The best example of this phenomenon might be the obstruction of the legislative process by blocking the seat of the speaker of the Parliament to make it impossible to enact a new bill in December 2018. The Constitutional Court did not attribute any legal value to the circumstance that the speaker could not reach his conventional place and conduct parliamentary business as usual.[26]

Therefore, the overwhelming majority of scholarship in Hungary is rather descriptive and analyzes the case law of the Constitutional Court primarily from a doctrinal point of view. This scholarship does not pay much attention to practices, usages, or conventions because they are regarded as simple facts or habits without any normative effect (Petrétei, 2013 161–162; Sólyom, 2001, 296–299). In this respect, the positivist legal tradition has retained its powerful influence. The gap between normative and living constitutionalism has not been examined thoroughly in legal literature. Likewise, sociological constitutionalism and empirical methods have not found traction in Hungarian legal scholarship. Only recently has some empirical research emerged focusing on how institutions actually work (Jakab, 2021) and how constitutional conventions influence the actual practice of institutions (Vincze, 2021a, 2021b).

Why Czechia and Hungary Approach Constitutional Conventions Differently: Tentative Explanations

We have shown in this chapter that Czechia and Hungary diverge significantly regarding the conceptualization, utilization, and level of judicialization of constitutional conventions. Czechia has – albeit in relatively few areas – embraced constitutional conventions, and its Constitutional Court as well as its Supreme Administrative Court has found some of them justiciable and even decisive for the outcome of some cases. In contrast, Hungary has so far resisted the meaningful use – as well as thorough discussion – of constitutional conventions.

This divergent development begs the question of why there are such huge differences between the two countries, despite their common legal culture and similar communist heritage. We provide three tentative explanations for divergent approaches to constitutional conventions in these Visegrad countries: (1) the level of majoritarianism; (2) the level of stability of the written constitutional law and the surrounding political landscape; and (3) the

26 Decision 15/2019. (IV. 17.) AB. Critically, see Zoltán Szente (2019).

existence of an explicit rule of recognition that includes an exhaustive list of sources of law.

The first explanation is a different level of majoritarianism in the two countries under study, which results from a complex interplay of the voting system, the number of chambers of Parliament, the relative strength of the President and the PM of the country, the strength of the major political parties, and the pre-communist legacies.

Czechia is clearly the least majoritarian by institutional design, as well as in practice. It features a bicameral Parliament, each chamber being elected in a different cycle and via a different voting system, and a very proportional voting system for the Chamber of Deputies which is vigorously guarded by the Constitutional Court.[27] Moreover, its President is much stronger de facto than "on paper". This feature, inherited from the interwar First Czechoslovak Republic, weakens the PM and results in a two-headed executive. The country has also inherited a relatively strong democratic tradition from the interwar era, which is still perceived as a "golden age" of Czechoslovak constitutionalism (Kosař, Baroš & Dufek, 2019). Moreover, no political party since Czech independent statehood began in 1993 has managed to win a majority of seats in the Chamber of Deputies, which has resulted in rather fragile coalitions. Only one such coalition had a constitutional majority in both chambers of the Parliament in the late 1990s, but it lost it before it could achieve anything. In such an environment, it is almost impossible to change the status quo through constitutional amendment. The political actors thus must play according to the existing rules and find a reasonably predictable way to interact with their opponents. Since there are several relatively strong competing actors and a high degree of uncertainty regarding future development, they have to create, invoke, and eventually uphold constitutional conventions.

Contrary to Czechia, Hungary had limited democratic experience to follow in 1989, since interwar Hungary had strong authoritarian features. The Parliament, also contrary to the historical past, has only one chamber that decides every important question from constitution-making to appointments, without any proper checks and balances apart from those of the Constitutional Court (this, of course, made the court an ideal target for capture). The members of the Parliament have always been elected by means of a mixed (but not proportional) electoral system preferring and producing stable majorities, which has of course reduced the need to make compromises and as such to establish a conventional modus operandi. Some decisions required a two-thirds majority – appointing some key functionaries, adopting some special acts – and requested the consent of the minority. This logically fostered the adoption of some conventional rules (like the nomination

27 We cannot discuss these features in detail here (but see Kosař & Vyhnánek, 2021).

of constitutional justices). Moreover, the President was rather weak (Vincze, 2021a), and therefore, there were very few constraints on the dominant position of the Parliament. All in all, Hungary has always had a majoritarian democracy. Since 2010, Viktor Orbán has commanded a two-thirds majority in the Parliament, enabling him to tailor-make the legal framework according to his current needs. His charisma is built on the perception that he can bend the legal system to his will, and therefore unwritten conventional rules have no role to play other than as window dressing (Vincze, 2020). The few conventions that are still observed – like those regarding the formation of the government, or the limited role of the President – serve mainly as the façade of democratic legitimacy, and do not constrain the PM at all (Brunclík et al., 2023).

The second and related factor is the relative stability of written constitutional law and the surrounding political landscape. When it comes to written constitutional law, Czechia differs from the other three Visegrad countries, as its 1993 Constitution is almost untouched,[28] and apart from the introduction of the direct presidential elections in 2013, no major constitutional amendment[29] has been adopted (Kosař & Vyhnánek, 2021). In contrast, Hungary undertook major constitutional overhauls. Orbán's Hungary in 2011 adopted a brand new constitution, which explicitly stresses discontinuity with the previous regime (Vincze, 2012). This major overhaul enabled the capture of key institutions like the Constitutional Court and the Supreme Court, redesigning electoral laws and cementing the power of the governing party.

These changes in written constitutional law often reflect broader changes in the political landscape. Orbán's takeover of power in 2010, the meltdown of his opposition, and the subsequent democratic backsliding are well-known and documented (Halmai, 2012; Uitz, 2015; Scheppele, 2022). We cannot delve into more details of the political development of each of these two countries. Here it suffices to say that constitutional conventions need legal and political stability to emerge and flourish. Since 1993, such a convention-friendly environment has existed only in Czechia. In contrast, Hungary has witnessed major regime changes that complicated or stalled emerging constitutional conventions and may even have killed off existing ones.

Third, it seems to matter whether the given constitutional system has an explicit "rule of recognition" in its constitution that exhaustively determines the permissible sources of law. Recall that Hart's "rule of recognition" is a rule that determines which rules are binding (Hart, 1994). This (secondary)

28 As of 31 March 2023, it has been amended 8 times.

29 We leave aside here the so-called Euro Amendments that had a profound impact on both Visegrad countries by embracing EU membership and EU law, because they were adopted in all Visegrad countries and because the Euro Amendments did not in themselves affect the domestic political landscape.

meta-rule underlying any legal system sets out the criteria for the legal validity of other (primary) rules and also specifies the order of precedence among the sources of law (Shapiro, 2009; Raz, 1992). It thus determines what counts as law in a given system.

If we turn back to the comparison between Czechia and Hungary, we can see that the country that is more hostile to constitutional conventions has an explicit constitutional provision that stipulates the sources of law, which do not include conventions. This is the case with Hungary. Article T(1) of the Hungarian Constitution stipulates that "A generally binding rule of conduct may be laid down by a piece of legislation which is made by a body with legislative competence".[30]

In contrast, Czechia's Constitution does not contain a similar provision. This makes the Czech legal system far more open to embracing constitutional conventions, as their use by law-applying officials does not violate the constitutional norm. Importantly, the lack of a binding list of sources of law on the constitutional level also widens the playing field for unwritten sources of law such as conventions and customs on the statutory level. This eventually materialized in Czechia, where the new 2013 Civil Code acknowledges and embraces conventions as relevant sources of law in disputes between individuals, as well as in business disputes.[31] This development on the statutory level may – in the long run – change the way Czech lawyers think about unwritten law such as conventions and customs more generally and increase the acceptance of constitutional conventions. In Hungary, such development is highly unlikely, as Article T(1) is engraved in the minds of Hungarian lawyers and blocks a lot of thinking about constitutional conventions.

Conclusion

The experience from two countries in Central Europe shows that constitutional conventions may play an important role in constitutional architecture within post-communist democracies belonging to the civil law family, but

30 Article T(2) then specifies what is meant by "legislation":

> Legislation shall include Acts of Parliament, government decrees, orders by the Governor of the National Bank of Hungary, orders by the Prime Minister, ministerial decrees, orders by autonomous regulatory bodies and local ordinances. Legislation shall also include orders issued by the National Defence Council and the President of the Republic during any state of national crisis or state of emergency.

31 See Arts. 9(2), 10(2) and 558 of the New Civil Code (Law no. 89/2013 Coll.). This has resulted in a burgeoning literature on the role of customs and conventions in Czech civil law see Horák (2022) and virtually any leading commentary on the abovementioned articles of the New Civil Code.

only under certain conditions. Based on the divergent developments regarding constitutional conventions in Czechia and Hungary, we identified three factors that contribute to the emergence and embeddedness of constitutional conventions: lower level of majoritarianism that requires greater cooperation between different constitutional actors, stable political landscape and constitutional text, and non-existence of an explicit rule of recognition in the constitution (that limits the sources of law to written law).

Hence, Czechia features the least majoritarian political system (featuring a strong upper chamber of Parliament, a strong President, and a strong Constitutional Court), has not witnessed any major constitutional amendment nor democratic backsliding, does not have an explicit rule of recognition containing the permissible sources of law in the constitution, and is most open to constitutional conventions. In contrast, constitutional conventions face a far more hostile environment in Hungary, which features a more majoritarian democracy, has witnessed democratic backsliding since 2010, has a brand new constitution, and stipulates an explicit rule of recognition in its constitution that prioritizes written law.

The conceptual debates about constitutional conventions in Central Europe are still rather basic. Both Czechia and Hungary struggled with how to make constitutional conventions, transplanted from the Anglophone context, "fit" into the categorization of sources of law in Germanic legal culture. In Central Europe, constitutional conventions are more than a settled practice, but at the same time, something less than a constitutional custom (Brunclík et al., 2023). Yet, by finding constitutional conventions justiciable, the Czech Constitutional Court blurred these categories and moved away from the traditional Westminster understanding of conventions.

At the same time, recent Anglo-American scholarship has challenged the outdated Diceyan understanding of conventions and has shown that there is no shared "Commonwealth approach" to the treatment of constitutional conventions and that some Commonwealth courts do and even should enforce conventions (Ahmed et al., 2019a, 2019b; Harding, 2022). This new strand of scholarship changed the anchor of debates on constitutional conventions in Central Europe but has not been so far – to our knowledge – properly reflected in Czech or Hungarian legal scholarship. Hopefully, Central European scholars and courts start soon engaging with this new scholarship and carefully adjusting conventions to their legal culture. If that happens, we believe that Central European countries may contribute to the global debates on constitutional conventions.[32]

32 This is already happening (see Brunclík et al., 2023).

Funding Statement

The research leading to this article (since all other articles you lowercase a) has received funding from the European Research Council (ERC) under the European Union's Horizon 2020 research and innovation program (INFINITY, grant agreement no. 101002660).

References

Ahmed, F, Albert, R & Perry, A, 2019a, 'Judging Constitutional Conventions', *International Journal of Constitutional Law*, vol. 17, no. 3, pp. 787–806.

Ahmed, F, Albert, R & Perry, A, 2019b, 'Enforcing Constitutional Conventions', *International Journal of Constitutional Law*, vol. 17, no. 4, pp. 1146–1165.

Albert, R, 2014, 'Constitutional Amendment by Constitutional Desuetude', *American Journal of Comparative Law*, vol. 62, no. 3, pp. 641–686.

Balthasar, A, & Vincze, A (eds.), 2021, *Hundert Jahre österreichisches Bundes-Verfassungsgesetz: Die Perspektive von außen*, Wien: Jan Sramek Verlag.

Boguszak, Jiří, et al., 2004, *Teorie práva*, 2. vydání, Praha: ASPI.

Bradley, CA & Morrison, TW, 2013, 'Presidential Power, Historical Practice, and Legal Constraint', *Columbia Law Review*, vol. 113, no. 7, pp. 1097–1162.

Brunclík, M, 2021, 'Three-Fold Gap: Researching Constitutional Conventions in the Czech Republic', *Politologický časopis – Czech Journal of Political Science*, vol. 28, no. 1, pp. 20–36.

Brunclík, M & Kubát, M, 2021, 'Constitutional Conventions in Central Europe: Presidents in Government Formation Process', *Problems of Post-Communism*, vol. 42, no. 1, pp. 42–54.

Brunclík, M, et al., 2023, *Power Beyond Constitutions: Presidential Constitutional Conventions in Central Europe*, Palgrave Macmillan.

Cianetti, L & Hanley, S, 2021, 'The End of the Backsliding Paradigm', *Journal of Democracy*, vol. 32, no. 1, pp. 66–80.

Drinóczi, T, 2020, *Informális alkotmánymódosítás alkotmányértelmezéssel az alkotmánybíráskodás és a kormányzás összehasonlító és alkotmánytani elemzése*, Budapest: Dialóg Campus.

Filip, J, 2003, *Ústavní právo České republiky. 1. Základní pojmy a instituce. Ústavní základy ČR*, 4. vydání, Brno: Masarykova univerzita – Doplněk.

Gerloch, A, 2021, *Teorie práva*, Plzeň: Aleš Čeněk.

Hájek, L, 2023, 'Idiotic or Columbo's Wife? Constitutional Conventions in the Czech Republic', *East European Politics and Societies*, vol. 37, no. 4, pp. 1425–1447.

Halmai, G, 2012, 'From the 'Rule of Law Revolution' to the Constitutional Counter-Revolution in Hungary', in Benedek, W & Benoît-Rohmer, F (eds.), *European Yearbook of Human Rights*, Vienna: Neuer Wissenschaftlicher Verlag, pp. 367–384.

Harding, A, 2022, 'Conventions and Practical Interpretation in Westminster-Type Constitutional Systems', *International Journal of Constitutional Law*, vol. 20, no. 5, pp. 1914–1936.

Hart, HLA, 1994, *The Concept of Law*, 2nd ed., Oxford: Clarendon Press.

Hesse, K, 1959, *Die normative Kraft der Verfassung*, Tübingen: Mohr Siebeck.

Hirschl, R, 2005, 'The Question of Case Selection in Comparative Constitutional Law', *The American Journal of Comparative Law*, vol. 53, no. 1, pp. 125–156.

Horák, O, 2022, 'Obyčejové právo v českém právním řádu', *Právník*, vol. 161, no. 5, pp. 442–452.

Horváth, P, 2014, *Pártok és koalíciók,* Budapest: Gondolat.
Hufeld, U, 2014, 'Urkundlichkeit und Publizität der Verfassung', in Isensee, J & Kirchhof, P (eds.), *Handbuch des Staatsrechts 12: Normativität und Schutz der Verfassung*, C. F. Müller.
Jakab, A, 2020, 'A jogforrási rendszer', in Csink, L, Schanda, B & Varga, ZSA (eds.), *A magyar közjog alapintézményei*, Budapest: Pázmány Press, pp. 865–918.
Jakab, A, 2021, 'Informal Institutional Elements as Both Preconditions and Consequences of Effective Formal Legal Rules: The Failure of Constitutional Institution Building in Hungary', *The American Journal of Comparative Law*, vol. 20, no. 1, pp. 1–41.
Jakab, A & Sonnevend, P, 2013, 'Continuity with Deficiencies: The New Basic Law of Hungary', *European Constitutional Law Review*, vol. 9, no. 1, pp. 102–138.
Jellinek, G, 1914, *Allgemeine Staatslehre,* 3rd ed., Berlin: O. Häring.
Jellinek, G, 1906, *Verfassungsänderung und Verfassungswandlung,* Berlin: O. Häring.
Kazai, VZ & Kovács, A, 2020, 'The Last Days of the Independent Supreme Court of Hungary?' *Verfassungsblog*, https://verfassungsblog.de/the-last-days-of-the-independent-supreme-court-of-hungary/
Khaitan, T, 2021, 'Guarantor Institutions', *Asian Journal of Comparative Law*, vol. 16, no. 1, pp. 1–20.
Kindlová, M, 2008, 'Ústavní zvyklosti jako součást ústavy (komparace commonwealthského přístupu a judikatury Ústavního soudu ČR)', in Klíma, K & Jirásek, J (eds.), *Pocta Jánu Gronskému,* Plzeň: Vydavatelství a nakladatelství Aleš Čeněk, pp. 300–317.
Kischel, U, 2015, *Rechtsvergleichung*, C. H. Beck.
Klíma, K, 2016, *Ústavní právo 5. aktualizované vydání,* Plzeň: Vydavatelství a nakladatelství Aleš Čeněk.
Klíma, K, et al., 2005, *Komentář k Ústavě a Listině*, Plzeň: Vydavatelství a nakladatelství Aleš Čeněk.
Knapp,V, 1995, *Teorie práva*, Praha: C. H. Beck.
Kosař, D, Baroš, J & Dufek, P, 2019, 'The Twin Challenges to Separation of Powers in Central Europe: Technocratic Governance and Populism', *European Constitutional Law Review*, vol. 15, no. 3, pp. 427–461.
Kosař, D & Vyhnánek, L, 2021, *The Constitution of Czechia: A Contextual Analysis*, Oxford: Oxford University Press.
Kysela, J, 2008, 'Ústavní principy, ústavní konvence a ústavní inženýrství', in Klíma, K & Jirásek, J (eds.), *Pocta Jánu Gronskému,* Plzeň: Vydavatelství a nakladatelství Aleš Čeněk, pp. 121–136.
Kysela, J, 2014, *Ústava mezi právem a politikou. Úvod do ústavní teorie*, Praha: Leges.
Lavický, P, 2014, 'Komentář k § 9', in Lavický, P, et al. (eds.), *Občanský zákoník I. Obecná část § 1–654. Komentář,* Praha: C. H. Beck.
Lechner, H & Zuck, R, 2011, *Bundesverfassungsgerichtsgesetz: BVerfGG*, C. H. Beck.
Masing, J, 2005, 'Zwischen Kontinuität und Diskontinuität: Die Verfassungsänderung', *Der Staat*, vol. 44, no. 1, pp. 1–17.
McCormack, T, 2019, *Britain's War Powers*, Palgrave.
Melzer, F, 2011, *Metodologie nalézání práva. Úvod do právní argumentace*, 2. vydání, Praha: C. H. Beck.
Melzer, F & Tégl, P, 2013, 'Komentář k § 9', in Melzer, F & Tégl, P (eds.), *Občanský zákoník – velký komentář. Svazek I – § 1–117 Obecná ustanovení*, Praha: Leges.
Merryman, JH & Pérez-Perdomo, R, 2007, *The Civil Law Tradition*, 3rd ed., Stanford: Stanford University Press.
Morlok, M, 2002, *Leistungsgrenzen des Verfassungsrechts. Informalisierung und Entparlamentarisierung politischer Entscheidungen als Gefährdungen der Verfassung? [Performance Limits of Constitutional Law. Informalization and De*

Parliamentarization of Political Decisions as Threats to the Constitution?], Veröffentlichungen der Vereinigung der Deutschen Staatsrechtslehrer, vol. 62, De Gruyter.

Pavlíček, V, et al., 2015, *Ústavní právo a státověda II. díl: Ústavní právo České republiky*, Praha: Leges.

Petrétei, J, 2013, *Magyarország alkotmányjoga I. Alapvetés, alkotmányos intézmények*, Pécs: Kodifikátor Alapítvány.

Píša, R, 2014, 'Ústavní konvence komparativně', in Wintr, J & Antoš, M (eds.), *Ústavní právo v mezinárodním kontextu*, Praha: Univerzita Karlova v Praze, pp. 17–26.

Pithart, P, 2013, 'Svoboda a odpovědnost v čase rozčilení', in Gerloch, A (ed.), *Odpovědnost v demokratickém právním státě*, Univerzita Karlova v Praze, Právnická fakulta, pp. 16–21.

Quigley, J, 1989, 'Socialist Law and the Civil Law Tradition', *The American Journal of Comparative Law*, vol. 37, no. 4, pp. 781–808.

Raz, J, 1992, *Practical Reason and Norms*, Princeton, NJ: Princeton University Press.

Scheppele, KL, 2005, 'Democracy by Judiciary: Or, Why Courts Can Be More Democratic Than Parliaments', in Czarnota, A, Krygier, M & Sadurski, S (eds.), *Rethinking the Rule of Law after Communism*, Budapest, Hungary: Central European University Press, pp. 24–59.

Scheppele, KL, 2007, 'Chapter Thirteen. Constitutional Negotiations: Political Contexts of Judicial Activism in Post-Soviet Europe', in Arjomand, SA, et al. (eds.), *Constitutionalism and Political Reconstruction*, Leiden, The Netherlands: Brill, pp. 315–336.

Scheppele, KL, 2018, 'Autocratic Legalism', *University of Chicago Law Review*, vol. 85, no. 2, pp. 545–583.

Scheppele, KL, 2022, 'How Viktor Orbán Wins', *Journal of Democracy*, vol. 33, no. 3, pp. 45–61.

Shapiro, S, 2009, 'What Is the Rule of Recognition (and Does it Exist)?', in Adler, MD & Himma, K (eds.), *The Rule of Recognition and the U.S. Constitution*, Oxford University Press.

Škop, M, 2018, 'Legislativní zvyklosti', *Právník*, vol. 157, no. 9, pp. 723–737.

Škop, M, Malaník, M, Smejkalová, T, Štěpáníková, M & Vacková, B, 2019, *Tvorba práva – empirické studie*, 1. vydání, Brno: Masarykova univerzita. Spisy Právnické fakulty Masarykovy univerzity, Edice Scientia.

Slater, D, 2013, 'Democratic Careening', *World Politics*, vol. 65, no. 4, pp. 729–763.

Sobek, T, 2008, *Argumenty teorie práva*, Plzeň: Aleš Čeněk.

Sólyom, L, 2001, *Az alkotmánybíráskodás kezdetei Magyarországon*, Budapest: Osiris.

Szente, Z, 2019, 'How Populism Destroys Political Representation (Anti-)Parliamentary Reforms in Hungary After 2010', *Saggi – DPCE Online*, vol. 39, no. 2, pp. 1609–1618.

Tichý, l, 2014, *Obecná část občanského práva*, Praha: C. H. Beck.

Tushnet, T, 2021, *The New Fourth Branch: Institutions for Protecting Constitutional Democracy*, Cambridge University Press.

Uitz, R, 2015, 'Can You Tell When an Illiberal Democracy Is in the Making? An Appeal to Comparative Constitutional Scholarship from Hungary', *International Journal of Constitutional Law*, vol. 13, no. 1, pp. 279–300.

Vincze, A, 2009, 'Egy félreértett alkotmánybírósági hatáskörről: a hatásköri összeütközés megszüntetése', *Közjogi Szemle*, vol. 2, no. 4, pp. 14–19.

Vincze, A, 2012, 'The New Hungarian Constitution: Redrafting, Rebranding or Revolution?', *Vienna Journal on International Constitutional Law*, vol. 6, no. 1, pp. 88–105.

Vincze, A, 2020, 'Die Interpretationsregeln des ungarischen Grundgesetzes: Zwischen Konvention, Tradition und Voluntarismus', *Zeitschrift für ausländisches öffentliches Recht und Völkerrecht*, vol. 80, no. 4, pp. 973–988.

Vincze, A, 2021a, 'Shaping Presidential Powers in Hungary: Convention, Tradition and Informal Constitutional Amendments', *Review of Central and East European Law*, vol. 46, no. 3–4, pp. 307–320.
Vincze, A, 2021b, 'Szokás, szokásjog és konvenció az alkotmányjogban', *Közjogi Szemle*, vol. 14, no. 1, pp. 1–11.
Werner, L & Wirnitzer, J, 2013, 'Pojem ústavní zvyklosti je idiotský, řekl Zeman. Němcové nechal naději', *iDNES.cz*, https://www.idnes.cz/zpravy/domaci/zeman-sance-na-vladu-pro-cssd-a-byvalou-koalici.A130711_071534_domaci_wlk
Wintr, J, 2010, *Česká parlamentní kultura*, Praha: Auditorium.
Wintr, J, 2022, *Proměny parlamentní kultury*, Praha: Auditorium.
Wintr, J, Antoš, M & Kysela, J, 2016, 'Direct Election of the President and Its Constitutional and Political Consequences', *Acta Politologica*, vol. 8, no. 2, pp. 145–163.

Index

Note: Page numbers in **bold** indicate a table on the corresponding page.

For Product Safety Concerns and Information please contact our EU representative GPSR@taylorandfrancis.com
Taylor & Francis Verlag GmbH, Kaufingerstraße 24, 80331 München, Germany

www.ingramcontent.com/pod-product-compliance
Lightning Source LLC
LaVergne TN
LVHW021127300926
849160LV00010B/900

* 9 7 8 1 0 3 2 8 2 8 3 6 7 *